Making Peasants into Kings

To: Amy
Thank you!
Jay Powell
6/29/10

Dr. Jay C. Powell
Founder of
Better Schooling Systems

authorHOUSE®

AuthorHouse™
1663 Liberty Drive
Bloomington, IN 47403
www.authorhouse.com
Phone: 1-800-839-8640

© 2010 Better Schooling and Information Systems. All rights reserved.

No part of this book may be reproduced, stored in a retrieval system, or transmitted by any means without the written permission of the author.

First published by AuthorHouse 1/22/2010

ISBN: 978-1-4490-0634-1 (sc)

Printed in the United States of America
Bloomington, Indiana

This book is printed on acid-free paper.

Front Cover from:
The Education of the Children of Clovis (1868)
by Sir Lawrence Alma-Tadena
Oil on panel - M. Knoedler & Co.

Table of Contents

Mission Statement	xi
Acknowledgements	xiii
Dedication	xv

In the Beginning … The Old One		1
Remarks		5

Chapter 1; Developing Compassion		7
Box ends	A frightening incident	7
Playing in the water	An unexpected reprimand	9
Being teased in school	Bullied	10
The day it all changed	My first intuitive leap	11
Larn me teach, I dare yuh!	A challenge from the floor	13
Toward challenging others	Seeking 100% in reading	15
Samurai sword	The threat that failed	16
Missed opportunities	She leaves the bed	17
Painting in black	A teacher creates a problem	19
Hiding behind coats	Managing classroom upsets	21
Individualized Educational Programs	Doodling or creative art	23
Jack	Echoes from the past	26
Another view of the school	My stepson's experience	26
Remarks		27

Chapter 2; Developing Cooperation		29
The purloined cap	Was it stealing?	29
Standing my ground	Self-defense	30
Keep your options open	A father's advice	31
Enforcer	A dubious victory	33
A bargain with infinity	To whom is heaven open?	34
Getting accepted	A short career as an entertainer	36
Dealing with death	A popular student commits suicide	37
Yearbook	I challenge authority	38
The dropout	Stay in school or quit?	41
Cheating	One student writes everyone's stories	42
Working together with compassion	Helping others to help each other	45
Transitions	Watching a loved one die	46
Cooperation	A student discussion group	48

Chapter 3: Developing Comprehension — 53

Lawn mower	A model from experience	53
Failing Grade 2	Poor progress in school	53
A new outlook	Beginning junior high	55
A "practical" joke	A toad in the desk	55
Learning how to learn	Home-schooling experience	56
Linking to the community	Comparative shopping	58
Spares and strikes	Becoming self-competitive	59
My ice cream summer	Summer employment	60
Classroom antics	Back to high school in Alberta	63
Dropping out of high school	Bureaucratic decisions	66
Into the land of the great unwashed	Employment for a drop-out	67
Adventures in the world of journalism	Copy boy at a newspaper	70
Remarks		72
Glimpses of the future	Sewer cleaner and more	73
More bureaucratic bungling	Becoming a flunk-out	75
Road to nowhere	Becoming a banker	75
Endlessly in trouble	An uncivil servant	77
The flunkout goes back to school	Training to be a teacher	81
Castles in the Sand	Imitation in learning	86
The dog through the hoop	Identifying my dyslexia	90

Chapter 4: Developing Communication — 93

Theories of Education	Artisan vs. Shaman	93
Remarks		94
Flight contest	Anticipatory discipline	94
The staff meeting	Where does cooperation begin?	96
Teaching how to learn	History as a vehicle to thinking skills	98
Step one:	Directed observation	100
Step two:	Developing initial independence	100
Step three:	Looking more deeply into the text	101
Step four:	How to write an essay from textual themes	101
Step five:	Moving toward independence in text analysis skills	102
Step six:	Applying their new skills	103
Learning from writing	My "Reading to Write" program	103
Raising school performance	Gaining two years in one	107
Broadening horizons	Teaching for mastery	112

A Learning Environment — 113

What about classroom atmosphere?	Effects upon personal worthiness	113
The teaching act under a microscope		114
First alternative ending	"Doing to"	115

Second Alternative Ending	"Doing for"	116
Third alternative ending	"Doing with"	118
Remarks		120
The next step beyond my P.h.D. into the school system		120
Identifying needs		121
Working with existing programs		122
Community liaison		123
Special projects		123
The outcome		124
Multi-tasking	Integrating many skills into learning activities	125
Listening skills	Getting students to pay attention	125
The incredible shrinking log	Developing obsevation skills	127
Concrete experiences from difficult language		129
The substitute teacher	What a self-directing class looks like	130

Chapter 5: Developing connectedness — 133
Going beyond the material — 133
What is Reality? — 134

What is non-locality?	A timeless, spaceless realty	135
The transient nature of matter		136
The role of the observer		137
Energy resources		138

A life beyond belief — 140
Escape from logic — 140

Genealogy of Jesus	Challenges from Scripture	141

Does time as we usually conceive of it actually exist? — 143

Baby robin	A ceremony from the past	143
Prophetic dreams		145
Was this a voice from the past?		145
Knowing a military secret?		146
Who took a moonwalk?		146
The cave of challenge and mystery		147
The impossible trip		149

Does matter actually exist? — 151

Where did the bell come from?	Objects from nowhere	151
A healing touch	Restoring a sense of smell	153

Does space actually exist? — 154

Vinny's message	Who goes to heaven?	154
Reconciliation	Life after life	155

A spectacular display	Connectedness	157
Passing through solid walls	The transmigrating dog	157

What does all this mean?   159
Are we created in God's image?	The spirit in the car	159
Creating my own "hell"	At war with myself	161
Soul mates	Frances, my first wife	165
Forming connections	Are we alone?	167
Becoming a scholar	Intellectual connectedness	173
To hell and back	An encounter with Ouija	175
The second love of my life	Wedding "Merry England"	182

A message from Mary   191
And now Valerie	My current wife	192
Responding to our Soul's imperatives	Finding our way	194

Chapter 6: Developing Consciousness   199
The meeting that changed the nation	Horace Mann	199
Should we be fighting the tests?	Whose standards	201
Discovering my mission	Called to be a teacher educator	202
Robin's nest	What is a "right" answer?	202
Plug-in theory of learning	The brain as a telephone exchange	204
The math behind the theory	The bell-shaped curve	205
"X" marks the spot	Information loss	206
Opening the door to post-secondary education		214
Improving teaching effectiveness	Raising student performance	216
Becoming a special educator	Up from far behind	219
Beginning a research program	My first publication	225
On the move again		226
Teaching bookkeeping		227
Teaching typing:		227

Now the fundamental question   229
Breakthrough or disaster?	Unexpected results	232
Studying children at last!	Developmental errors	235
The dilemma	Where do choice changes fit?	238
A leap into the possible	A new way to investigate performance	241

The end of an era   243
Alternative answers	More than one way	243
The extraordinary challenge	What do answers mean?	245
The Souvenir Shop	Many ways to answer	246
A new scoring technology	Recovering lost information	248
A light at the end of the tunnel	Could it be an approaching train?	252

A paradigm shift 255
  A possible solution   Adding dimensions 258
  The key to this approach   Using every answer 264
  The Heavenly circle   What might they say? 268
  What did you do to my kid?   How well does it work? 272

Epilogue: Unanswered Questions 275
  A defining choice   From Peasants to Kings 275
  How should we teach what we teach?   Recitation vs. exploration 278
  How about the teachers' workloads?   Let your students do the work 282
  Marks and grades   Helping students meet expectations 283
  Financial considerations   How much will it cost? 286
  The last few words   Meeting the challenge 287

Our company   **Better Schooling and Information Systems**   288

Afterword   **Good Luck! We'll help**   288

Appendix A   **The souvenir shop**   289
              Francine's Group   289
              Gregory's Group   290
              Abdul's Group   291
              Amit's Group   291
  Recapitulation   293

Endnotes 297

Mission Statement

"Peasants" are people that are responding to the imperatives of their cultures. They have been dumbed down by their educational system (or lack thereof) to become vassals (slaves) to the culture in which they live. They may be able to read but they don't. They may be able to think independently but they usually rely upon influential others to tell them what to think and what to do.

"Kings" are people that are responding to their Souls' imperatives; to the "Kingdom within." These are people whose talents have emerged to become gifts to others and a source for personal power. They create their own futures in concert with everyone and everything around them, recognizing and honoring the interconnectedness of all things.

If we intend to educate in a way that all peasants can become kings, to provide equal opportunity, we need to do something different than we are now doing. More of the same has not worked for more than 150 years and there is no good reason to expect it to work any better for the next 150. What is our alternative? That is the subject of this book.

Acknowledgements

This book has been more than two decades in the making and is now in its tenth revision. It would be impossible to thank all those who have contributed importantly to this effort over these many years. However, special thanks must go to Allan Clapp, whose tireless efforts and programming skills have made it possible to continue this research after my retirement and to make some of the most important discoveries reported here.

I must also, of course, give a deep heart-felt thank you to each of my three wives for their encouragement and support to the fullest extent possible. I am delighted that in the case of Frances and of Mary, this support is continuing from their side of the veil. Now Valerie is doing wonders with her editing, intellectual and emotional support.

I cannot neglect mentioning Roxane Christ, my former editor, over the last several drafts. It was her suggestion that led to my removing most of the didactic discussion about the emerging theory behind this approach and posing the questions that begin and end each anecdote to provide the flow of thought. Her suggestions about narrative flow made a writer out of a stogy academic.

I must also thank the Association for Supervision and Curriculum Development (ASCD) (pp. 45-46), The Ontario English Catholic Teachers' Association (OECTA) *Review* (pp. 86-90) and the Psychological Tests Specialists (p.222) for permission to use their Copyrighted materials in this book.

Finally, I wish to express my thanks to the Benevolent Universe in which we live for allowing me to undertake this mission of my choice and providing the support and resources needed, including my three wives, Frances, Mary and Valerie, empowering me to move this far on the world transformation so desperately needed today.

Dedication

To all those who would seek to express the imperatives of their Souls without regard to personal and social consequences as long as they have succeeded in leaving the world a little better off than they found it.

In the Beginning ... The Old One

And God saw every thing that he had made, and, behold, it <u>was</u> very good. (KJV:[1] Ge. 1.31)

There was a soft rustle among the leaves outside my hut. Did I have a visitor?

I pushed the skin door-flap to one side and peered out into the blinding sunlight. No one was there.

As my eyes adjusted to the brilliance, they fell upon an iridescent green feather hanging from a notch on my doorpost.

"The old one wants to see me," I mused. "I wonder why."

Putting on my feathered cap and woven alpaca cape of many colors, my ceremonial dress for such occasions, I strode across the common area between the huts.

Mine was a small unpretentious hut at the sunset end of the village. The old one lived in the much larger hut we called "the lodge" next to the gathering place at the sunrise end of the village.

I nodded to my number-two wife working by the stream in the vegetable patch to the high noon side of the village. Recognizing where I was going from my robes, she fell silently in stride behind me as I crossed the common.

The jubilant laughter of the younger children delighted my ears as they chased each other among the huts. The boys were playing a hunting game, the girls pretending to be homemakers.

My number one wife had a group of young girls surrounding her. Their breasts were just beginning to bud. She was showing them how to weave floor mats from reeds. She acknowledged my passing but did not leave her task and charges.

A breeze rippled the wheat in the plot to the left as I turned the corner toward the gathering place.

Dr. Jay C. Powell

The old one's wives sat in a huddled curve in front of the door opening to the old one's lodge. They moaned softly. This meant that he was dying. Was he going to nominate me as his successor? My number-two wife squatted among the mourners and joined with them in their soft lament.

I entered the incense-filled chamber. His number-one wife stood up from his side. She picked up the ornate bowl from which she had been dipping a white pasty liquid and wiping it on his brow. She scurried out the door. In the background the soft moaning continued.

The old one signaled me to squat beside him close to his head.

"I'll be leaving soon." His voice was thin, like the rustle of wind in the reeds. "I am the last of the first ones. I have trained you in all the lore I know. I now wish to give you my parting instructions.

"I have chosen you because you have been my best student. You have learned the recipes well. You don't seem to have done as well with the craft skills but the women will help to preserve them. It is extremely important that the herbal recipes for medicines be preserved.

"Why did he not mention the incantations?" I wondered under my breath. Those incantations were something, I could say proudly, at which I was good. Memorization was my strength. Understanding the explanations was not so much my strength.

"There are four things you must understand. First, you must honor the women.

"Over these many seasons they have improved the crude living items that began our stay here almost beyond belief. We no longer need hollowed logs for containers, piles of straw for bedding, sharpened sticks for hunting, or raw animal skins for clothing. In addition to giving us comfort and bearing our children, they have made this very good life possible.

"Second, be careful not to lose your sense of connection with everything. I have watched the more recent generations slowly lose their sense of deeper being. If it continues, this loss will be the source of much sorrow. If we come to see ourselves as separate instead of being a part of everything, our desire to have more, at the expense of others, will produce much harm."

I said nothing but my mind raced. "Was this all nonsense – the ravings of a senile old man?" I dared not give voice to my thoughts.

"Third, beware of those who would take from us what we have built. Now that we can live in one place, we no longer need to confine our possessions to what we can carry. As our riches grow, so does their greed. There are already signs that some of the Akkai are planning to take over this river valley.

"This increase in possessions, which we all share, is the source of envy for those not as successful. Their men have learned to ride their alpacas and to herd people the way they herd their animals. They have lost their sense of connectedness. They now intend to take with force the things we could share with them and help them to make. Hunting people is replacing hunting for food. This descent into meanness could last for many, many seasons, if it is not stopped.

"Fourth, you must know about our origins. I am the last of the first ones, so I am the only one who can tell the tale. We did not start in this place. We began from a group of beings that came from the candles of the night sky. They could not live for long in this air and water place. To provide us with the ability to survive, they had some way of changing the babies in their mothers so that the babies could live here. It killed the mothers to do this.

"They taught us as much as they could before they had to leave. They may contact us again in the future. I don't know whether or when. All I know is that there is more to living than just this time and place. We are part of a bigger plan than just this village and this river valley."

With this last statement, he handed me the eagle talon staff that was the symbol of his office. "Carry this honorably, my son," he croaked.

Then he reached out both of his leathery hands to grasp mine. His grasp was stronger than I expected. "The future is now up to you." He sighed, fell back upon the blankets that formed his bed, and became still. His rasping breathing slowed and finally stopped altogether. A ball of soft blue light formed at the top of his head, lifted slowly as it turned to white. Then it was gone.

I arranged his hands across his chest, closed his eyes gently and stood up. I left the lodge slowly, a heavy stone in my chest. I carried the staff awkwardly. I couldn't feel the connection with power that I expected.

The wailing of the women became louder and shriller. My second wife stood slowly. Usually she walked with her head bowed. This time she lifted her chin and our eyes met. It was as though she could see right through me. I shivered. For a moment my knees felt weak. "Did she know?" My thoughts were a mass of confusion. "What was all this about connectedness and greed?"

She fell in behind me once again, knowing that we would now be moving from our hut to the lodge.

The pain inside me was very sharp and deep. How was I going to tell the people that in the end The Old One was quite mad?

Remarks

This fictional account of the origins of humanity sets the stage for what is to come.

Have you ever felt that you had a mission – a purpose for being alive – but you didn't know what that purpose might be?

Have you ever felt at the core of your being that there is an immense power, like a volcano? A vitality that is sometimes quiet – sometimes restless – sometimes throwing off smoke and steam – sometimes erupting with intense heat and dazzling color – that overwhelms you and possibly even those around you?

It is an up-swelling of just such an internal power that has driven me all of my life. It has made me into what I have become – through a tumultuous childhood, an extraordinarily difficult education and a topsy-turvy professional career.

In the largely autobiographical account that follows, I will elaborate upon the six themes that this short story contains.

The themes that will form the chapters of this account are:

Compassion,
Cooperation,
Comprehension,
Communication,
Connectedness and
Consciousness.

I make no apologies for what I will tell you about myself or for those who have influenced my life for better or for worse. I have changed the names of some of the participants so that I will not be pointing fingers at others who are unable to speak in their own defense.

I have made a startling discovery that has profound implications for the way we educate each other. By the time you have finished reading how I untangled the mystery of

Dr. Jay C. Powell

where education has gone astray, perhaps you will have come to the same conclusion.

Come walk with me as I tell my tale. Perhaps you too will discover how to tame this power within you – to participate with its demands and challenges – and ultimately, how each of us can use this vitality to generate, for the benefit of all, what we are designed to become.

Chapter 1; Developing Compassion

If you have a 'killer instinct' inside you, is it a good idea to become a teacher? That's what I did!

Box ends

The pain inside me was very sharp and deep.

It was the fall of 1941, precursor of another cold winter in Edmonton, Alberta. I was almost ten years old. My sister Grace, who had turned six in March and just begun school. We were home alone when a deliveryman arrived at the door with a load of wooden box-ends. These were scraps of apple wood that were left over from the manufacture of produce boxes at a local factory. We used this wood for our wood-burning kitchen stove and as kindling to start up our coal-burning furnace.

We opened the window above the coal bin in our cellar. The deliveryman dumped the box-ends through it on top of our coal pile. Once the unloading was completed, Grace and I decided to remove the wood from atop the pile and stack it on our residual kindling supply along the cellar wall beside the furnace.

First, we cleared away the stray pieces that had fallen to the floor around the bin. Then we tackled the knotted tangle of board fragments on top of the coal. Grace was more agile than I, so she offered to dislodge the tangle by pushing the pile apart with her feet. She braced herself by holding on to the ceiling joists. With a deft kick she sent a section of the wood cascading to the floor.

I picked up armloads of wood, carrying it to the stacking pile. There I dropped the bundle and straightened it out. This procedure worked well for a while. Then, after an unusually small load, I got a bit ahead of her. I returned to the edge of the pile more quickly than either of us anticipated. With her back to me, she gave a mighty kick to the woodpile under her feet.

I had just bent over to pick up a few stray sticks. A large section of the remaining box ends dislodged and flew outward with the force of her effort. It crashed down on the back of my bowed head.

The violent pain was so severe that a red film of anguish obscured my vision. Suddenly, blind rage directed at her carelessness invaded me. I was overwhelmed with desire to kill her. My eyes fell upon the hatchet we used to split the larger pieces—and I then froze. Something deep inside me stopped me.

"This is the sister you love, and she's just a little girl." This gentle, quiet voice pushed back at the furor dominating and blurring my thoughts. As quickly as the rage erupted it abated; to be replaced by panic at the realization that I was capable of killing someone I love.

My breath was now rising in huge gulping gasps. I was shaking. I reached for the back of my head where the load had landed. I felt a large lump bulging under my hair. I withdrew my hand, looked at it bewildered; there was no blood on it.

My knees went weak and buckled under me, sitting me down with a thump on the cellar floor.

"I'm s-s-sorry," Grace stammered. "D-d-did I hurt you?"

I grunted something meaningless in reply, scrambling awkwardly back to my feet. Distractedly, I bent down to pick up the scattered pieces of wood. Amid the pain, the fear and the astonishment I realized that a killer instinct laid in wait deep within me. I could do nothing but groan a few words expressing incoherent thoughts.

It took about twenty minutes for the gasping and trembling to cease and for my breathing and vision to return to normal.

I was a mere boy, yet my limited knowledge allowed me to recognize that something monstrous within me had to be controlled — controlled at all cost. From that moment on, I vowed I would never allow myself to get that angry at anyone again. I was determined not to let the monster within me emerge; although, in the future, there were occasions when I might have good reasons to let go of this resolve. In my rage I had lost my connectedness. Fortunately for both of us, I had recovered this link with All That Is, before I took action.

Does understanding self provide the personal depth needed to understand others?

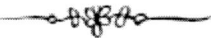

Playing in the water

Does valuing obedience over seeking understanding create unintended learning problems?

"James, I told you not to play in the water." Mr. Carmichael, the principal of MacKenzie Elementary School grabbed me by my jacket collar and dragged me into his office. Out came the black rubber strap with the embedded strands of rough cotton. My palms were soon red from the impacts. "In the future, I suggest that you follow instructions."

I don't remember ever telling my parents that I had been given the strap in the first grade. I wasn't sure what I had done wrong. To me, standing beside water rivulets formed by melting ice, while trying to divert the current flow one way or another with a stick, was a source of delightful exploration.

I was enthralled with the light and dark streaks of sediment that rolled along the channels I was creating. It was interesting to watch the larger dark chunks move more slowly with the flow of the stream than the smaller and lighter colored ones.

When the principal grabbed me, I thought he was concerned about my health—at six years of age, I tended to think that adults were always concerned with your well being, but he seemed more concerned with my obedience to his instructions. What's more, as I recall, he made no effort to enquire what I was finding so interesting in the flow of water.

My dad's approach has always been, "Go and find out." Perhaps not consciously, or deliberately, that's all I was doing, finding out about how water currents flow. In my many years of working with children and adults, I am saddened to see how often the skill of careful observation has been lost by middle childhood.

Such treatment as this strapping may have caused many children to curb, or lose their natural curiosity. Humiliation from not being able to give expected answers in school or at home can be as devastating as physical punishment. This problem can be seen in the conflict between memorizing and understanding introduced in "The Old One."

I have never lost my desire to explore by watching what is happening around me. This event was the beginning of my realization that others around me might possibly be acting for reasons different from my own.[2]

Is this recognition of differences the basis for our sense of individuality?

Being teased in school

Is being different in the classroom and playground a social 'sin'?

"Jamie can't run yet!" Freddie Slater taunted as he slowed his cycling pace to be even more tantalizing. I quit trying to chase him and headed back across the school grounds towards the Boy's entrance.

There was a "clank" behind me as his bicycle bounced over the edge of the concrete sidewalk in front of the school. I jumped out of his way just in time to avoid being run over. It was bad enough that I was the butt of jokes in the classroom where my consistently poor oral reading was repeatedly humiliating.

My small stature and physical clumsiness also led to endless ridicule in the playground as well as the classroom.

I survived by staying away from the people who were tormenting me. I found a haven at the outside edge of the school grounds by the fence. There I could while away the recess time in a comfortable imaginary world drawn from the strange dreams I had, which kept coming true.

I did not fit the school environment. All I knew was that I felt driven by this sense of being more than I was showing. Something somewhere had to change.

To put it simply, "Elementary school was hell!"

How many children feel this way about their school experiences?

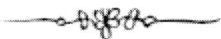

The day it all changed

Is providing for insight the way to give students appreciation of their own capabilities?

The streamers from the fan lolled lazily on that hot afternoon in May of 1943. The huge fan blowing cool air from the basement was not accomplishing much toward cooling the school because most of the teachers had opened their classroom windows.

It was the class before afternoon recess. Mr. Franklin was teaching science to his sixth grade.

"Here is how sound is created," he explained. He put his left elbow on his lectern and moved his forearm across in front of him.

Pointing to his palm, as it descended in an arc, he said, "As the tine of the tuning fork moves toward the air it compresses it. This produces a condensation that travels outward in all directions from the fork."

He then swung his arm in the other direction. Once again pointing to his palm he explained, "As the tine swings the other way, it stretches the air reducing its pressure. This rarefaction follows the condensation out into the air. When such changes in air pressure reach our ears we hear a sound."

He continued his explanation, "Of course, if something should happen that two such waves are produced, so that the condensation in one exactly coincides with the rarefaction of the other, the pressure differences cancel each other out. We won't hear anything. This event is called being in *counter phase.*"

"There is something wrong here," I told myself. From what Mr. Franklin had just demonstrated, I visualized *both* sides of his hand. As the palm descended, and his palm was squashing the air the back of his hand was stretching it. The opposite was true on the reverse swing. "If the air on both sides of the tine is responding as a unit, they should cancel each other out. The opposite sides of the tine would be in *counter phase.* Therefore we should hear nothing!"

I tested this idea by placing a piece of paper on my palm. I waved my arm through the air toward the paper. I then moved my palm away from the paper. It fell to the floor. I tried the same movements on the back of my hand, with identical results.

"Pick up that paper!" Mr. Franklin reprimanded as the recess bell rang.

I stopped at his desk and tried to explain my observation.

"Go out to play!" he growled by way of reply. I shrugged and headed for the playground.

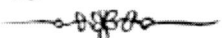

This incident changed me forever. I had seen a contradiction in the logic of that explanation. I *knew* the explanation he had given was *wrong*. I had just had my first truly independent thought. I had also just learned that I could not trust teachers to be "right" all the time. I realized that I could now think for myself. To get to the truth I would have to work step by step through the logic of an explanation *on my own!*

With these realizations I became insulated from the inanities and cruelties of schooling. School was no longer 'hell,' merely mostly silly.

I taught myself how to read and from that skill how to learn. This realization was my first major step toward the idea that people are often unaware of what they do not know.

Is the unimaginable invisible? Like the threat of war from the Akkai to that peaceful village by the river?

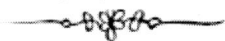

Larn me teach, I dare yuh!

What makes people turn to intimidation to obtain recognition and personal control?

In my second year of teaching, after returning a test, a fair amount of paper appeared on the floor. For some reason, much of this arrived under Roger's desk. I asked him to pick it up and put it into the wastebasket. He yelled, "I didn't put that (@*%) paper there, an' I ain't gonna pick it up!"

"Who put it there was not the issue," I replied. "It was now your responsibility because I just gave you the job." He stood up angrily. Immediately the students around him moved their desks away, creating an open space.

To my own and everyone else's amazement, I managed to remain calm and could think clearly. Doing battle with a student would be pointless. Had I quelled the rage reflex? I stepped to the blackboard and pressed the "Call" button on the intercom.

There was no response. I tried again; still no response.

He smirked to his buddies and became more hostile.

"Soon the period will be over," I pointed out. "Another class will gather outside the door. The commotion they will make will bring someone. There is no way you can win this one, Roger. You might just as well give in to the inevitable, pick up the paper and end the affair."

Roger persisted. The next class assembled in the corridor, and the principal came to investigate, escorting him away. It turned out later that he had knocked down more than one teacher in elementary school and a fellow teacher in this high school in similar circumstances.

He was suspended from classes and did not return to school that year. I now understand that I learned and taught only part of the non-violence lesson that day. The fact that I didn't resort to violence relieved much of the tension in this class. Roger may have learned this same lesson, at least in my classroom. In my view, suspension was inappropriate.

Later, I realized that he had been set up. I had seen Roger's actions in the same way as Mr. Carmichael had viewed my playing in the water, as an issue about who is in control. I could have handled this situation much better. I could have picked up the wastebasket, starting the disposal operation myself, asking for everyone's help in the cleanup.

Recalling my feelings when I was strapped for disobedience at MacKenzie Elementary, I am not surprised at the amount of pent-up anger Roger must have been carrying. Recalling my feelings at being the butt of teasing, I now suspect the motive that made him so ready to resort to physical violence was to maintain his self-esteem. He must be carrying a monster like mine, but he had less control over his.

Of course, this resentment could also have come from his home and the community the school served. But the school was not a haven for him or he would have responded differently.

Are these some of the factors behind discipline problems in schools?

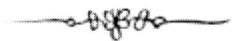

Toward challenging others

Does providing for success help build students' self-confidence, stimulating their effort?

In the early 1960s I became one of the first special education teachers in Ontario, Canada in high schools. There were 16 students in my ninth-grade special-program group. An important aspect of this program was the reading and writing components I had developed. Assuming that these "special" students were poor readers and unaccomplished writers, my plan was to encourage fluent reading and extensive writing.

The program I designed used high-interest low-vocabulary condensations of classics of English literature.[3] I prepared a ten-question multiple-choice "comprehension check" for each book to assess their understanding of what they read. These students could get 5 percent on their reading mark for each check on which they scored 8 out of 10. Ten books would give 50% for a thirteen-week term.[4]

One day in late October, Brian Richardson, one of these students, asked me, "Is it true, Mr. Powell? Is all I need to do is to read 20 of these books in this term to get 100 per cent?"

"Provided that you pass the comprehension checks, yes," I replied.

"You know, I just read *The Thirty-Nine Steps*. It was the first book I have ever read from cover to cover in my life. I really enjoyed it. I just got all the comprehension check questions correct. This is *fun!* Getting 100 per cent should be easy!"

"Go for it young man!" I encouraged.

Brian was as good as his word. By the end of the term, he had successfully read 20 books. By the end of the second term, he had read another 20. However, after he had read 30 books he complained that he was finding the low-vocabulary books too easy. For a couple of the titles he tried the original versions. At this stage in his skill development, he found *A Tale of Two Cities* too difficult.

With his complaint in mind, I added forty adult-vocabulary books from a librarian's list of titles of high interest topics for teenaged boys. To extend the program in this way, I had to prepare comprehension checks for all these books as well. Off and running again, Brian read another 20 books in the third term, finishing with *A Tale of Two Cities* once again and enjoyed it thoroughly.

Does such an approach create a deeper self-awareness in students?

Samurai sword

Is self-awareness and self-assurance needed to resolve the conflicts arising from our differences?

In the 1980s and 1990s I ran a small non-profit interfaith magazine. As part of our growth we needed to provide computers for several of our volunteer workers. I found a local provider of reconditioned used computers and placed an order with him.

When he delivered the order, it didn't fulfill our agreement. After several attempts to get adjustments, my board decided to return the equipment, requesting a refund. All the while he maintained that the "as is" clause in our contract held, even when we had not received what we had paid for.

Finally I phoned him to tell him that I intended to return the entire order. I would arrive at his residence (and place of business) at a certain time on a certain day. I would have two independent witnesses to verify the inventory and I expected to have my payment refunded.

He told me that he would be away at that time on that day. I said, "That's fine with me. I'll put the equipment in a safe place. I'll have my witnesses sign copies of the inventory. I'd leave the equipment there with a copy of the inventory."

The three of us went to his place at the appointed time and finished our business as arranged. We had just finished inspecting equipment and signing the inventory when he arrived on the scene. He had a souvenir from Japan, a sheathed Samurai sword in his hand.

"You're trespassing!" he exclaimed menacingly.

"No we're not," I replied. "I told you when and why we would be here. These are my two witnesses. You can inspect the equipment in their presence if you wish."

He moved a step closer, drew the sword, and repeated, "You're trespassing!"

"No, we're not," I responded. "I told you exactly when and why we would be here."

He took another step forward, waving the sword menacingly. "I'm going to call the police."

"Please do," I rejoined, as a deep sense of inner peace flooded over me.

He called the police, who handled the affair graciously, and we settled the issue without further fuss. I bought the equipment he had supplied correctly. He refunded the difference.

I now knew that I had quelled the murderous monster within me, not by will power, but by *finding peace within myself.*

Should this be a skill we teach people like Roger in school?

Missed opportunities

How many of the problems that arise between people come from the simple failure to communicate?

It was about three in the morning in the mid 1980s. I had been working many extra hours to strengthen my pension and, as usual, I was very tired.

This time I awoke feeling more refreshed than usual and a strong desire to make love with my wife Frances. I touched her tentatively and she mumbled something so I knew she was awake.

She had her back to me so I cuddled up to her and put my arm around her. As I moved closer, she flinched, scrambled from under my arm and stood up. "I've had all of this I can take," she said. She walked into the spare bedroom and crawled under the covers. Soon she was fast asleep.

I was devastated. She was older than I. Her much beloved sister had passed away several years before. That had closed off the whole of her life before our marriage in 1954. I thought I had given her a good life in our thirty years of marriage. And now she was leaving our bed; never to return?

I assumed that at her age she had decided she had had enough of sex. I bore my humiliation in silence for several years. Trying to be honorable, I remained celibate. During this time she began to show signs of advancing senile dementia.

Then an opportunity came for us to visit Swampscott, MA for a couple of weeks in 1992. Our landlord of the apartment we had rented while I was at Harvard doing post-Doctoral work had invited us to visit for a week or so. The visit to familiar, favorite settings seemed to clear her mind.

In addition, I found a book in a local store by Deborah Tannen *You Just Don't Understand*.[5] I read it and realized that I had been contributing to her diminishing functioning. I finally understood her fits of anger. With this in mind, I confronted her about leaving our bed.

"The bed was too narrow," she complained. "I had to put a box along the wall so that I could brace myself. Otherwise, I ran the risk of falling out of bed whenever you got too close."

Of course, she was right. The bedrooms in our apartment were too small for double beds. We used three-quarter beds that were only four feet wide. It was not my amorous intent that put her off. It was more than ten years of discomfort from our sleeping arrangements.

Why had I not asked her about it that very night? I assumed that she had realized my intention and was rejecting me! When we don't understand motives, we often make invalid judgments. This is what the hero did about the old one. I now realize how much she must have adored me to tolerate this discomfort for so long.

Our relationship improved dramatically over the remaining nine months of her life. Her last words to me were, "You're the most wonderful man I have ever met."

How often do we miss opportunities by making assumptions instead of asking questions?

Painting in black

Are the things we don't realize we are doing creating wrong impressions in our minds and inappropriate actions in response?

"It's Mrs. Prentice on the phone, Dr. Powell," my secretary advised. "She seems very upset."

"Hello! How may I help you?" I said into the receiver, having no idea what the woman wanted.

"It's my son, Ralph," the harried sounding voice explained. "I went to a parent-teacher's meeting last Friday at Orton Central Elementary School." By this time, she was on the verge of tears. "His fifth grade teacher, Mrs. Schmidt, said she was concerned because she thought that Ralph might have schizophrenic tendencies."

After several minutes of hearing more of the story and helping Mrs. Prentice to calm down, I assured her that I would look into the matter and get back to her.

Such are the strange things that can happen to a school psychologist. I looked at my calendar and decided that I could swing by Orton Central at 10:00 AM tomorrow (Tuesday), when Mrs. Schmidt had an open hour.

When we were comfortably seated in the Nurse's Room that served as a private office for visitors, I addressed the issue. "What can you tell me about Ralph Prentice?"

"Did Clara Prentice contact you?" Mrs. Schmidt enquired. "I'm not surprised. I talked to her last Friday evening during Parents' Night."

"What happened?"

"I'm taking an Art History course at Easton College toward my Masters Degree," she continued. "I have an assignment of writing a paper in art interpretation. I have become fascinated with the psychological meanings of artistic symbology and style. One of the things I discovered is that schizophrenics tend to paint most of their pictures in black. Nearly all of Ralph's paintings are in black.

"Of course, I am alarmed, and I shared this alarm with Clara Prentice."

I called the school secretary on the school's intercom, "Would you have Ralph Prentice come to the Nurse's Room?"

Looking puzzled and a bit scared, Ralph knocked on the frame of the open door.

Once he settled in a chair, I asked, "What's this about your painting in black?"

"Oh that?" Ralph relaxed. "Well … you see I sit in the back of the row by the windows. Mrs. Schmidt always hands out the paints beginning at the front of the row by the door. When the box gets to me there is seldom anything but black crayons or paints left. I'd rather not use black but I don't have much choice."

Mrs. Schmidt gulped and then grinned. "I misunderstood your actions," she said to Ralph with only a trace of embarrassment in her voice.

"Thank you, Ralph," I smiled reassuringly. "You may return to your class."

"Is that all?" Ralph muttered as he beat a hasty retreat.

"Do you want to explain the situation to Mrs. Prentice, or do you want me to talk to her?" I asked.

"I'll be happy to put her mind at ease," Mrs. Schmidt chortled. "And I'll start varying the way I hand out the colors!"

How do we give control away in ways that encourages self-control in others?

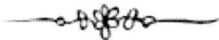

Hiding behind coats

Is the ability to view a situation from the other person's point-of-view a critical skill in interpersonal relations?

Melissa Santiago was one of my better pre-service teacher trainees. Her discussion in class and her assignments showed unusual sensitivity. For this reason, I was delighted to be her practice-teaching supervisor in her last round of classroom preparation before graduation.

It was a balmy Wednesday afternoon, in early spring. The fifth grade class she was teaching was a bit restless. She skillfully refocused their attention when it wandered. It seemed that everything was going smoothly.

From the back of the room, I saw Grace Minden pass a note to Sharon Little. Sharon opened it cautiously behind her propped-up social studies text. I noticed that Melissa had seen the event as well and wondered what she would do.

She seemed to ignore the event until suddenly Sharon burst into a giggling fit.

"Take your chair and go to the back of the room, Sharon," Melissa said gently but firmly.

Sharon complied, struggling to swallow her laughter as she went. The coats of the class members hung on hooks along the back wall. As soon as Sharon was seated, she hid her face behind some coats.

"Uncover your face and pay attention," Melissa instructed, a bit sharply.

"Yes, Miss Santiago," Sharon replied as she poked her head out from behind the coats. Soon, however, her face contorted with constrained mirth, and she ducked behind the coats again.

"What did I tell you to do, Sharon?" Melissa's voice had a definite edge this time.

The head reappeared from behind the coats for a minute or two and then disappeared once again. By this time, Melissa was visibly becoming annoyed. She strode to the back of the room and forcibly moved the chair away from the wall.

Fortunately, at that moment, the bell that ended the day rang. Melissa, with a sigh of relief, instructed the class to put on their coats and line up for dismissal.

When all was cleared away, the three of us, Melissa, Mrs. Overstreet, the Associate Teacher, and I sat down to recap the events during the afternoon's class.

"How do you think this session went?" Mrs. O. asked.

"Fairly well, for the most part," Melissa remarked.

We two agreed.

"How would you have handled Sharon's episode differently?" I asked.

"I don't know. I lost patience with her when she covered her head."

"Why?"

"Because she wasn't paying attention to the lesson," Melissa answered.

"Which was more important *for her*, attending to the lesson or regaining her composure?" Mrs. O. asked.

"Which was more important *to you*, having her attend to the lesson or having *her* regain her composure?" I added.

"I guess, when you put it that way, maybe having her regain her composure," Melissa replied looking at both of us with some dismay.

"Good for you!" Mrs. O.'s voice showed her pleasure.

"Think about it for the moment, could you have paid attention to a teacher in the middle of a giggle fit?"

"No, I don't think I could have."

"You have learned a valuable lesson about teaching today, Melissa," Mrs. O. continued, "One that took me a couple of years to achieve. When children lose it, their ability to concentrate disappears. At that point they need some time to themselves."

"What does this school do about time out?" I asked.

"We don't have a separate place where we can send someone. As you have noticed, we don't even have separate coatrooms. I usually send the children to the back of the room the way Melissa did."

"And if they hide their heads, you let them?"

"Of course, that is usually the end of the disturbance. Carrying it further disrupts the rest of the class."

"I see," Melissa nodded. "It is important not only that I think about what I am teaching, but also how my students are responding. There is much more to teaching than I thought."

Do we pay so much attention to our own objectives that we become disconnected from others?

Individualized Educational Programs

How much of under-learning comes from students being unable to deal effectively with their emotions when harried teaches feel they cannot take time to deal individually with their students?

Bruce Lipton's[6] research into epigenetics suggests that our biological system has two modes of operation, growth and protection. The protective mode shuts down the higher mental processes. It doesn't matter whether this shutdown comes from severe pain, substance abuse, loud noises, emotional or physical trauma – including giggling fits – the resulting reduced capabilities are severe.

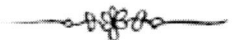

"Bill is on an IEP," Susan, his classmate, told Mrs. Fraser.[7] "He is permitted to draw whenever he wishes."

Mrs. Fraser had started substitute teaching after a couple of years of retirement because she found that she missed the contact with young people. She was unfamiliar with this particular school system because she moved from Wisconsin to Colorado to be closer to her grandchildren after her husband had passed away.

She thanked Susan and decided to observe Bill's learning strategies more closely. He had a coil-bound notebook open at the first page. It exposed a pattern of doodles.

As the day progressed, she observed him switching frequently from attending to the lesson to adding to the doodles. From her background as a special programs teacher, and a major in Fine Arts, she was perplexed. Drawing is a creative activity that requires nearly full engagement of both hemispheres of the brain. Doodling, on the other hand, often requires virtually no conscious brain engagement at all.

Knowing that she would be the teacher for about six weeks while their regular teacher was recovering from surgery, what should she do? She approached Bill at the first opportunity. 'Would you show me some of your best drawings?" she asked.

He produced a shabby notebook from the bottom of his disorderly desk and handed it to her without comment. She leafed through it in amazement.

"These drawings are very good!" she exclaimed. "Tell me something about this one." She showed him a line drawing of a young boy busily writing or drawing something. Above the boy's head was a balloon caption that said, "Mom, what time is my birthday party?"

"That's my baby brother. He's seven," Bill explained, pointing at the boy in the drawing. "The other day he was drawing a picture when he asked this question. Mom told him that this was only November and his birthday wasn't until April. When he asked again, Mom finally gave him a time of day."

When we looked at his drawing, it was an invitation to a little girl in his second grade class. It read, "You are *so* invited to my birthday party."

"That's a nice story to go with the picture. Would you draw me a story picture?"

"Yes," Bill replied as his eyes lit up.

By the end of the day, she had a three-picture story sequence on her desk.

She then started him on illustrating the stories in the readers they were using. At first he merely copied the illustrations already in the book. By the end of the sixth week however, his drawings were original. They showed that he had picked up nuances in the text that the illustrators did not include. This observation showed that he was reading with understanding.

We have all experienced moments when we were so upset that we couldn't think straight. If our situation at home is continually upsetting, by uncooperative children, by a nagging wife or an overbearing husband, or at work by an insensitive boss or coworker – we know the feeling. Instinctively either we 'fight to the death' to establish our side of the problem or we 'withdraw into our shell.' Is the third option engaging in a constructive alternative activity?

Did Mrs. Fraser's knowledge of the psycho-physiology of art help her deal with Bill effectively?

Jack

Does the sheer volume of facts students must learn overwhelm them?

"So I say," cried Jack, pleased with the new idea, ... "I do hate to be driven so I don't half understand, because there is no time to have things explained ... making a fellow learn eighty questions in geography [in] one day, [only to] forget them the next (From: *Jack and Jill*, by Louisa May Alcott; 1880)."[8]

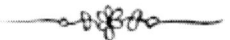

How soon we forget! Horace Mann borrowed the educational system we are using today from Prussia in the 1840s; a system intended to make managers and army officers of a literate elite. These people were already well read and well traveled. Geography was a way to increase their appreciation of where they had been. It means nothing to a boy in Idaho who has never ventured more than twenty miles from home, or to a teenaged gang member from the Bronx with even narrower travel horizons.

How often do teachers fail to take their students' backgrounds and emotional states into account?

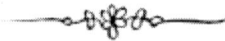

Another view of the school

Is success in school the result of hard work?

"I paid close attention to what the teachers said or stressed in the textbook and gave that back to them. I did very little homework, but did all right in school. At home I pursued my other interests, as you know."[9]

These remarks came from my stepson, Chris Tramp; he showed the same educational emphases in this second half of the century just past. Chris, of course, had his own agenda. From the age of twelve he wanted to be in the US Coast Guard and to sail as crew on the USCG's tall ship "Eagle." At the age of twelve he began learning the skills he needed to be a superb sailor. After high school he realized both dreams.

Compare his statement with the remark made by Jack in the nineteenth Century and the events I have reported about my own school experiences. Schooling can either be trivial or challenging, boring or engaging. It can also be downright cruel.

Why do most dropouts report school as "boring?"

Remarks

We have asked a whole series of questions, all of them related in some way to the emotions being experienced. May we now suggest that an important component of teaching is *compassion*?

Putting the ideas presented together, we get a picture of what I mean by compassion. It combines self-knowledge, self-awareness and self-confidence with careful observation and a willingness to view reality from the other person's point-of-view.

About two thousand years ago one of the champions of compassion put it this way, "Forgive them Father, they know not what they do." (KJV: Lu. 23.34) This problem continues today. People always do the best they can, based on what they know. Is the problem many people are facing that they do not have a deep enough understanding of their surroundings, and the people around them, to be able to respond to each other, or the environment, with compassion?

Compassion requires the ability to delay judgment, to support others' needs and desires without jeopardizing progress. It requires us to care enough to pay calm attention. It does not try to control others but encourages self-control instead.

Dr. Jay C. Powell

We can now move on to discussing how to put compassion into effective action through *cooperation*.

Are global warming and the energy crisis the result of this lack of compassionate awareness?

Chapter 2; Developing Cooperation

Having once learned that we can interrupt rage before we retaliate, we can gradually replace the rage reflex with calmness.[10]

Daniel Goleman

The purloined cap

"They now intend to take with force the things we could share with them and help them to make." (Old One, page 3.)

Before I even started school I was fitted with glasses because I was so far sighted I could not see clearly. My father realized something was wrong when I couldn't catch a ball.

We had a friend who was an optometrist who lived with his wife about a half-mile away. We sometimes visited them, using the trip as one of our regular Sunday walks.

I had been given a rubber ball that needed to be inflated through a tube. The tube could then be tied down into a laced pocket. I enjoyed blowing it up and then listening to the squeals it made as I stretched the mouth of the tube. I was playing this game the day we went to visit our family friends.

When we arrived at their house I saw the cup shaped end of a pull-down window blind lying on the porch floor. "Oh boy!" I thought, "A mouthpiece for my bagpipe." The pin fitted nicely into the tube. I tucked the ball under my arm pretending I was a piper. Just imagine the fun I had with this new toy. As I marched into our house my mother spotted the "mouthpiece" I had fashioned.

"What do you have there?" she demanded.

"It's my mouthpiece for my bagpipes."

"Where did you get it?"

"It was on the floor on the porch at the Satchwells."

"Did you ask if you could have it?"

"No."

"Then it doesn't belong to you. Take it back and apologize to them for taking it."

I was probably four years old at the time. That half-mile was the longest walk I have ever made. It was here that I learned not to steal. The "Old One" points this out as well.

Is one of our important lessons to protect others from the detrimental results of our actions?

Standing my ground

How do boys develop respect for the new kid on the block?

In 1938 our family moved from Edmonton to Lamont, a town 42 miles northeast of Edmonton. Daddy had been hired into a full-time job after several years of part-time employment during the Great Depression.

I began the second grade in a one-room school a short walk from our house.

Shortly after school started we had a heavy rainfall during one weekend. The lot behind the garage, across the street from us, was churned into huge clumps of clay that quickly dried into rock hardness. On the way home for lunch on Monday, several of the local boys decided to test the mettle of this *intruder* from the big city. They jumped on me behind the garage.

The clumps of clay made wonderful defensive weapons and I managed to hold them at bay until I could run across the street to our home. Because I defended myself so well, I became an accepted member of the mob. This was the first half of my lesson.

The boy who sat behind me in class had a habit of poking me in the back during work periods. I protested but he didn't stop. Finally, I asked my new friends to help me teach him a lesson. We waylaid him. He was overwhelmed but not seriously hurt physically.

On the other hand, although the poking ceased, he now approached me with fear. My intention was to stop an annoyance. The effect was to intimidate. I have regretted this action all my life. It was the beginning of my understanding of the importance of intention and the disastrous impact that can come from misdirected goals. Such are the consequences when we do not protect others from our actions.

Does intimidation create slaves, enemies or both? Could this be the source of terrorism?

Keep your options open
Is this yet another way to look at the birds and the bees?

I was in the sixth grade. The art teacher had given us an assignment to draw some people. I decided to draw two standing figures in two separate panels on a single page. The figure on the left was a woman in a bathing suit. The one on the right was a man dressed in the uniform of the Royal Canadian Mounted Police. My father was a "Mountie" and I was very proud of him. He told wonderful stories of the early days in western Canada.

When I was satisfied that my work was up to par, I showed my drawings to my dad. He admired them both. Then he told me the corrections I should make to the Mountie uniform. Finally he told me the errors I had made when drawing the woman, who was as shapeless as a telephone post.

He provided me with some pictures that helped me adjust my drawings. Then, he smiled in an odd way and said, "I guess it's about time I told you about the birds and the bees."

He gave me a brief explanation as to how babies were created. Then he recounted an adventure from his youth:

"I was on patrol on horseback in southern Alberta. I arrived at a rancher's house in mid afternoon. He was unloading a wagon full of hay into the loft of the barn. I offered to help him.

"'Sure, if you'll stay the night,' he offered.

"The nearest neighbor was more than an hour's ride away. I accepted the offer and picked up the second pitchfork. We both worked lustily for about an hour and the hayrack was now empty and the loft half full.

"Having worked up a sweat, we both reclined on then new-mown hay to get our breath. The softness of the hay and its pungent smell sent me into a reverie. 'It would be nice to have a beautiful woman about now.'

"'Sound like a good idea,' he replied. 'I'll send my daughter out to you.'

"Realizing that he had taken me seriously, I objected strongly to the suggestion.

"Several months later, I was investigating the stealing of some cattle. The evidence pointed to this same rancher. When she heard about my investigation, his daughter turned him in.

"I asked her why she had done so. She reminded me of the hay loft incident and said that after that her father had remarked repeatedly, while making his usual suggestions that she get married, that, 'Maybe you're not going to get married after all. You're not even good enough for a Mountie.' Can you imagine anything more devastating to a single girl?

"If I had accepted his offer, it could have compromised my ability to carry his crime to prosecution.

"Keep this situation in mind, my son. You never know what the outcome of your actions might be. Keep your options open."

My respect for him overwhelmed me at that point. Treating people with compassion was the hallmark of his character. I have been true to his advice and not had sex with anyone other than my three wives.[11]

Is this illustration of proper behavior, by showing the respect we display toward others, the best way to teach social responsibility?

Does this illustrate the need to "Protect ourselves from our own inclinations and to protect others from us?"

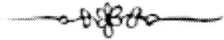

Enforcer

Is youth violence an inevitable outcome of "city-center" culture?

With the advent of World War II my father was invited to return to the Royal Canadian Mounted Police in order to release a younger man to go overseas. As a result we moved from Lamont back to Edmonton in 1939.

Because Daddy did not like driving, we bought a house that was within walking distance of his work, in the bottom cycle area of the city. Violence was common. There were occasional knife fights. Guns were not easily available in Canada. Most commonly the fights involved the use of bare fists. These fights occurred most frequently between public school children and Roman Catholic school children.

Here was where the teasing I experienced in elementary school, which I reported earlier, also occurred. My elementary school experience was a social disaster. I avoided social contact as much as I could.

By the time I reached grade seven and went to the toughest junior high school in the city, the clique divisions among students within the public school were beginning to harden into gangs.

Some of the youth in the roughest group were suspected of stealing hubcaps from luxury cars to purchase "reefers" or marijuana cigarettes.

Although I became involved in the city youth marching band and began to be more academically successful, my reputation for being an easy mark moved with me to this new school. By the time that I was in the eighth grade the tension between that group and me had become extreme.

Our school system provided shop courses one day a week. The shop classes were held in an elementary school several miles away. We convened each Friday. One such morning, their "enforcer" challenged me in a way I could no longer avoid. Early in the exchange his fist hit me squarely in the mouth and broke a tooth.

The sudden pain was reminiscent of the box end incident I related earlier. My rage erupted and I flew at him as though I were crazy. Then I saw the fear in his face. There was a flash memory of the person I tormented in Lamont.

My rage broke. I stepped back. My adversary was almost unconscious. He had to be supported by his friends in order to get into the industrial arts shop.

It took me the better part of the morning for my breathing to return to normal. Wisely the teacher asked no questions. I was ecstatic. I had broken my rage in full bloom.

To my surprise my victory over the gang's champion made me their new enforcer. For the balance of the year I was expected to settle disputes within and between gangs. My approach was to try to resolve these issues without violence. Was it my reputation as a fighter that made this non-violent approach successful?

The following year we moved to Bermuda. I still don't know how long this approach could be maintained in that setting. More recently my attempts toward win-win solutions almost always have been successful.

Do we need to conquer the rage reflex in order to find inner peace, or does finding inner peace conquer the rage reflex?

A bargain with infinity
To whom is heaven open?

It was now 1945. My sister's recurring rheumatic fever caused her doctor to suggest a change of climate. My father was a Certified Health Inspector. He used these skills to seek an alternative place for us to live.

We wound up moving to Bermuda. We were advised to arrange for Grace's and my education on our own. We enrolled in correspondence courses from Alberta before we left and withdrew from the public school system. The fact that we were being schooled at home meant that we had very little contact with other young people our own age.

I don't remember what Grace did for friends. We did have some contacts through the local church. In my case, I developed a friendship with the son of an American civilian worker at Fort Bell. This was a United States Army Air Force base on St. David's Island, across the harbor from St. George's Island where we were living.

He was of the Roman Catholic persuasion. I was Protestant. Along with many swimming trips, we shared a variety of boy's games and board games. We enjoyed each other's company.

We also had some interesting discussions. One such discussion was about whether only Catholics went to heaven. After many sessions, sometimes with reference to Scriptures, we reached an impasse. We found no basis, other than doctrine or personal opinion, to answer this question.

We ended the issue with a typical teenager solution. We made a bargain. We agreed that whoever passed away first should look for something close to the Pearly Gates. If that person found a *pear tree with four apples on it*, Protestants also had access to heaven.[12] We must then find a way to get this message back to the survivor.

Unlike the rancor that drove the battle between Protestants and Catholics in Edmonton, we were able to arrive at this resolution in good humor. Finding the ability to disagree with humor bypassed the rage reflex and helped to protect us from each other.

On the other hand, I had much more difficulty with group social skills by lacking contacts at this age.

Dr. Jay C. Powell

Are we entitled to carry our version of the "Truth" to others by the Book, the sword, intimidation, persuasion or only by our life-success example?

Getting accepted

How does a teenager connect with a closed social group?

We stayed in Bermuda for nearly two years. I took my ninth and tenth grades using correspondence courses.

We then moved to Roanoke, Virginia where I began the eleventh grade. I don't know whether it was southern hospitality or something about me, but I seemed to be accepted immediately in Jefferson High School.

I recall overhearing a conversation about me on a stairway. "Did you say he came from Bermuda?"

"Yes."

"He's got a good tan but he looks just like us!"

Within a week or so, I had a girl friend and had settled into my classes quite easily.

Family financial problems however had us on the road again. This time we moved to Enumclaw, Washington. My acceptance into this other community was very different this time. The social groups were well established and I was an outsider once again.

One of my classes was the mixed chorus. I have a reasonably good baritone voice. One day several of us decided to practice one of our songs during the lunch hour. In this particular song, I had the lead. Soon I found that the others had stopped singing. I was doing solos and a crowd was gathering around me.

I was flattered when some of them began making requests. I obliged. Soon I was entertaining my fellow students at lunchtime on a regular basis. I made a point of learning many of the popular songs of the day. I seemed to be gaining recognition. But I was not being invited to any of their social gatherings.

At the spring dance there was a "kissing booth." I watched the booth for a while. Some were getting physical kisses and some candy kisses. I decided to pay the fee to see what happened. A crowd collected around me as I walked toward the booth. You guessed it. The girl gave me some candy kisses. The crowd had a good laugh at my expense.

Apparently my efforts to become accepted had been unsuccessful. Was this the result of lack of social skills caused by home schooling? Was it a result of the socially closed nature of the community? How do we develop respect for diversity in a "closed" community?

How do people succeed in establishing healthy social skills without guided practice?

Dealing with death

Are there times when students' needs are more important than the usual teaching activities?

It was my first year teaching in this particular small high school. I was finding this Monday morning's lessons very frustrating. The first period had gone poorly. Most of the students had not completed their homework in business practice from the Friday before.

After several false starts I gave them the period to work through the weekend's assignments and went around the classroom checking their work. There were murmurs all over the room behind my back. The assignment saw little or no progress.

Now in the second period, the math class was going no better. "What is the first step we must take to solve this equation, Gary?" I asked. Silence was my reply — an unusual response for Gary.

"Okay, look at the list on the side board. What does it say?"

"Collect like terms," Gary replied in a small thin voice.

"Let's try to do this problem then." I pointed to the equation he had written on the front board. I got no response.

"All right," I sighed with exasperation. "What's going on here? Please, won't someone tell me?"

Linda took a deep breath; "It's about Jessie!" she gasped and burst into tears.

"Who's Jessie?"

Frank chimed in, "You weren't here last year when she graduated so you don't know her. She was the student president last year. She was the most popular girl in the school. *She committed suicide last night!*"

With this revelation I abandoned my math lesson and began helping them to talk about this highly emotional issue in their lives. What would other teachers have done? The easiest way would have been to carry on with the lesson and pretend that the expressed and upsetting event did not exist.

Is stepping forward with effective help, as needed, the way teachers earn respect?

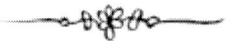

Yearbook

How do we get students to work together for their mutual benefit?

"May we talk to you, sir?" There were three senior students at my door.

"Of course," I replied as I opened the door wide as they crowded through it.

"We heard that Mr. Simonsen, the Principal, has cancelled the yearbook this year," Tessa explained.

"That's what he asked us to do at our staff meeting before school started this fall," I agreed.

"Well we seniors, and several juniors, really want a yearbook as a keepsake of our high school classmates and activities," Bob interjected. "It's particularly important for us because we will graduate this year. If we don't have a yearbook, we'll have nothing to look back upon."

"Our friends and our activities are part of what has kept us in school," Muriel added.

"What can we do to get the yearbook reinstated?" Tessa's voice trembled and her eyes glistened with the beginnings of tears.

"Let's take Mr. Simonsen at his word. He has two concerns," I explained. "First, that enthusiasm wanes quickly and too often the yearbook winds up as a teacher's chore instead of a valuable student project. The other was that the emphasis upon social matters was interfering with academics objectives. Is this the picture you have?"

"Last year Mrs. Christiansen, the journalism teacher, took it over in mid January when she raised objections about some of the editorial content."

"I don't want to get into the past politics. If this criticism is true, you students have some fence mending to do," I remarked.

"What do you suggest?"

"We are already into the third week of the fall term. Our first basketball game was last Friday evening. Can you get a picture or two from that game? Have you started setting up your editorial board? Have you begun to seek advertising? Show Mr. Simonsen that this year is different and that you mean business by your actions. You might get him to change his mind."

Their enthusiasm for getting to work on it drove their anxiety and hostility away. They left my room with bright faces and eager steps, exchanging plans as they went.

About an hour later, Mr. Simonsen called me to his office.

"What's this about you encouraging our seniors to set up a yearbook? I told everyone at the staff meeting that I didn't want one this year. I'm retiring at the end of this year and I want as hassle-free a year as I can get."

"You said that teachers wound up doing all the work. I figured that if I told them the truth and challenged them to take more responsibility the results would be hassle free for you and a good learning experience for them. After all, a high school yearbook is a lifelong souvenir."

"They asked that you be their staff advisor," Mr. Simonsen countered determinedly. "You've exceeded your authority. I am adamant that there will be no yearbook this year. I want you to stand up in front of the assembly on Friday morning and tell the entire school that, as a first year teacher, you are too busy to be staff advisor. There will be no yearbook."

"I'm sorry you feel that way, Mr. Simonsen," I stood firm in my resolve. "However, I'm not going to destroy any respect I might have earned from the students in this school by taking the blame for *your* decision. If there is to be no yearbook -- you tell them!"

With that remark I left the sputtering Mr. Simonsen seated behind his desk and returned to my classroom.

Needless to say, I did not teach in that school system the following year. On the other hand, the teacher who supervised them praised the cooperation of these students showed to produce the yearbook.

Does helping people to surmount unreasonable demands from people in authority, without adverse consequences on those who have a reasonable position, open important doors to the future?

What is the role of such extra-curricular activities in teaching life's skills?

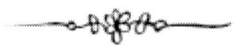

The dropout

What does it mean to fail in school?

"May I talk to you, Mr. Powell?" Bobby's unkempt long blonde hair, the earring in his left ear, and the stubble that was not yet a beard was a source of irritation to many of his teachers.

"Of course, what is your problem?"

"It's almost Christmas time and I'm thinking about quitting school."

"You're in Grade 11 aren't you?" I asked, "Why quit with a year and a half to go?"

"I'm bored out of my skull in most classes.

I looked at Bobby's marks records. "You're not doing very well in Bookkeeping 10, I see. Mostly you are not getting your assignments turned in."

"I'm enjoying your class more than most. But my life in school and outside of it is a mess."

"You'll get a mark of 35 in bookkeeping for the year so far. How are you doing in your other subjects?"

"About the same ... or worse," Bobby avoided my eyes with this confession.

"It's possible that you could get more out of your life, earning $35 a week as a janitor than 35 marks in a half year at school. Do you want to say anything more about the mess your life is in?"

"No."

"Then, just one word of advice, keep your options open," I suggested. "I left high school with failing grades. After a series of nowhere jobs and stretches of unemployment, I went back to school. I'm now working on my Ph.D. and teaching half time to pay for my schooling."

"Really, I didn't know that?" Bobby said looking astonished at what he just heard.

"I'm only telling you this because I recognized your intelligence. You are wasting your time here. If you find yourself wasting yourself in the kinds of work you can get without your diploma, you can always change your mind about the value of an education."

Two years later, I met Bobby in a drugstore and he told me that he had returned to school after being unemployed for most of the eighteen months since our last encounter. He had had time to evaluate the circumstances surrounding his schooling and certainly felt that returning to class was the right thing for him to do. I shall add here that Bobby was not only doing well in all subjects, but seemed to enjoy being back in school.

Is promoting change in attitude an important way to help people to help themselves?

Cheating

What is the role of the school in teaching about socially unacceptable behavior?

This event comes from the writing portion of the of the same classroom program in which Brian did so well in reading. I had the class produce a written magazine weekly. We started with each student filling a quarter-page on Mondays with a creative writing piece. These pages were then duplicated for distribution to the class members – two sheets printed on both sides – on Tuesdays. On Thursdays as a group we marked each composition.[13]

Initially, there was a 10-point maximum for any composition. During the last week of September, after getting two thirds of the way through the class, one composition stood out as being very far above the rest.

"What are we to do?" Sam asked. "If this composition by Harry is to be given a 10, we will have to lower the marks on the 9 samples we have already marked!"

"Are there any other options?" I asked. In the painful silence that followed they all looked at me pleadingly.

"How about leaving the others marked out of 10 and mark this one out of 15?"

"Can we do that?" Tracey wondered.

"Why not?" I replied. "What's so sacred about 10 marks?"

They were all much relieved.

About a week later we were, once again, marking compositions when the following problem arose...

"There's no question about it," Tracy insisted. "This is the best story we have ever looked at." The rest of the class indicated their agreement.

"Why not give this story 20 points out of a possible 20?" I asked. They all agreed.

"But …" sputtered Harry. His embarrassment showed. Harry's story received only 9 points and was in fifth place.

"What's the problem, Harry?" I asked.

"I wrote the story that Sam is claiming to be his. It's my story that is now earning 20 points!" Harry admitted sheepishly. "In fact, I wrote all the stories for the class today!"

"As if that ain't bad enough," Pauline protested. "I'm usually third, and the story that is supposed to be mine is in ninth place." With sixteen in the class, her score had dropped from the top quarter to below the middle.

"Please explain." I did my best to conceal a knowing smile.

Ruby spoke up, "You let us give fifteen points instead of ten for Harry's story last week. It was so much better than everyone else's that we would all have had to lower our scores to credit Harry's properly."

"Yeah," Bill added, "so we figured that we would all get better marks if we had Harry write all our stories. We all brought Harry's stories into the room and copied them for our weekly assignment."

"And now," I mused, "You see that even the person who sometimes produces the best stories does not write every piece with the same level of quality."

"Yes," Freddie continued. "But more than this, some of us usually get better marks than the ones that Harry's stories earned for us."

"Worst of all," Harry groaned, "the story I kept for myself was not considered the best one this time."

"Let me ask you two questions." I now took on the mediator role. "First, is it reasonable to think that writers will always produce stories of consistent quality?"

"I guess not," Mabel remarked. "I love Will Durant's stories, but I like some better than others." The rest of them agreed, with several giving examples.

"When we work on editing skills later, we will see how we can improve the quality of a story, but even then, our writing will remain inconsistent," I explained.

"Second, if you let other students write your stories for you, how are you going to learn to write better?"

"Did you set us up?" Harry asked.

"No, you set yourselves up. Eventually, the temptation to take credit for someone else's work comes to all of us. The sooner the better because, as we have just seen, everyone loses when we replace achievement with pretense." When this lesson is learned, people can start to learn how to protect themselves from themselves.

Is schooling intended to be a training ground for effective living?

Working together with compassion

How do we create opportunities for helping others?[14]

In our opening "council" meeting [of 22 high school students on a mountain retreat], they each stated what nourishment they hoped to receive during the next five days and the nourishment they hoped to give. But then one of the students broke down. "I want so much to give my love to Felicia—I know we don't have much time left, and there's so much I want to tell her …" [her outburst triggered similar responses from other students.]

[Felicia, a fellow student, who was dying of bone cancer, was not present at the council meeting. She came to the retreat shortly thereafter and participated as fully as she could with her crutches, avidly maintaining her independence all the while.]

[The time came for the closing ceremonies on a beautiful spot downhill from the meeting rooms. The teacher agreed before she realized that Felicia would not be able to navigate the hill.]

Suddenly I [as the teacher] have an idea. I approach a group of boys hanging out together and lower my voice. "Would one of you guys be willing to carry Felicia down the hill if we need you?" Two young men volunteer immediately. One—Jimmy—is probably our tallest, strongest student. He also has a reputation outside this class for being a good-for-nothing cut-up. He has been a disappointment to his father, who had raised him and an older brother, who was a star athlete and academic success. But in our work in this class, Jimmy has proved himself trustworthy, even of this delicate task. Since the first day of the semester, Jimmy has seen this class as a place that was safe enough to expose his pain, his longing, his wisdom. Our group has loved and acknowledged the beauty of this struggling young man.

I ask Jimmy and Will, the other volunteer, to go inside. Then I ask Felicia and her best friend, May, to join me for a moment in our meeting room.

"Felicia, you have a choice to make. The walk we're about to take is too far for you to do on crutches. Would you be comfortable letting either Jimmy or Willy carry you on his shoulders? It would mean a lot to these guys and to all of us if you would accept our help." Our days together have made it easier for her to face the truth, to let go, and to let us in. But still she hesitates, she cannot decide.

"Do it, Licia!" May says gleefully. "You can ride on Jimmy, and I'll ride on Will. We'll be side by side, riding in style. It will feel like a parade!"

Felicia's eyes light up with a girlish joy I had seen only in photos from before the cancer. "Yes!" she shouts, high-fiving May, and then Will and Jimmy. "Let's do it—it will be a blast!"

The rest of us tromp behind them down the hill as Felicia and May ride like prom queens on the shoulders of these proud young boys-becoming-men. They are carrying her for all of us—allowing her to surrender to our love and care.

In our hearts we all know that this is truly a moment of "passage" for Felicia—and for all of us. Despite our continuing hopes and prayers that this young senior will make it to graduation, we sense that a much more challenging graduation awaits her.

A month later, on her 18th birthday, Felicia died.

What is the role of the heart in academic education?

Transitions

Can watching a loved one die be a beautiful experience?

As with Frances, I was guided into my second marriage. We were doing church work together. During this time we came to a mutual realization of a deep link between us and we decided to marry.

Our marriage was a very good one as well. Many of her friends observed that Mary, whose life had been very difficult, "blossomed" during our relationship. My friends made similar observations about me. Being a Canadian of British background, I tended to be reserved. With her help I came out of myself.

We had a bit more than twelve wonderful years together. The last four of which were marred by Mary's contracting lung cancer. Boosting her immune system worked for a while, but the cancer spread to her brain. The Doctors took her off chemotherapy, started radiation treatments and put her on steroids to keep her brain from swelling.

The steroids made her hyper and eventually burned her out.

Our last vacation together was a delightful schooner cruise along the coast of Maine, just before the radiation treatments began. She was at the best she had been in the last couple of years.

When chemotherapy was resumed it didn't seem to be working. We went to Zion, Illinois to the Cancer Treatment Centers of America clinic there. Their service was exceptionally fine. However after two treatments with a new drug, that didn't work either and we returned home in mid March of 2006.

At that point she decided not to continue therapy. She began to fail very rapidly. She did not have the strength, upon our arrival at home to climb the five steps from the front door to our living level in our bi-level house. She sat on the stairs and I lifted her bodily, one step at a time.

I called a friend who was a professional care-giver. She took one look at Mary and took me aside to say, "You know that she is dying."

"I know," I replied. "I guess I'd better call our family physician and Hospice."

She was able to get out of bed for about three days and lucid for about ten. I slept in her room at the hospice center.

I contacted all her children and step children to tell them the situation.

Two of her sons and their families lived about sixty miles away. Chris and Paul visited her regularly. Mark her oldest son took off from work in Denver and came as soon as he could.

Her step-daughter and family lived in Jacksonville, Florida. After a marathon drive, they arrived about 9 PM on March 23rd, 2006. This date incidentally was Chris Tramp's birthday.

Although her eyes were closed and her breathing somewhat ragged, she twitched one eyebrow when the Florida party arrived. And so her entire family, including the grandchildren, was at her bedside when she passed at 6:04 AM on March 24th. It was like her not to want to spoil Chris's birthday.

Her final breath was peaceful and gentle, as her life with me had been. Her ashes were distributed on the site of the homestead where she had grown up, as she requested and with the permission of the current owners of the property.

But this story is not finished at this point, as we will see, in Chapter 5.

Do relationships with the ones we love end with death?

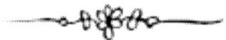

Cooperation

What is cooperation?

Jason Cook sighed deeply. He was uncertain where to turn next. For several weeks he and a group of his college friends had been meeting to work with the spiritual development lessons from the Association for Research and Enlightenment (A. R. E.) as built upon the readings of Edgar Cayce. "Maybe Dr. Powell, my Psych. Prof. can help?" he mused.

The office door was open. "Dr. P.," Jason asked, "Would you visit our discussion group? We seem to have reached a dead end and I suggested to our group that you might be able to help us out." The young man was a teacher in training who was in my leadership seminar.

"Of course," I replied, intrigued by the invitation. "When and where are you meeting?"

Jason went on to explain that his group was meeting every Tuesday evening in the lounge of his dorm and that they were working with some study material from the A. R. E.

At the appointed time, the group gathered in a quiet corner of the lounge.

With the introductions over, their discussion began.

"What can you tell us about the concept of cooperation, Dr. P.?" Jason asked.

"I'd sooner hear what your friends have to say before I say anything," I replied.

Clarence spoke first. "We are hung up on the concept of cooperation," he explained.

"My girlfriend is telling me I'm being uncooperative when I refuse to go to her parents' house with her over a long weekend," Jason began.

"Well, my mother says I'm being uncooperative when I don't clean up my room," Susan chimed in.

"My Dad expects me to carry my share of the yard work," Bill added, "even when I'm loaded with assignments. I feel guilty if I don't work with him because he has a bad back and the work in the yard is difficult for him.

"You don't know the half of it," Clarence insisted, "my folks are up in arms because I switched from pre-med to theater arts. They are accusing me of throwing my life away."

"How do you feel about it?" I asked.

"There's something … I don't know … when I'm on stage … portraying a character … it's like I'm alive for the first time in my life!"

"I get cold feet when my boyfriend tries to make out with me," Sarah added. "He says I don't love him or I would let him. That's not true. But is he simply trying to take advantage?"

"I'm chewed out frequently by my Mother," Linda put in, "when I'm helping at the store and I miss some detail that she would not have missed."

The discussion continued in this manner until all six of them had expressed their opinions.

"What do all of these complaints you have been making have in common?" I inquired at the first lull in the conversation.

"They are all situations were we feel hard done by," Larry offered.

"That goes without saying," I replied. "Is there anything else?"

Bill scratched his head. "It seems to me that they are all expectations from someone else."

"What sort of someone else?" I asked.

"Parents, teachers, employers . . . people in authority." Frank grinned at his insight.

"Now you're on track!" I encouraged. "What else?"

"I guess," Harry blurted, "We are talking about being upset by being told what to do."

"Is this how you define 'cooperation'?" I leaned forward encouragingly.

"If doing as you are expected is not cooperation, then what is?" Susan asked.

"Before we try to answer that question, I hear you saying something else," I said. "This other part of your discussion is the issue of trust. Either you feel that others do not trust you, or you do not trust someone else."

"Well, that is certainly true in my case." Clarence nodded his agreement.

"How can you cooperate with someone where there is a lack of trust?" Nathan asked.

"But you cannot trust everyone all the time," Jason objected. "I trust Herbert to help me with statistics. I'm not so sure that I would trust him with my girlfriend though."

"Okay, can we agree that trust is not absolute? When can we trust others anyway?"

"We can trust people in areas of recognized accomplishments or skills," Susan suggested.

"That's not good enough," Frank objected. "The person must do what they agreed to do."

"Are you saying that you are being cooperative when you are doing something someone else wants you to do?" I continued. "Is this what you really mean?"

"I hadn't thought about it that way before," Sarah mused. "I guess we have been thinking in a wrong direction."

"Not necessarily. Cooperation is often used as a synonym for obedience. Is there another way of looking at it?"

"Well," Jason remarked thoughtfully, "if I said that Herbert and I were cooperating when he helped me with my statistics and I proofread his themes."

"Let me ask you all, this question," I redirected the discussion. "Is there a common goal in the service exchanges Jason has just described?"

"They are both helping each other to do better in their studies," Frank suggested.

"But it won't help Jason in the long run if Herbert does his statistics for him. Nor will it help Herbert if Jason doesn't show him why something needs changing," Susan speculated.

"Now you are on to it," I encouraged. "Cooperation, not only must have a common goal, the exchange must be of mutual benefit as part of a mutual agreement. It must add to the capabilities of each as well to provide for greater success for both than each could have achieved alone."

"I guess we haven't been talking about cooperation after all," Sarah smiled. "Can you work with us, Dr. P., to help us become more cooperative?"

The conversation took a new turn. Soon they were defining cooperation in terms of willingly sharing a project to help each other, or exchanging skills, or planning and working together toward a common goal; willingly among the group by mutual agreement.

"But are we not in competition with each other?" I asked. "Isn't everyone our enemy?"

There was a chorus of "No" to that remark.

"We aren't enemies with our friends!" Susan objected.

"Then when, where, and how do we learn to behave differently? Isn't that what the A. R. E. material is getting at?"

There was general agreement at this suggestion and the discussion then turned to the development of cooperative skills. Here we see the leader working toward helping others to help each other. Acquiring this skill is an important part of learning compassion.

Is developing cooperative skills a way to acknowledge diversity?

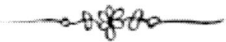

We now move from the emotional aspects of development to the intellectual ones. These will be the topic for Chapter 3.

Chapter 3: Developing Comprehension

The very idea of freedom carries with it the obligations of ignorance and the rewards of understanding.[15]

Ernest Holmes

Lawn mower

What do we do when something doesn't work?

I was probably about four years of age. I know it was before I started school. My parents had given me a Mechano˙ set for Christmas. It was now summer and I enjoyed working with my Dad in our garden and raking up the grass behind his reel lawn mower. I was still too small and light to push it myself.

Later that afternoon I got out my construction set and built a model of a reel mower. With considerable pride I took my model to show my Mother. She noticed that the way I had built it the cutting reel would not turn. I had struggled with this problem as I built it.

Feeling ashamed but challenged, I went back to the set and rebuilt the mower so that the reel would turn inside the frame. I figured out how to solve it without help. Mother complimented me on my ability to fix the problem but my greatest compliment came from my own satisfaction of having resolved it for myself.

What do parents or teachers do today that makes such intellectual challenges possible?

Failing Grade 2

My mother looked angry. She dropped the letter on the dining room table and turned to Daddy. "Can you imagine?" she snarled. "Miss Parslow wants to keep James in the second grade for another year. She says that he is not reading at the second grade level and that he is fidgety and would sooner draw pictures than do his work."

"Well," my dad replied, "he is young. He was only five when he started school. "

"No way! He's not stupid. This would put him a year behind when Grace starts school. We need to do something."

"I'll talk to Mr. Ross, the principal. Maybe he has a suggestion."

Subsequently, Mr. Ross invited me to his office. I had to walk a half mile to the building where Mr. Ross had his office because the first and second grades were in a separate building, a one-room school.

"Sit down," he said, pointing to a chair facing him beside the desk. He proceeded to ask me a series of questions. I must have done all right because he modified Miss Parslow's decision and arranged that I be given a "conditional pass" to Grade 3. This decision meant that if I did poorly I would be put back into Grade 2.

That fall, however, the family moved from Lamont to Edmonton, so I stayed in Grade 3 in Alex Taylor School. Unfortunately, I didn't do much better in any of the subsequent elementary school grades. Reading remained painfully difficult. My spelling was atrocious, and I would still sooner draw pictures than do written assignments.

Besides, I usually understood what the teacher said the first time she said it. The other two or three repetitions were a waste of my time. Why not draw? It was more fun. When my sister started school that fall, she was immediately at the top of her class.

Why was I doing so poorly in school when my sister Grace was doing so well?

A new outlook

Was this the beginning of the new me?

The picture changed dramatically following my awakening in the sixth grade. The following September I went to junior high school. I was terrible at arithmetic because it didn't make any sense to me. It was a collection of incomprehensible rules. Besides, I had difficulty remembering my number facts. I would count on my fingers to get the number I needed.

Algebra was a very different story. It had patterns to it that I could understand very clearly. Also I was now aware that I could think. That meant I had a new confidence in my schoolwork.

With my father proofreading my compositions because I was still a terrible speller, my marks improved from borderline to middle scores. I later realized that part of the reason why I was a poor speller was that he proofread my work. He meant the best for me and I honor him for that. But I have now realized that learning is intensely personal and can be done only by the learner.

Does excessive support, from the sidelines, even when well intentioned, make learning unnecessary?

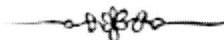

A "Practical" joke

How might unanticipated outcome teach unexpected lessons?

Much of what I remember about this time suggests that I was a normal bratty teenager. I recall the incident when I found a large toad under a hedge beside the sidewalk while walking to school. I put it carefully into my book bag. Miss Laramie was a substitute for our homeroom teacher. She was mean-mouthed and grouchy. My fellow classmates despised her.

At school I put the toad into the desk drawer on top of the attendance book. When she opened the drawer to take attendance book out it hopped. She screamed, jumped to the top of the desk yelling, "Get that beast out of here!" She pulled her skirt over her head and went into hysterics. What as sight that was! The class was doubled over with laughter.

The principal came in response to the commotion, helped her down and led her gently away. She did not return to that school. We had a number of substitutes who were little better before Mr. James arrived to take us in hand. They never did find out who put the toad into the desk.

My feelings were a strange mixture of satisfaction because of the gratitude my fellow class members expressed to me and shame for having terrified Miss Laramie so dreadfully. When I became the enforcer I remembered this event and tried to act accordingly.

Is this how we learn from our mistakes?

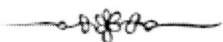

Learning how to learn

What situations make supreme effort in school worthwhile?

As mentioned earlier, our family migrated to Bermuda in 1945. My sister's recurring rheumatic fever led her doctor to suggest a change of climate to avoid winter colds. My father was a Certified Health Inspector. He used these skills to seek an alternative place for us to live.

He received a letter from Dr. Henry Wilkinson, the Chief Medical Officer for the government of Bermuda. Dr. Wilkinson offered Daddy a job in Bermuda. He pointed out however that the schooling in Bermuda was not very good.

With this latter comment in mind Grace and I quit attending Edmonton's schools in October of 1945, enrolling instead in the Alberta Correspondence School courses. This was when we finalized the details of our move. These courses were designed to provide education to isolated communities. I was in the ninth grade and Grace in the fifth.

At that time the Alberta education system had province-wide government examinations in Grades 9 and 12. I needed to pass seven Grade 9 exams, which were tightly prescheduled for June, and take two other courses in order to enter an academic high school program from Alberta.

We were to fly to Hamilton, Bermuda from New York City late in December. Our household effects were to be crated by a mover in Edmonton and would follow us by freighter. This turn of affairs created a huge problem, especially for me.

Because we were to go to Bermuda by plane, we had to leave most of our belongings in Edmonton, including our textbooks and course materials. These were to be packed by a moving company to follow us later. Our household effects did not arrive until February.

The program from the Alberta Correspondence Schools was organized into 20 lessons; two a month for the year. I was required to complete at least 16 of them to qualify for the finals. This meant that I had about 70 lessons to complete in 75 days.

The arithmetic of this problem suggested a lesson a day, five days a week. I would be doing two weeks' work in one course each day. Although there were no similar finals for the fifth grade, Grace agreed to follow the same work schedule.

The program required reading text or performing small projects and science experiments and answering questions. We then mailed our answers to the Correspondence School Branch offices in Edmonton, where they were marked, commented upon and returned. The turn around time was usually at least two weeks, which meant that I would be working on the second lesson after the one I just received back. The comments, suggestions and error corrections would be coming in late for my continuing the program.

Having taught myself how to read following my insight in the sixth grade, I now had to add text analysis to text interpretation skills. The comments from the teachers were sometimes helpful. More frequently than not, I figured out on my own how to correct the errors because I usually started my next two-week set of lessons before the commentary returned.

It was a wonderful challenge! We divided our workdays into three units, morning, afternoon and evening. We swam every day that the weather was decent, choosing the time of the high tide. We did our work on the other two time blocks.

When the lesson was done, our day was done. Soon, our weekends were free. I found myself learning with increasing speed as the weeks went by. I finished the course requirements in time and did better on the exams than my previous history would have predicted. I had learned how to learn.

We continued with correspondence courses the following year. I particularly enjoyed Latin and mathematics in grade ten. Otherwise, I loafed through the tenth grade, figuring that I had a full year this time. I had worked hard enough in my ninth grade year. Also, Alberta's regulations did not permit taking more than one school year's work in a calendar year. Had I been permitted, I believe I could easily have completed both the tenth and eleventh grades in one year.

I now was a quite different student from the day when I squeaked by in the second grade. I was still a slow reader. I had to take frequent breaks when reading because, even when I found it absorbing, reading was very tiring. Reading for more than an hour at a time would put me to sleep.

Is learning how to learn a critical personal skill for school success?

Linking to the community

Does the school need to be isolated from daily life?

One of the assignments I gave to my Business Practice classes was comparative shopping. I arranged with the local supermarket that they would let my students get some information from the store.

The students were asked to find at least one product from every continent except Antarctica, to compare price to size in costs per ounce, and to look for unhealthy ingredients on the labels. For the cost per ounce, they had to find at least one item where the larger item was more expensive than a smaller one.

I also asked them to take in a recipe with them and price out the ingredients.

In all, they had a worksheet with 20 questions on it that were designed to help them become more knowledgeable shoppers.

Is this a good way to get the community involved in the school and the students in school involved in the community?

Spares and strikes

How does self-competition affect school success?

While I was in Enumclaw I began going to the local ten-pin bowling alley for recreation. There was a sign on the bulletin board asking for pinsetters. This was a chance for me to make a little pocket money so I applied and was hired on the spot.

It was heavy work and required speed as well as strength. The bowlers did not like waiting for the pins to be set.

I picked up the pins that had been knocked over with each ball, placing them into the setting machine. I would then return the ball along the track that took it back to the bowlers. Each bowler had two tries to knock down all the pins. After that I needed to reset the pins for the next bowler by pressing the lever on the setting rack. It dropped to the alley to set the pins. The rack released them and rose to the rest position when I let the lever go.

I would arrive shortly after school was out, having had a quick supper. Often there were few bowlers this early so I could bowl a few lines of ten pins just for fun. The boss gave me a discount for my bowling if I set my own pins.

Bowling was a real joy for me. I did not try for high scores. Instead I tried to create difficult combinations of pins with the first ball and to take the rest of them out with the second ball. I kept a record of my ridiculously low scores to show how much I owed.

After several months I became quite good at this self-competitive game. I set increasingly difficult tasks and worked progressively to achieve them. It takes considerable skill to deliberately leave pins 5 and 10 standing while knocking down all the rest.

After this experience I decided not to take up golf as that might have become an obsession, taking more of my time than I might be willing to spend.

Is self-competition the best way to learn?

My ice cream summer

What is the best way for a high school student to find a summer job?

Our family moved from Enumclaw, Washington back to Edmonton Alberta at the end of the 1947 - '48 school year. Daddy had gone ahead to find work with the City of Edmonton and had bought us a house.

Schooling in Washington State ended early in June, whereas in Alberta it ended three weeks later. This was a good time for me to find summer employment before the high-school students' rush.

At my father's suggestion I went to the Canadian government employment office to find work. The employing officer interviewed me, found my interest in chemistry and sent me to a job in a feed mill. From pin setting I was a fairly strong 18 year-old who weighed 165 lbs.

My job at the feed mill was to fill a fabric bag with 198 lbs. of feed from a hopper. I had to make sure that this weight was correct on the scale under the hopper. I then had to lift the bag from the scale to a conveyor. This conveyor then drew the bag under a sewing machine that closed the bag. The bag then slid down a chute to the storage and loading area.

In spite of my physical strength, the bags were far too heavy for me. I spilled the third bag. That was the end of my experience working in a feed mill.

Back at the employment office I was sent to a chemical plant to make an arsenic-based weed killer. This job involved more "chemistry." I was to mix several chemicals in a big vat. I would then drain the mixture into 55-gallon steel drums for shipment, clean out the vat and start all over again. The arsenic came in 350 lb. wooden barrels but there was a chain hoist to lift them.

I took one look at the job and said, "Thanks, but no thanks."

At this point I carefully reviewed the "Help Wanted" ads in the newspaper. Most of them required experience on the job. Reading between the lines, I decided that employers listed jobs with the government employment office that they could not fill in any other way.

I needed a new strategy. I made a list of all the things I might like on a job. One of the things I put on the list was, "All the ice cream I can eat." I then looked in the telephone book for distributors of ice cream. A local dairy manufactured this commodity, so I hopped on my bicycle and rode to their plant.

The manager invited me into his office. "Were you sent here by the government employment office?"

"No."

"Are you looking for full time employment, or only for the summer?"

"Summer only," I replied.

"What made you choose City Dairy?"

I told him what I had done. He laughed and said, "I like your attitude young man. Can you start at 8 o'clock Monday morning?"

"Yes."

I worked there until Labor Day when the fall term began at the local high school.

My first job was as a "butter printer." This meant that I was to feed 30 pound chunks of butter from the storage cooler into the hopper of a machine.

The machine put one-pound wrappers onto a large circular table. It then squeezed one pound of butter through a rectangular spout and cut it off with a piano-wire slicer. The cube dropped onto the wrapper on the rotating table where little arms folded the paper around the cube and pushed it off onto a conveyor where two women hand-packed it into 50 lb. waxed boxes. One of the women periodically put a package of butter onto a trip scale to make sure that the package was exactly one pound. I found the machine fascinating to watch as I ran it.

It was fast work, but not very hard. I had a quart of ice cream along with my lunch every day and I had a ball! The three of us who ran the machine kidded and joked around. I heard all about family issues in the intimate way that women talk about such things.

My skin became very smooth and soft from handling all that butter.

When the regular butter-printer operator returned from an extended leave, I moved to the churn room where I helped make the butter. Two men staffed this operation. It was "men's talk." here. I heard about hunting and fishing expeditions, about athletic competitions and about sons learning to shoot or to ride bicycles.

Finally I was transferred to the egg-grading station in another building. Here there was no ice cream and I was stacking 30 dozen wooden crates of eggs six high. This presented a problem because I had broken my elbow playing football in Roanoke and my right arm was not always secure. Fortunately the fall school term was soon to begin so I stuck it out to Labor Day without serious mishap. Except for the egg-grading station, these jobs were most enjoyable.

Is this a good way to self-create employment opportunities?

Classroom antics

How do school systems compare?

This time we were living in the west end of Edmonton, close to public transportation so that my father did not need to drive a car to work. In his opinion, when public officials, such as health inspectors or police officers used automobiles, they separated themselves from the people they were hired to serve. My dad had been a Mountie before the Great Depression. He had patrolled a large section of Southern Alberta on horseback. His view of his role was that, to do his job well, he needed to be a respected servant of the community.

We now lived close to the wealthier part of town and the sons and daughters of the local establishment attended the high school where I would be going. The atmosphere of this school was very different from the city-center junior high school I attended before we moved to Bermuda three years earlier.

I had already taken chemistry in Enumclaw. However Alberta required two years of chemistry, the first year being inorganic chemistry and the second year being organic chemistry. The Enumclaw course covered both topics in one year. I had already done quite well in Enumclaw so that my time, though the course was somewhat interesting, was largely wasted.

My advanced algebra teacher was a delight. She gave a weekly test. If we passed it with 80% or better, we were invited to aid students who were having difficulties. I learned a lot about teaching mathematics as a peer tutor. When not helping others, our time was our own, as long as we kept our scores up and didn't disturb anyone.

Although she didn't explicitly teach us how to use the textbook to teach ourselves, I figured out how to do this on my own. In this way I maintained my grades by teaching myself the mathematical skills I needed. This was the model I borrowed and adapted in my high school and college math teaching. I enjoyed her course very much.

My trigonometry teacher was a sarcastic bore. I spent the year trying to avoid doing any work and he spent the year trying to catch me without my work done. For the most part, I would simply take the text to the board when he asked me to solve a problem and work it for the first time in front of the class. I did not often get the answer wrong.

As they had been for the ninth grade, the provincial government set the final examinations for the twelfth grade courses. I was less confident about trigonometry than algebra at the end of the year.

This is why I copied all the formulas into the center of my booklet of mathematics tables I was allowed to use to help with the final exam. The questions were simple enough that I didn't need this crib to make an 82%. I felt guilty having planned to cheat and was relieved when I didn't need to do it. I was relieved that the teacher did not look at the booklet he had allowed us to bring in. My algebra mark was much better than this.

My history teacher had written a book on the subject. His method of teaching was to copy his book onto the blackboard. He would fill four or five boards every period and he expected us to recopy what he had written. If there is a less interesting way to teach history than this I have yet to encounter it.

My Latin teacher was a delight. She was full of interesting and often humorous stories about Roman times. She often illustrated the course lavishly with slides of her visits to Italy. I had not studied any language in Enumclaw; this was my second of three years of Latin. I took my first year during Grade 10 in Bermuda.

She reminded me of Grace, my sister, who also became a college teacher. Grace accumulated 40,000 slides over the years from her worldwide travels. She used these to illustrate her courses in geography.

My English teacher was ruthlessly sarcastic. At the end of the year she publicly predicted everyone's grade of each student, embarrassing the whole class. She claimed that she was seldom more than 10 points off. She predicted my mark as, "No more than 60." When I finished the year with a 75, I was jubilant.

The seventh class was the first of two years of physics. As an avid reader (though a very slow one) of *Scientific American* and other science-based magazines, I breezed through that course. Mr. Gray gave the same explanation for the propagation of sound as Mr. Franklin did six years earlier. I didn't try to persuade him differently.

There are two events in that school year that stand out for me. The first was my part in the school's annual play. I played the high school principal in *What a Life*, the original Henry Aldrich story. This gave me a taste for the theater that has stayed with me all my life. I haven't been on stage as often as I might have liked. However I have produced a number of stage plays during my high school teaching career. Everyone had a good time.

The other was a public speaking contest held by Lions International. I wrote a speech of which I am still very proud. Unfortunately I didn't read the fine print. The rules were that the speech was to be delivered from memory. I missed this requirement and read my speech. Quite rightly, I was disqualified. The principal of the school (who also taught third-year Latin from a textbook he had written) said that he liked my speech and asked to look at it more closely.

I agreed and gave him my only copy. Several weeks later some of my friends attended the citywide contest. I was unable to attend. They told me that Saul Reichmann, my competitor in the contest at the school, had used *my* speech for the citywide run-off.

To my chagrin he won the Canada-wide contest in Toronto and came in third at the international run-off in Washington, D.C. I have no way of knowing whether I would have done as well, or better, but at least my speech stood up well. If the principal had asked me to let Saul use it, I believe I would have said, "Yes," and felt that I shared his glory. To have it stolen, put me at odds with the principal.

Upon completion of that year, because of my year in Enumclaw, I still needed 13 credits to finish the twelfth grade; the second year of physics, the third of Latin and some trivial option.

How would I manage to return to this school to have the person who stole my speech as my Latin teacher?

Dropping out of high school

What might be the disastrous impact of arbitrary rules on someone's future?

I went to work for the summer at a local pharmacy as sales clerk and delivery boy. After about three weeks on this job, the owner told me that he would have to let me go because he wanted an apprentice pharmacist in my position. In the course of our discussions he told me that the University of Alberta provided special college entrance examinations in September. These were intended for people who wanted to start college without completing high school.

This information sounded like a "God send." I could avoid another boring year doing only three subjects at that high school. All I needed to matriculate was to complete my third year of Latin and a couple of senior science courses. The principal taught senior Latin. By reputation he was dreadfully dull. Because he stole my speech I didn't respect him. Spending a year in his classroom didn't appeal to me one little bit.

I applied for these special examinations, undertook Latin, physics and biology from the Alberta Correspondence School Branch. I started my one lesson per day routine all over again. By late August I was two-thirds of the way through these three courses when I received two letters. One was from the University telling me that I could only apply for one examination, not three.

The other was from the Alberta government Department of Education, telling me that I had already earned 35 credits for seven courses in 1948-'49. Their regulations made this the maximum allowable. I could not earn any additional credits before January of 1950.

So there I was two-thirds of the way through three courses and at least four months to wait before I could do anything about it. Would it not be pointless to go back to that high school, to be even more bored than I would otherwise have been, because I had already done much of the work *and* I would have as one of my three teachers the person for whom I had lost all respect?

How many students leave high school before finishing because of the prospect of boredom?

Into the land of the great unwashed
What sort of work can a high school dropout find?

I decided to look for work instead of returning to school. I found employment selling furniture and floor coverings in a department store. Once again I liked the work. It was great fun looking at the merchandise and speculating how it might fit into various decors. My artistic interests were reawakened.

As a salaried junior trainee I had the advantage of having the run of the entire floor. This included lamps, carpets and draperies as well as furniture. I could service people in any or all of these departments.

Most of the regular sales staff were confined to just one department and were on commission. The salespeople who survived in this setting did very well. The strongest survivor was the floor manager who collected a slice for every sale on the floor. His arrogance irritated me. He had been with the company for more than fifteen years and had an ego that would fill a city block.

I particularly liked one of the younger salesmen; I'll call him Jeff. We often chatted when traffic was slow. I would turn the better prospects over to him, whenever I could.

As part of my job, whenever we had a remnant from a roll of floor coverings, I would spread it out and measure it. I would then put a tag on it showing how many square yards it contained. One day a couple of gentlemen came to our department. They were dressed in ill-fitting chalk-striped business suits. They were olive skinned and reminded me of the typical gangsters from the "B" movies I so much enjoyed.

The manager maneuvered them in my direction. As I began working with them, they explained their mission. They were representatives from a local ethnic club and were seeking to buy a hard floor covering for the basement of their club hall. They wanted about 200 square yards of material.

We had several remnants in a popular pattern that they liked. If they bought them all, they could cover the area and save quite a bit of money. At least, that was what seemed possible to me when I added up the tags on the remnants.

Apparently I made some mistake in my calculations. I'll never know what it was. All I remember is that they came back saying that there was not enough to finish the job and they wanted to buy more of the pattern. The pattern had been back-ordered.

Remember, 200 square yards at $5 a square yard is *a thousand dollars*. This was a lot of money in 1950. I gave them

Jeff's card instead of the manager's card because I was disgusted that he let their appearance interfere with his judgment about potential purchasers. A customer is a customer. He berated me for making whatever error I had made and was particularly annoyed that I had not given *his* card to them instead of Jeff's.

About three weeks later a scruffy looking little old lady came wandering around the floor. Once again the manager sent me to service her. Her story was that her husband had been a conductor on the railroad where he had worked for 45 years. They had just bought their retirement dream home and wanted to decorate it from top to bottom.

I introduced her to the store's interior decorator. We had a very pleasant day. She said she would return on Friday with her husband and they would then make their final decisions. I gave her Jeff's card for the same reason as before.

On Friday the manager sent me to the store's warehouse to help unload a boxcar full of furniture. I spent the better part of the day unloading the boxcar. At about four o'clock I returned to the main store and asked the manager if I could take time for lunch. I had left it behind, thinking I would only be at the warehouse for the morning, as he had suggested. He reluctantly agreed, and I picked up my lunch bag from my locker and headed for the lunchroom.

At the lunchroom I met Jeff, who was taking a break. He was aglow. "Thank you, thank you, thank you!" he exclaimed, nearly crushing my hand with his shake of it.

"What happened?"

"That conductor and his wife came into the store late this morning. They used my card to introduce themselves. 'Where is that nice young man who talked to me the other day,' the wife had asked. I explained that you had gone to the warehouse to unload some furniture."

"'Well let me show you what we talked about.' She led us all over the floor. They spent nearly $10,000 on furniture alone!" That was more than 50 years ago; it would be more than $50,000.00 today.

"My commission will be wonderful! Thank you again."

I returned to the floor where the manager told me not to bother returning to the store on Monday except to collect my last check. I guess it was not my place, in the business world, to teach the floor manager a lesson about the nature of quality service.

Are such experiences usual for people who have not graduated from high school or college?

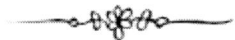

Adventures in the world of journalism

When is a contract not a contract?

I then found a job as a "junior reporter" at a local newspaper. I was actually a copy boy. The fancy title was made possible because I obtained the grain and cattle market prices each day. This meant that the newspaper could pay apprentice wages at a rate below the legal minimum wage.

Once again I enjoyed the job. The operation of a daily newspaper opened many insights for me. It was late 1949 and the paper was still using typeset technology. Each line of type in the paper was a separate sliver of shiny typemetal. It was usually an inch and a half long with the letters on its top in a mirror image of the print it would produce.

These were set up in the composing room on the top floor, loaded into small frames and printed out on a small press upon six-inch wide strips of newsprint paper. My job was to go up one flight of 22 stairs, collect these strips from the composing room, and go down these same steps to deliver them to the proofreaders. The proofreaders would indicate the errors. I would then deliver the proofed copy to the composing room for correction.

Once they were corrected these slivers of type were then assembled into a page-sized frame. Pictures were chemically etched onto metal plates and mounted on wooden blocks to be the same depth as the type. Drawings were treated similarly.

These frames were rolled on carts into the plate room where they had a thick piece of rice paper pressed into their surfaces. These were then curled into a semi-cylinder and placed in a machine that poured typemetal onto them. The result that emerged was half of a drum that would be attached to the press rollers on the high-speed printing presses in the basement. Four pages would be printed at a time, the front and the back of either aside of the centerfold.

The pressmen mounted as many drums as there were sheets in the edition to be printed. They matched these drums with large rolls of newsprint, fed the paper through the machine and checked everything before starting the presses. When the presses started an alarm bell sounded, which we could hear all over the building.

I don't remember how fast they went; my guess would be at least 100 copies a minute. Anyway they were cut, folded twice, stacked and tied into bundles of 100, all by the machine. The pressroom was noisy. However there was an air of excitement in the basement as the men scrambled to keep the flood of newspapers removed from the machine and carted off to the circulation dock.

Another thing that captivated me was the process of gathering news. National and international news came in from the wire services by Teletype. An editor decided which stories to use, condensing them as needed and had me deliver them to the composing room. Staff reporters usually wrote local stories. They would call the local police and fire departments for events that occurred in past twenty-four hours.

Another source was the activities of the city council, the school board and the provincial legislature. Phone calls from local citizens sometimes also led to stories. Investigative reporting was rare. With daily deadlines and space limitations to meet, such reporting consumed too much time and space.

Bad news is easier to collect than good news so reports were biased toward catastrophe. This fact is obvious to people in the business but is rarely brought to public awareness.

When I was hired by the city editor, he told me that if I did well in six weeks or so, I would receive a raise in pay. After nearly three months on the job and several "gentle hints," I made an appointment with the publisher to find out when I would be getting my raise in pay.

I knew that a position in the proof reading room was opening. Although I don't know how I would have handled it because I was such a poor speller. My idea was to ask about the proofreading job instead of criticizing the city editor for breaking his promise. Boy was I naïve! I was not permitted to see the publisher.

Instead I was introduced to the "bear pit" procedure. This is where several senior people surround the miscreant to badger him or her into submission. I stood my ground in this hopeless situation and resigned before I left the room.

That was the end of my venture into professional journalism.

Is the breaking of such verbal agreements common practice in business?

Remarks

I abandoned my studies while I was working and did not learn as quickly as I might have done what it meant not to have graduated from high school. The main reason was that I attacked each new position with enthusiasm and enjoyed the variety of experiences each new job had to offer.

Looking back, I also realize that I responded to these challenges in unconventional ways. I did not stroke the floor manager when he violated my ethical principles of fair treatment to customers. I did not sit quietly and docilely by when I knew that I was being underpaid by a sham apprenticeship.

I gave the best I had and that was not good enough because I would not do the "politically correct" thing. Individuality leads to divergence, which seems to be unacceptable in the main stream of our society.

These consequences temporarily were about to change.

How similar is this employment history to others who left high school before graduating?

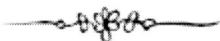

Glimpses of the future

Is there another way to look at the employment world?

It was February of 1950. I was on my fourth job after withdrawing from high school the previous June. This job with the Research Council of Alberta was a temporary one; supposed to last only six weeks.

There were two assignments for me to complete in these six weeks. First I was to dismantle a carbonizer that had been used to study ways of reducing the sulfur content of high-sulfur coal. I had to disassemble it in such a manner that it could be rebuilt if need be. Because the interior of this chimney-like device was full of soot, this was a very dirty job.

Working out a code system for the order of the parts, I removed them and packaged them effectively in less than ten days. I gave a copy of my code to my supervisor.

Second, I was shown where a grease kettle from a residence kitchen had overflowed into the basement laboratory section of the Council's premises, rendering the area unusable. The flood had coated the walls, floor, and much of the equipment with now rancid grease. The smell was unbelievable.

I experimented with mixtures of detergents. I found a combination that removed the grease fairly easily. I completed this task and had the basement smelling sweetly in two weeks.

There were still two and a half weeks left in the contract. My supervisor was so pleased that he found me a third job to do.

This time I was to scrub all of the dirty glassware. Tight budgets prevented the Council from hiring a full-time lab assistant. The Provincial Treasurer had insisted that it was more economical to use new glassware for each experiment than to hire an assistant to clean used equipment.

I now faced a huge stack of dirty laboratory glassware. The manager found some extra money and extended my contract for two weeks. Those two extra weeks saved the Council thousands of dollars by making this glassware reusable.

While working in the main laboratory, my interest in science was expanded. As I scrubbed away I talked to these researchers and listened in on their conversations with each other. Although oil had been discovered at Leduc only about a year earlier, there was a well-known oil deposit in the Athabasca Tar Sands.

The problem with the tar sands was the difficulty of extracting this heavy oil from the sand. These researchers estimated that there was enough oil in those sands to extend then known oil reserves of the world from 50 to 75 years by about another 150 years.

Of course, all these numbers were speculative and many new finds and consumption increases since then have changed the time-line. However, what I found so fascinating was the fact that these people were working on a problem that might not materialize in their own lifetimes. It was extraordinary to find people working on problems 60 years into the future!

How might these researchers have been working if climate change had been a recognized issue in 1950?

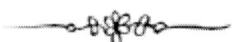

More bureaucratic bungling

What is the rationale behind government regulations?

After leaving the Research Council I found work with the Alberta government as a clerk in a government operated bank. This meant that I had to leave home. I took up residence in a rural community and began to settle into its social life. I did not even take my schoolbooks with me to that job.

There was not a dance within fifty miles that I did not attend. This life away from home was fun! Many of my new friends were in the local high school. At their encouragement I applied to write my three exams at that school. I brought the books from home about three weeks before the exams and spent my evenings reviewing the work.

I made the mistake of not submitting any more lessons. My thought was that I was now learning fairly efficiently and that I would have no problems with these exams. Little did I know!

Finally, in August, I received the anticipated letter with my marks. I had made 35 in Latin, 45 in physics and 55 in biology. Certain that I had done better than that, I wrote a letter of enquiry. In response I was told that because I had not submitted at least sixteen of the lessons in any of the three subjects. The markers had penalized me 25 marks on each exam! I had actually passed all three subjects before the penalty. I was livid, both at myself and at the educational system!

How many students have been devastated by such silly rules?

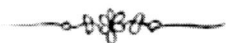

Road to nowhere

Why was I such a slow learner?

It was now June of 1950. ... I had found a job as a bookkeeper with a government-operated bank and moved away from home. I was boarding in a rural community near the Saskatchewan border. I was responsible for keeping records in two huge ledger books. One was a part of the main branch records. The other held all the records from a satellite branch we opened two days a week.

I was hired because the satellite books were $1,000 short. The bank had let the previous bookkeeper go. They wanted me to find the error. After several months of checking the balance on every account and wearing out the adding machine, I found it. I had one of the other bookkeepers call back to me all the entries for the month that was short. We found a $500 deposit that had been entered as a check and subtracted from the account. I told the accountant what I had found, presuming he would tell the manager.

Because, when I started, my arithmetic was so poor; there was also a $10 error in my work that I never found. I continued to look for that for another couple of months.

One day the manager called me into his office to ask about the status of my records. I had told the accountant about finding the $1,000 error two months earlier. Apparently he had not told the manager. Once he knew that there was only a small overage left he remarked, "If that's all, I'll make a general journal entry to square everything away."

I blew up, "Do you mean to say that you have let me come back to the office every evening for the past two months when you could have fixed it so simply?"

Because of this outburst, he sent in a negative report on me. Shortly after this an opening came up in a branch closer to home and I transferred.

Was my tendency to do things differently and to be self-righteous getting in the way of employment success?

Endlessly in trouble

How might I get myself out of this predicament I had created?

My stint in the next bank branch placed me once again in a predominantly female setting. The small city of the branch had a shortage of men in their mid twenties because an entire brigade from that city had been wiped out in one of the unsuccessful ventures early in World War II. There were nine workers in the branch, only the Manager and I were male. The manager usually stayed in his office.

I find it fascinating to contrast the views of these women with those of the feminist movement of a decade or so later. In their view, circumstances had condemned them to being career women. As a result they were torn between the social need for appealing to men and to be the sole financial providers for their futures. Interestingly, none of them considered moving elsewhere.

Being single and under twenty, I was treated as genderless. They tended to forget that I was male. Their transition to genderless roles opened my mind to the underlying humanity of people before any social and cultural distinctions are drawn. Beyond this, my social life was much more restricted here than previously.

I rented a room in a garage and lived by myself. I often awoke through the winter with snow on my bed. My general discomforts led to me spend many weekends at home with my family in Edmonton.

One winter day I was delivering the checks that had been deposited in our bank from the other banks. While scurrying through the minus 20 temperatures, I was amazed to see a man leading a lion cub on a leash through the cold. I was full of this event when I returned to my office. The girls didn't believe a word of it until he brought the cub into the bank.

After that I became more deeply involved in their conversations. My stay there became much more pleasant.

The following spring, an opening for a teller came up. I asked the manager about it. By now my ability to do arithmetic was nearly perfect, so I believed I could manage the promotion. The manager accepted my application. A few days later he told me that I couldn't get the job. The previous manager's negative report had made such a promotion impossible.

I arranged to take a couple of days off. I went home to Edmonton that weekend. On Monday I went to the head of the personnel department for the Alberta government to ask about a transfer. On the basis of a recommendation from my present manager, he arranged for a transfer from the Treasury Branch to the Department of Lands and Forests.

Beginning on June 1st I returned home to Edmonton and began working at the Aerial Survey section of that department. During the six years since World War II, the province had funded an aerial photographic survey of the entire province. These had to be catalogued. The photos were all 9 inches square and overlapped 60% east-west so that they could be used stereoscopically. They overlapped by 20% north south so that the flights could be linked together.

My job was to locate the centers of these photos on regional maps. Many of the regional maps were topographical sheets from the Canadian government. These maps were made from physical land surveys. A few were sketchy maps based on verbal reports.

Looking at the terrain of the entire province in black and white from 20,000 feet was enthralling. Sometimes I needed to use the stereoscopic capabilities of the pictures to pinpoint the location of a photo's center-point. Seeing the valleys fall away, the hills stand up toward me, and even silos poking up from fields by the houses captivated me beyond description.

On some occasions I even helped the engineer who was making new maps for the regions where top sheets were not available. This was by far the most interesting and challenging long-term job I had ever held. The projected time value of these photographs was much shorter than the time-line for the Athabasca tar sands. An aireal photo is immediately out of date when it is taken. However their engineering and land development value was clearly evident to me.

After about a year on the job, the government decided to photocopy all of the land-title books that were made in the late 1800s. Their concern was the deterioration of these critical archives. Our photocopying room went to double shift work. There were two women who ran this part of the department. Another junior clerk and I were assigned to form the second shift. We alternated day and evening shifts on a weekly basis.

It took about six months to finish this assignment. I was greatly relieved to return to my map-making role. Then the senior woman in the photocopying room announced that she was remarrying. The head of our division asked both the other junior and me to apply for this position, because we both knew how to do it.

I had two problems with accepting this job. First, I found that the chemicals irritated my skin and lungs. Second, although the starting salary was higher than mine, the ceiling was much lower. This range was typical of jobs intended for women.

I took my associate aside and suggested that we stand together and ask for improvements in pay and working conditions. He agreed to do this. I presented my position to the department head.

When my co-worker made the same presentation they subjected him to the "bear pit" I had experienced at the newspaper. He got the job without any improvements. I had not violated anything, so they could not fire me. As a result my supervisor was instructed to make life so miserable for me that I would quit.

I went to the Personnel Manager to arrange for another transfer. This made matters worse. Every day or so, my supervisor would call me into his office to criticize me about some trivial matter. I would wait until he finished his tirade and then explain my action in as calm a manner as I could muster. At least by now I had learned to control my temper.

Each time he called me into his office he usually became so angry that he lost his voice. I waited until he could no longer talk and then explained calmly what I had done and why I did it. There was never anything that I did for which I could be fired.

It was now 1952. As the months passed it was clear that I was going nowhere. By now I was approaching 21 years old. I could now apply for admission to the University of Alberta as an adult student. I didn't have the language requirement (Latin) to go into my first choice of honors physics.

I found that I could enter the Faculty of Education, to become a teacher, without the language requirement. Because I had passed biology, I now needed 8 credits for admission. I rewrote physics with a quick review and earned a 65%. This mark, after two years away from the books, vindicated the mark I should have received. I also enrolled in a 3-credit art course and completed that in July. This gave me my admission requirements.

I then went back to the Personnel Manager to ask about evening or night work. He sent me to the head of Public Works. I began as a janitor on August 1st, 1952, cleaning up after the very people I had been working with and making 30% more money!

The people I was leaving gave me a departure party. Their gift was a bag full of toilet paper. There was a card with it that had a drawing of a winged camera over a landscape. The card was inscribed with the message, "*Semper in Excreta.*" I wept at the sentiment.

Was this the intervention of Destiny?

The flunkout goes back to school

Was this where all the previous events of my life began to come together?

I didn't expect college to be so much like my previous high school experiences. I had anticipated that we would finally be working with ideas. Instead, the focus was still upon the acquiring of information. In the methodology courses it was on the "how to" of giving information.

This approach to teaching had not worked for me in elementary school. It was the basis of my boredom in high school. I was no longer surprised with myself for having taken more than three years to get myself back into the classroom.

There were a few notable exceptions to this general rule. My calculus teacher was asked a question one day in class about the relationship between trigonometry and calculus. He paused for a moment and did a quick calculation at the corner of the board. He then gave a lucid explanation.

"This is something you need to remember about mathematics," he continued. "Mathematics is the language of numerical and logical relationships. You don't need to memorize formulas if you understand how they were developed." I loved it! Here was the beauty I had first observed from my algebra teacher in high school.

In another course we learned how to run a music appreciation program in elementary school. As a potential high school teacher I would be certified from the third grade onward. One of the books I read for this course was by Dr. Leslie Bell. I don't remember the title but I was thrilled by his approach.[16]

His premise was that he would explain how to get boys to sing. Girls had sweet voices and would go along with most songs. Boys were another matter. He then went on to explain how to identify the voice type of each boy and to explain what to do to accommodate each type.

"Wow! If I had been taught that way in reading, I wouldn't have had so much trouble," was my first thought. I later learned better and that teaching reading was more complex than that. However, this diagnostic approach still appeals to me. It stood in stark contrast to everything else I was being taught about how to teach. I did reasonably well that first year.

Grace graduated from high school with high honors in 1953. I was between my first and second year of college. My parents offered to take us on a trip to Europe for the summer. Thus began 75 days of eye-opening amazement. For me to take this trip, I had to quit my job as janitor.

Upon my return I went to the government employment office to try to find another janitorial position. This time I came in with a record of experience and was immediately hired by the Alberta Government Telephones (AGT) to work in their brand new head-office building.

During my second year, with more of the same dull stuff, a group of us migrated to the cafeteria to discuss all sorts of things, including alternative ways of teaching. It was here that I realized that many of the young women in college were not looking for an education but for their "Mrs." degree. Most of the aspiring wives struck me as being the social climber I regarded my mother to be. In this my judgment was unfair, but it insulated me from making a serious error.

On November 11th, 1953, Canada's Memorial Day, there was no school, no work and a parade in which I could play trombone during the morning. It was a relief to take a midweek break.

By the end of the day I was at loose ends. I decided to take in a movie at my favorite theater, which specialized in British films. It was located on the south side of the river that divided the city. The show was over about nine-thirty. Going home this early would almost certainly have led to yet another round of endless arguments at home. I decided to go to a nearby dance hall to top off the evening.

I arrived at the 10 PM intermission. As I cruised around the floor, I saw a co-worker from AGT talking vigorously to an attractive woman. He was a strong believer in conspiracy theory, which belief he supported by spending his days observing activities at the local courthouse. His views about women were similarly off the wall. Knowing what he was like and seeing how irritated she was becoming, I decided to rescue her. He introduced us to each other. When the music began, we danced away from him.

I took her to a late dinner after the dance. She was fascinating. She was not like any of the other women I had met in my life. She had a sweet gentleness about her. She was not out for bed or board or both, like so many college students.

We started to date and after about a month I realized that I had fallen deeply in love. The flow between us brought sunshine into my life and a spring into my step. She did not attack my ideas as my mother and sister did. Instead she listened intently and made gentle suggestions.

She cautioned me that she was older than I, twenty-three years, in fact. This didn't matter. Here was a woman, although was married once before, who displayed a deep innocence. I could honor and respect her like no other.

I asked Frances to marry me on January 19th and we were married on May 5th of 1954.

This event was a major turning point in my life. If I hadn't married her I would probably have accepted the two-year certificate and started teaching to get away from all the inanities of the program. Instead, I settled down to business and wound up taking three more years of college.

In my Junior year, I was allowed into the stacks at the library. This was a whole new world for me. The range of professional books was beyond my imagining. Also, the students who frequented the stacks were in college for an education, not a jolly time.

As a major in mathematics and a minor in English, I began taking advantage of this interdisciplinary mix to engineer a good education. I found out who the very best teachers were and haunted the Deans' offices to get these courses allowed on my transcript.

One obligatory course for my math major was a course in mechanics. The professor was a real dud. He had been a champion in earlier days but he was now becoming senile. The Dean would not allow students to leave his class on the grounds that, "A mass exodus from his class would probably kill him."

The other students began to audit a course on the same subject from the engineering faculty. I could not do this because that course was in the evening and I was working from 4:30 PM. I failed the course and had to switch my major to English with a minor in mathematics.

This move proved very beneficial. I was now able to take the "Nature of Mathematics" course from my former calculus professor. This course was open to math teachers but closed to math majors. It laid the foundation for my understanding of mathematics as a language.[17] It is a descriptive communication system using numbers or their equivalents instead of words.

I also began to love English and American literature even though reading was still difficult. My courses steadily enriched my understanding of the world around me.

The course I took on Shakespearean literature was particularly eventful. One of the professor's term papers was to be on, "Undisplayed action in Shakespearean plays." I decide to write on "Undisplayed Action as a Vehicle of Plot Development." My friend, Saul who did so well with my speech, asked me what I was writing about. I shared my idea.

The professor failed me on this paper. I went to see him. He explained, "Whenever I give an assignment to freshmen, all I get is the story back. I expect more writing maturity from upperclassmen." I asked him to go into more detail. After about 20 minutes he ended, "The only excuse you might have is when you are dealing specifically about the plots of the stories."

I pointed out my title on the paper. He shrugged, but refused to change my mark. There was some consolation in the fact that Saul also failed this assignment. Using my ideas the first time brought him international recognition. Using them the second time caused him to fail that paper but not the course. Was that poetic justice?

Another course of value to me was "Diagnosis and Remedial Instruction." It was a very unpopular course because the Professor required a lot of work and it was contra-cultural to the general trend of teaching as the transmission of information. She was a severe taskmaster. The students in her course did a lot more work than for most other courses for only middle level grades. However, I lapped it up. I was seeking an education, not high marks.

I completed my Bachelor of Education degree in 1956 and went on to take seven additional courses to complete a Bachelor of Arts degree in my fifth year. There were two notable courses in that year. The first was a statistics course given by the then head of the mathematics department. He stressed underlying patterns and principles. His themes were to consider the size of measurement error when making statistical comparisons and understanding over formula memorization.

I will always remember an incidental remark he made about the Gaussian (or bell-shaped) curve. "The important thing to remember about this curve is that it is the upper limit of the binomial distribution when the exponents approach infinity. The events being observed *must* have only two values. If they have more than two values the curve can create the impression that we are observing purely random events, when we are not." We will return to this idea in Chapter 6.

The other class was one in American literature. The professor made a remark about Emily Dickenson's use of half rhymes. An author suggested that the editing of her poetry caused this poetic device. I found a copy of her complete works and showed that indeed these rhymes were intentional; a deliberate poetic device in her poetry.

My professor liked my work and suggested that I consider taking a Masters Degree in English literature. He said he might get me a scholarship. He also said that there were only five people in the English department in Alberta. It might be better for me to go elsewhere.

"Where do you suggest?" I asked.

"The University of Toronto has the best program in Canada," he replied.

It was on the strength of this recommendation that Frances and I moved to Toronto, where I began my teaching career.

How different I had become from being a high school flunkout in 1950 to becoming a budding scholar in 1957?

Castles in the Sand [18]

What is the role of imitation in learning?

In my roughly forty years of life[19] I have gazed in awe at the world's two greatest oceans, stood breathless among some of the world's greatest mountains, and on a clear frosty night have contemplated the vastness of the universe, and marveled at nature's fiery winter display.

For all of these things I claim no special status. In this there are many more fortunate and eloquent than I. But of all the things I have done, there is one thing of which I am particularly proud. That thing is the sand castle I built at Lake Simcoe in the summer of 1958.

The building of a sand castle is quite an engineering feat. Often the sand is too lumpy or too sparse. If you dig your moat to the appropriate depth the water may come up into it and your whole effort then sags and slithers into a watery grave. Or the sand may be too dry and you wind up carrying cupfuls of water in little tin or plastic pails for miles across the sand from the water's edge just to get the sand to stick together.

Or perhaps the beach is too crowded with people to give room to build, or there may be too few children around to appreciate your efforts. But that summer while working on my master's degree at the University of Toronto, everything was just perfect. The sand was moist enough to stick and fine enough to smooth nicely. It was deep enough to provide an adequate supply of sand without flooding the moat, and there were just enough children around. So I built my sand castle -- the first one that really *looked* like a castle.

I was fortunate that fine summer morning. Someone the day before had been pouring water on the beach and had made a nice "gully" and seaward "cliff" overlooking the mirror waters of Ontario's jewel. The height of the cliff was about eight inches, which established my scale. I could see immediately that by deepening the gully another four inches and extending the cliff a foot or so to the southeast I could probably excavate enough damp sand for the entire project.

It was about 9 AM when I began my project. As the seaward wall began to take shape a sprinkling of youngsters appeared to bravely challenge the chilly morning waters and to laugh and shout as they splashed each other, sending ripples to trouble the perfect reflections of the sparkling morning.

Like a knight of old I planned as I built.

Since attack from seaward was most likely, it was here that I concentrated my heaviest fortifications. By making the walls stand six inches above the ridge of the cliff they would have an overall height of about eighteen inches from the base of my excavation. There would be three parapets arranged in a broad "V" about twelve inches apart at their centers along the crest of the cliff. Each parapet had cannon ports on the seaward face and a short wall between them with battlements for archers in case an attempt was made to scale the cliff.

Dr. Jay C. Powell

I was deeply engrossed in sculpturing the battlements and the first parapet with a Popsicle stick when a man and his two sons passed by on the seaward side. Full of the pleasure of my task I beamed a friendly "Good morning" at them. The man gazed at me with a puzzled expression. I could not begin to read the thoughts behind that look, though perhaps he thought I had arrived early at a second childhood.

As soon as the sea wall was finished I decided that the castle should be a pentagon and have a dry moat on the inside of the outer wall. I was busily fashioning the two landward parapets with sand scooped from the dry moat when I noticed I was acquiring a gallery of spectators. It was still nebulous and remote: composed of boys of all sizes up to the age of about twelve. There was only about half a dozen of them, all in swimsuits and tanned chocolate brown. None of them went into the water but chose to chase each other up and down the beach, always careful never to get out of sight of my project.

I had found a flat piece of driftwood about the size of a hunting knife, which made an excellent digger and smoother, and as I continued with walls and battlements I noticed that the vigorous chasing had ceased and the boys were standing in groups to watch. An occasional grownup went by. Most avoided my eyes. Some of them smiled wanly, perhaps secretly amused, others seemed quietly contemptuous. One expressed the thought that what I was doing was a good idea and looked like fun. Another suggested a misspent childhood.

With the aid of two Popsicle sticks and a piece of cardboard from a tissue box, I made an arched gateway in the centre of the landward leg of the castle. I had finally completed the outer walls, and the sun was not yet high. Their outer perimeter was in the neighborhood of five feet and the walls were about three inches in diameter at the base and one and a half inches in diameter at the top with the battlements about half that. The seaward wall rose about six inches above the cliff and the landward walls about four inches above the sandy terrain. The wall contained five parapets and a fortified close. In all, it was a formidable fortress.

During the completion of the landward wall, a little girl about five years old in a yellow swim-suit paraded back and forth past the sea wall as though on sentry duty. Each time I looked up she made a point of looking the other way. She couldn't take her eyes from the project so that in one of her passes she missed her footing and fell flat. "Crash," I said, and she fled in a flurry of tears, to return much later but never so close again.

I then began the central keep and tower.

By now the gallery had abandoned all caution. They stood around singly or in groups of two or three to gaze silently or utter the occasional "Oh!" or "Gee!" or "Man" in hushed tones. I had a couple of them collect Popsicle sticks for me for my drawbridge, which they did with enthusiasm. One passer-by told his father "I didn't know castles were for real. I always thought they were only something they put in comic books."

The grownups stayed in the background like sidewalk superintendents watching for a while and then moving on. They were always far enough away that I couldn't hear their comments.

Then an interesting change in the gallery occurred. No longer did they watch proceedings. Instead, they burst into a flurry of activity along the beach. At least a dozen castles sprang up around me. They referred to other castles as models for details but each was a unique creation.

By noon my castle was complete with wall, moat, and a central tower having five different levels, the highest rising about twelve inches above the highest outer walls! I topped it with an improvised flag and then gave it to my two helpers. They couldn't believe me at first, but when they did they were thrilled.

I do not even have a photograph of the finished result. But I have three witnesses. There are two boys probably in university now who had the pleasure of destroying something they had helped to build and in so doing, hopefully, learned that building is more challenging than tearing down. There is a little girl in a yellow swim suit, probably in high school now, who upon reading this, will finally realize that I meant to share rather than to scare, but did not know how.

That was the summer I *really* learned how to teach. I can thank the children and a "silly" impulse to do something I had always wanted but had never been quite able to do before. Is it possible that by becoming a child again for a few hours, I finally began to grow up?

This event occurred between my first and second year of high school teaching. Was this experience the beginning of my really paying attention to events beyond my own activities?

Was this event where I began involving others in my personal growth so that they could learn along with me?

The dog through the hoop

How important is self-discovery?

There is one more personal incident I must relate to finish this account of my intellectual development as I prepared to become a teacher of teachers.

My mother, who had been an elementary school teacher before she married Daddy, had no idea what my learning problem might be. It was not until I was working on my Ph.D., and took a battery of tests, which I would use as a school psychologist, that I discovered I was dyslexic.

One of these tests was an early screening for visual problems developed by Emmet Betts. A task on it required that I look through a stereoscope at some pictures. The stereoscope presents a different image to each eye. I had used this effect making maps for the Alberta government.

In one of them there was a picture of a dog shown to my right eye and a hoop shown to the left eye. If my visual fusion had been normal the dog would be jumping through the hoop. In my view, the dog was too far to the left of the hoop. There before my very eyes I saw why reading was so difficult and tiring for me. My eyes were not fusing images properly at reading distances!

Such learning problems were unknown during the 1920s when my mother taught school, nor was it acknowledged during the late 30s and early 40s of my elementary school days. Her efforts to help me were in vain through no fault of hers. I began to appreciate her efforts that had annoyed me because what she tried to push on me didn't help.

Now I understood that she was doing the very best she could with what she knew. This change in perspective has blessed me all the rest of my life.

What happened when my inclination to be unconventional; to look for reasons behind observations became the way I taught?

The answer to this question is the subject of the next chapter as we turn to issues of ways to manage communication within classrooms.

Chapter 4: Developing Communication

In many schools and districts, the local curriculum is a hodge-podge of individual initiatives knit together with collective good intentions.

Judy Carr and Douglas Harris[20]

Theories of Education

How should we be teaching?

The artisan form of instruction

My number one wife had a group of young girls surrounding her. Their breasts were just beginning to bud. She was showing them how to weave floor mats from reeds. She acknowledged my passing but did not leave her tasks and charges. (From: "The Old One," page 1.)

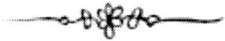

The shaman form of instruction

"I have chosen you because you have been my best student. You have learned the recipes well. You don't seem to have done as well with the craft skills but the women will help to preserve them. It is extremely important that the herbal recipes for medicines be preserved.

"Why did he not mention the incantations?" I wondered under my breath. Those incantations were something, I could say proudly, at which I was good. Memorization was my strength. Understanding the explanations was not my strength. (From: "The Old One," page 2.)

Dr. Jay C. Powell

Remarks

These two excerpts from the introduction, illustrate two different approaches to teaching. One is "hands-on." The teacher explains and demonstrates. The students practice the skills presented in this way. This way to teach is used in vocational education and in the arts. It is the way of the craftsman.

The other is based upon teacher talk. The teacher gives information and then asks questions to find out how well students remember what they were told. This way is more common in academic education. It is the way of the shaman. As just indicated, a huge problem in this second way of teaching is that remembering can occur without understanding.

When students are tested for their factual recall it is easier to teach them as if they are becoming shaman. This is the most effective way to teach for the *No Child Left Behind* initiative because the scoring procedure being used considers only *right* answers to be of value. Such answers can be memorized without understanding.

Should we be teaching in this way?

Flight contest

How might teachers undo situations they create?

As I matured as a teacher I learned to manage classrooms with much more skill. When Roger wished to do battle with me because of my decision to be in control I could have handled the situation better.

Similar results can be seen in the way Melissa acted when Sharon hid behind the coats. This control issue is subtler than the overt events in hiding behind coats. We saw these deeper implications in the conclusions Mrs. Schmidt drew when she misinterpreted Ralph's painting in black. In each of these cases, the *teacher's behavior* created the situation.

As teachers gain experience their ability to anticipate such outcomes improves. On one occasion, I was substitute teaching for a high school; psychology class. The teacher had left a twenty-item multiple-choice test for me to administer. No other instructions for the 55-minute class were provided. The students finished the test in 15 minutes.

At this point I needed to come up with alternative activities quickly in order to avoid a wasted and noisy 40 minutes. I told the class that I was a psychologist and would be willing to answer any questions they might have in psychology.

The second option was to have a study period. If they chose to use the time for studying, that was fine. I would find an activity for those who had nothing to do. This particular class chose the second option. Most of the class went to work, but about a dozen of them did not begin productive activities.

With a bundle of blank paper in hand I gave three or four sheets to the inactive ones and asked them to use the paper creatively. They were to show me what they were doing as the period progressed. Some drew pictures; a few wrote poetry and two boys behind each other in one row made paper airplanes.

These boys were done quickly. I realized that there would soon be an air war if I didn't intervene. I reminded them that airplanes had decorations of various kinds on them. They always had logos, airline names, insignias and numbers on them. I asked them to decorate the planes before flying them. I said that they could have a contest at the end of the period to see which flew best.

This plan put them back to work again with gusto. The planes were beautifully decorated by the end of the period.

The bell rang, the class left the room. The two boys flew their planes, put them into the wastebasket and left with big smiles of satisfaction on their faces.

I resolved these two problems by paying close attention to what the class members were doing with their time. The first problem was from the regular teacher who allowed too much time for the test without providing alternatives for those who finished early. The second problem came from the very open-ended option I had created by saying, "Be creative!" I had not anticipated the production of airplanes. Hence, I had to improvise on the spot. Getting them to decorate their planes and giving them a time to fly them after the class was over produced the win-win situation we all needed.

To avoid mayhem, what other courses of action might I have taken in this situation?

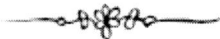

The staff meeting

Where does cooperation begin?

In 1958 I was in my second year of teaching. The staff meeting was almost over. Mr. Romanchuk, the school inspector, was stacking his papers to put them into his briefcase.

"Is there anything else?" Mr. Graves, the Principal, asked. It was clear to everyone but me that the meeting was over. I had been fidgeting all through the last half of the meeting. Ever since Mr. Romanchuk had indicated the provincial government wished to have curriculum committees operating in the schools, I had been itching to speak up.

"Yes," I said, "I have a concern. When I was teaching mathematics and science last year, there seemed to be little integration between these two subject areas. This year I discovered that my diploma students in their eleventh grade history class were unable to read their textbook with comprehension.

"Is there a possibility that we could set up a curriculum committee that would look at the skills needed by different students in various subjects? We could then decide who teaches which skills, in which sequence, and integrate every subject in the school into a single program."

"That is a good idea," Mrs. Cadieu chimed in. "Teachers of modern languages find that we must explain the *infinitives* of verbs to all of our freshman students. They don't seem to have any idea what an infinitive is. They seem to have trouble understanding the conjugation of Spanish verbs because they don't understand infinitives."

"Why don't we postpone this discussion until our next staff meeting?" Mr. Graves was impatient. "Mr. Romanchuk has to get back to Metropolis before dark."

"That's fine with me," I said, "as long as we do not drop this issue." The two administrators exchanged knowing frowns as they hurried out of the staff room.

"I like your suggestion, Jay," Marie Cadieu commented as she joined me at the coffee urn. "It's not just Spanish, either. All of the teachers of modern languages feel the same way. It is an issue that came up at our conference this past summer."

"I'll look into it," I promised. "I'll let you know what I find out."

That evening, before I went home, I borrowed the curriculum guides for English from the teachers' reference section of the school library.

On Monday morning I brought up the subject with Marie Cadieu again. "I've been right through all the guides for English," I told her. "There is no mention of infinitives in the first-year guide. It is an optional topic for sophomores. It is not until the junior year that it is a formal part of the grammar curriculum, so far as I can see."

"I'm not surprised," she replied. "The left hand never seems to know what the right hand is doing."

We find a similar situation being addressed when Mrs. Fraser persuaded Bill to draw meaningful pictures instead of doodles. The integration of students into the classroom must always be done in a meaningful manner. Teaching should be: –

Dr. Jay C. Powell

Hands on – Minds on – Eyes and Ears open – Heart open.

Is what Carr and Harris suggest about schooling correct? Is a lack of close integration of programs a serious problem in our schools?

Teaching how to learn

How do we teach information gathering skills through studying history?

As just mentioned, in my second year of teaching I was assigned to teach a history class in the eleventh grade.[21] These non-academic students needed a high school diploma to be employed in the local factory but did not need college entrance status. Being a mill town, the division between the management people, professionals and the workers was as sharp as if they had been from different planets.

The mill insisted that its workers have at least a twelfth grade education. Those that didn't get this far in school were employable only in the fringe jobs of the community. The other history class was for the academic group.

The academic students would continue through grade 13 to achieve college entrance requirements. They were destined for management positions. Many of them would leave the community to further their personal and professional development at a college or university, perhaps never to return.

With the goal of being a mill worker as their primary motivation for remaining in school, many of them were reluctant learners. Survival was their mode of relating to school as illustrated by Roger's defiant stance presented previously.

The teacher who dared to try to teach them more than enough to "get by" was in for a hard time. As you can gather, control of the class became a very strong issue for the first few weeks of my second year of teaching.

One Friday, in mid October, I reorganized my teaching plans for the third time. In this approach, I gave two pages from the history text to the students to read over the weekend. When asked at the beginning of the next class the following Monday, how many had read the assignment, most indicated that they had.

I then asked them a series of questions about the contents. They were unable to answer most of these questions. My first reaction was to accuse them of not having read the material. They insisted that they had.

To allay my doubts, I insisted that they open their books to the pages assigned, and find the answers to the questions I had set for them. They were, for the most part, unable to do this. They seemed to go blank, even when asked only to read the sentence aloud that contained certain key words in the question. In their oral reading, they were painfully slow and often stumbled over words of more than two or three syllables.

This class session was the turning point for me, for the class and for my teaching. *I realized that they could not read the textbook with comprehension.* There must be some other way. The obvious one for me was *to teach them how to read the text*. Having taught myself to read in junior high school, I had no doubts that they could learn how to read a history text in Grade 11.

I adopted the approach that had taught me how to learn while in Bermuda. The correspondence courses from Alberta used a "guided questioning" approach to self-study. I added some ideas from the remedial reading course I had taken in college.

To make this change, drawing from the book, I prepared a series of study questions. My discipline problem vanished. In its place began to emerge a sense of self-discovery among these "reluctant" students.

Step one: Directed observation

In the first several sessions, I handed out these questions at the beginning of each class. Step-by-step I showed them how to identify *key words* in the questions, and how to use these words to find the part of the text to which the questions referred. Ultimately, I showed them how to answer questions directly from the text, with proper referencing.

From this point onward, I planned my lessons and conducted my teaching based upon how my students were answering my questions. This approach to teaching is independent of the subject matter being taught. It focuses upon thinking skills and learning how to learn, using the course content as a vehicle for teaching. In effect, I taught them following the pattern of learning I had taught myself that immunized me from the nonsense that has gone on in my own classroom learning experiences.

Step two: Developing initial independence

Once they had acquired the ability to answer these questions from the textbook during class time, I gave them similar questions for homework. In this phase, I asked them to share their answers in class. We discussed their answers and identified the misreading that had occurred and the reasons for them. When I worded a question poorly, this fact came out in the discussion as well. Instead of my teaching being "from on high" we became mutual participants in the learning process.

I followed the identification of the text content with discussions about the passage they read. I encouraged them to try to relate things like "life in Rome" to "life in a mid 20th century mill town in Ontario." When this approach is taken the common elements of human life; food, clothing, shelter, rearing families and recreational activities stand out. The differences among cultures based upon climate, political structure, technology, *etc.* also made these studies more interesting.

Step three: Looking more deeply into the text

The next step was to give them questions that were more complex. For instance, I told them that such and such was an *effect* and asked them to identify the *cause*. This skill required that they read the text surrounding the location of the part identified by the key words in the question. Then they must pick out relationships among the concepts in this broader portion of text. They must now consider content beyond merely the ideas in a question itself. This progression of complexity among such questions led to a steady deepening of contextual comprehension. [22]

Their excitement about learning continued to increase. They were gaining confidence in their ability to learn.

Once they had acquired the ability to interconnect parts of the text, I began to show them how to look for *themes* in the text. They were to read the questions and identify all of them that related to only one topic; say for instance, "Life of a peasant in the Middle Ages."

Once they could identify major themes, I extended their classification skills by showing them how to subdivide these topics into secondary themes such as food, employment, entertainment, and so forth. In this way, I had the students integrate still larger pieces of text. In so doing, they were now considering the order and the structure of the material.

Step four: How to write an essay from textual themes

From here I showed them how to use these subtopics to write paragraphs for an essay, having them compare and contrast their own lives with those from the past. I had them write sample paragraphs on the board as we discussed the process. At this point, we were moving from comprehension to the application and analysis levels of understanding. Their view of themselves as a part of history was beginning to take shape.

The next stage of organization required them to integrate these paragraphs into a sequence, develop transitional sentences, and to write an introductory and closing paragraph to complete a formal essay. Thus, starting from rough notes, they developed the interconnection of ideas on a step-by-step basis. Here they were learning to read at the synthesis level of understanding. As we can see, this approach is independent of the particular subject being taught.[23]

The final step occurred when I helped them to write this essay on the similarities and differences between the lives of people today and those of this period of history. This last step took about six weeks of classroom time. This compare and contrast activity introduced them to the *evaluation* level of understanding.

Step five: Moving toward independence in text analysis skills

We then returned to reviewing the subsequent study questions, continuing with the course content. As the work became easier for them, the pace of coverage increased, their discussions grew livelier as their understanding deepened. Having demonstrated these skills, my plan then was to recycle through the skills with less direct support. The objective at these later stages was to help them to become independent in these skills.

Towards the end of the year, both my students and I began to tire of the "study-question" approach. There were occasions when I did not review the questions I had written before coming to class. The students caught me out because *I was inadequately prepared.*

This event improved our relationship even further because I acknowledged when I was in error, and admitted to my own negligence. Never again, did the exchanges returned to the power struggles we all had experienced at the beginning of the year. Is this the distinction between the "Sage-on-the-stage" and the "Guide-by-the-side" approach to teaching?

Step six: Applying their new skills

Once I had shown them how to write an essay, I asked them to plan and write an essay on their own topic, using the same approach and having them hand in their work as it progressed. Teaching them the editing process followed this. The final assignment for the year was a full-blown essay, for which only the finished and fully edited document was all that was to be submitted.

This discussion of how I taught the skills of reading an informational text, using history as a vehicle, illustrates the craftsman approach to teaching content. Here the text content becomes the "reeds" from which the "mats" were woven.

Besides resolving discipline problems, what other outcomes might you expect from this approach to teaching?

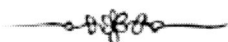

Learning from writing

What is "Reading to write?"

Also during this same year of high school teaching, I tried a similar experiment in English literature. This idea originated during my study of Shakespeare. A famous sidelight of his life was his exchange of love sonnets with a young man. My professor was part of the movement in the 1950s that suggested Shakespeare was gay. My reading of those sonnets and his letters gave me a different opinion. I think that he was teaching the young man how to write.

It is from the ability to experiment with ideas that the true ability to think creatively comes. About ten years later I read an interesting article by Pryor *et al.*[24] This paper gave an account of an experiment with porpoises that was conducted at Marineland of the Pacific in Hawaii. The researchers recognized that in behavior modification the objective is to produce a specific behavior by getting the learners to focus upon it, through systematic rewards.

Pryor's idea was to try rewarding divergent behavior instead of rewarding behavior that converged toward some specific actions predetermined by the experimenter. This experimental approach shifted the paradigm. The rewards were now being given to *behaviors initiated by the learners* instead of *behaviors predetermined by the trainer.*

For the first six weeks, these porpoises followed a behavior pattern that was very similar for all the creatures involved in the experiment. After six weeks, there was a dry period, in which they simply swam around and around their tank, refusing to eat or to engage in the experiment.

Then, one by one, they began making creative moves that were unique to each animal. After two or three more weeks their creativity-produced actions became so complex that two independent observers could no longer agree on the details. With this emergence of amazing creative complexity the experiment was terminated.

A similar sequence to the one observed with these porpoises emerged in my classroom. During the first six weeks in this grade 10 class, using themes they participated in choosing, their creative-writing stories became steadily more pornographic and violent. Each was trying to outdo the other in "shock value." I ignored the filth and the gore, and commented upon the story-telling merits each piece possessed.

My plan was to give a brief statement of a story line. The students, in groups of six, would discuss the story idea and then write a story within certain constraints. For instance, they might be asked to write their stories in a dialogue or conversational format. They would then share their stories and select one from among them to be submitted for marking.

With 36 students in the class, I needed to mark only six or so themes from their weekly assignments. I made sure that I had marked at least one story from every student each month. In this way, I greatly increased the amount of actual writing they did without a huge marking load. As a means of scaling the marks assigned by the students in their groups, I gave the marks, assigned by their peers. With their approval, I adjusted them to fit my mark on the sample from their group.

Once they became comfortable with the routine, I started assigning story lines. These were plot capsules from the literature they were expected to read during the year. After they had thought through and written their own stories, I had them read the same plot line from the literature the curriculum guide required them to study. Their response was remarkable.

Almost immediately they began to see how professional authors were creating stories. It gave them a whole new way to look at reading narrative material. They were learning how to write by seeing how professionals wrote. The result was creative imitation such as I had witnessed during the previous summer, which I recounted in "Castles in the Sand" (pp. 86-90).

After six weeks there was a three-week dry period, during which time the students complained bitterly that they had run out of ideas. Then, one by one, as though lightning had struck, great bursts of profound creativity began to emerge. One student caught fire to a huge extent. The assignment of about five pages and entirely written dialogue was about trying to decide whether or not to leave home. He turned into 89 typed (double spaced) pages of powerful introspection.

Since then I have used this same approach to teach creative writing and report writing with adults, only to observe the same pattern emerging with each group. I have also talked with many teachers about their experiences while trying to develop creativity. Most of them became so horrified by the gore and filth with which the experiment begins that they stopped the program in the first phase. By doing this, they reinforced the adolescent impression that adults will not allow young people "free expression" (see: Yearbook, pp.38-41).

Some became disillusioned by the "dry" period and, thinking that the experiment had *failed,* discontinued it. In this way they taught these young people what each of them had expected about themselves all along, namely, "I will never be creative." A few hang in there. The rewards of seeing students, of whatever age, take delight in their new found abilities, is a pleasure to behold.[25]

Here is an illustration of how this approach worked. The idea was to have the hero of the story alone in a boat that gets caught in white water, or a whirlpool or some similar life-threatening situation.

Once they had completed and marked this assignment they looked at Edgar Allen Poe's "Descent into the Maelstrom." Their first reaction was, "Do you mean that you can use scientific principles in story writing?"

The purpose behind this approach is to get them to *think their way through* such a situation with sufficient depth to write about it *before* they made comparisons with the writing of a successful author on the same theme. This technique gets our students to look beyond the story line into the writing techniques such authors use. Notice how this approach reverses the paradigm of "literary interpretation" commonly used in language arts.[26] It is exploratory instead of surveying.

At a later stage in the program, I would encourage them to set their own creative-writing goals in a sequence similar to learning-how-to-learn from a history text. The appreciation of literature that this strategy develops goes far beyond the more common, "What does this passage mean?" way of developing an understanding of literature.

As you can see, it was my second year of teaching where I truly learned how to teach. The summer adventure with the sand castle and the course in test construction converged with my best pre-service training to move me from subject matter-focus to student-learning focus.

How successful do you think this change in focus might have been?

Raising school performance
Can school performance actually be increased?

The next year I moved to a small rural high school. I returned to the teaching of mathematics and science courses. At the end of my first year in that school the test results I received on the Ontario Department of Education high stakes final exams for my Grade 13 students dropped 30 points from the scores I assigned.

Only one of seven papers received a passing mark. I was flabbergasted. I was certain that I had taught more effectively than this. When I found out that the principal of this school had a similar decline of 25 marks, I felt better. This 5-mark difference could be explained by my inexperience as a teacher of advanced subjects.

I decided that I would try to do better the next year. I spent the intervening summer reviewing the test papers I had given. My objective was to look for clues about how to change my teaching strategies. The scores on these tests were useless to me. They were within the usual range. They did not alert me to weaknesses. I had set them based on their demonstrated abilities.

I quickly realized that the best source for diagnostic information was the errors that students made in their work. Collecting these and summarizing them I found several weaknesses.

First, the students did not understand the concept of zero as a placeholder.

Second, they did not understand the concept of zero as the center of an infinite range of numbers.

Third, they did not understand the mathematical meaning of equality.

Fourth, they seemed to be applying rules that they had memorized but did not understand. They often confused rules because they did not know where these rules applied and why.

Finally, they made frequent calculation errors. In short they did not understand the number system.

My courses in the nature and the history of mathematics, my training in remediation, and my earlier success in teaching how to learn and how to think through history and creative writing came together. I now decided to try a similar approach to teaching mathematics.

On the first day of class in my ninth grade and tenth grade mathematics courses, and my twelfth grade algebra course I had eight problems on the board. There were four addition problems and four subtraction problems. All eight of them were supplied with answers, using the five-base number system, where all the counting is done on one hand and 4 + 1 = 10 (hand complete).

I began the class with a challenge. "If the answers I have supplied to these questions are correct," I asked. "What did I do?"

For the most part they all said that the answers must be wrong. "Take a closer look," I suggested.

After several minutes one of them spoke up, "Are you adding by fives rather than tens?" One of them asked.

"Please explain," I encouraged.

"Well, how else could 4 + 1 be 0, as you have shown on the right-hand side of the first addition problem?"

There were a few glimpses of recognition and many puzzled looks.

"Go on," I was delighted at the insight.

The young lady continued to explain how the answer for the first addition problem was found. I then asked other class members to explain the other problems in turn. The fourth problem I reserved for the student, who, I knew from the previous year, was weak in math. With some prompting he made it through correctly.

We then turned to the subtraction problems. They had more trouble with borrowing than with carrying. I made a note of that weakness. It reinforced my conclusion that they didn't understand place value, as I had surmised from their test papers.

Notice that this approach is similar to getting them to think through a story line before reading a professional's writing as I did in my "reading to write" program.

I then gave them a worksheet that had about a dozen more problems without the answers. One of the six addition problems required the adding of more than two numbers arranged in a column.

We exchanged papers and scored them at the end of the class. Most of them got most of the questions correct. I asked the students to indicate on the ones that were not correct the nature of the errors they had made. I collected the papers to summarize the error types. Doing the work in class and identifying errors was similar to the way I began my approach to teaching history.

The next session had more addition and subtraction problems. I went over the error types I had identified and reminded the classes to watch out for the types of errors they had made the previous day. Accuracy was much better on the second day.

As soon as most errors had disappeared, I introduced them to multiplication and division in the five-base number system. By this time I was giving them homework because the solution of these more complex problems required more thought and took longer.

After they were fluent with the five-base number system, I switched to the twelve-based system. This change showed them that they would need more than nine numerals and zero to write down a number. Then I went to the Mayan system. It is a twenty-based system but has only three symbols to produce all of the numerals required.

The binary system, in which there are only ones and zeros was next. I showed them how, in the binary system, there need to be only four operations; store, count, add and compare, to perform all the operations done in a computer.

Finally, I introduced them to calculation using Roman numerals. This was a huge challenge for them but they caught on quickly. To see the complexity of this task try multiplying VIII by IX.[27]

As we went along, I also showed them how to convert from one number system to another. They used this to check the accuracy of their calculations. The introduction of calculation with Roman numerals showed them that the same arithmetic processes apply without regard to the numeration system being used and the advantage of place value in the Arabic system.

This whole process took about six weeks. They found the mental activities required challenging enough to hang in there. The excitement was electric except when they tried using Roman numerals. Switching to different bases helped them appreciate the meaning of place value. Carrying ceased to be a problem but borrowing still presented some difficulties for them. The numerical practice also helped their accuracy.

It was now time for the switch. I put the following expression on the board.

$4x^2 + 12x + 9$

"What could the x in this expression possibly be?" I asked. It didn't take long for someone to suggest that it was a base for a number system of which we did not know the value. The light went on in their eyes all over the classroom.

"Can we figure out its value?" one student asked.
"What do you think?"
"No, you can't."
"Why not?"
"Because the relationship doesn't change whatever value for x you put into it."

I was delighted at this level of insight.
"Suppose that I changed it to:
"$4x^2 + 12x + 9 = 0$"

"Yes, you now can find a value for *x*," another student said, and all agreed.

From here I went on to solving equations in the ninth and tenth grades and to the equations for parabolas and other curves in the twelfth grade. Whenever we encountered a problem of understanding a process, we returned to arithmetic and then generalized it to algebra.

Another relationship needs clarification. When we started working with problems that called for the addition or subtraction of fractions we had a different problem. For instance, you cannot add 2/3 and 3/4 because the bases of these two numbers are different. One is in base 3 and the other in base 4. We must convert them to the same base (in this case a base of 12) before they can be added. Suddenly the mystery behind the finding of lowest common denominators disappeared.

As the year progressed they began to realize that mathematics is the language of numerical patterns. As such, it needs to be taught like a foreign language, through immersion. Notice that this is exactly the strategy I use to teach history and "reading to write."

Shortly after I introduced them to algebra in this way, I prepared a series of study questions such as those I had produced for history. These were designed to walk students through the procedural explanations in their textbooks. My idea was to show them how to use well-written mathematics textbooks to teach themselves mathematics.

Some learned this skill very quickly. For these students I adopted the technique used by my high school algebra teacher. If they passed the weekly tests with mastery, their class time was their own, once they helped those others to whom they were assigned who were having difficulties.[28]

In my science courses I used my history-text approach to teach them how to read science texts. When it came to doing "experiments" I worked like a shop teacher, getting the equipment out, to start with and getting them to find the equipment for themselves. Finally I required them to use equipment to show that it was functionally the same even though it looked different.

I always gave them tasks that required them to think their way through to the results that the books said they should expect. If it didn't work they had to figure out why not. Central to all these approaches is the amount of critical thinking I asked the students to undertake in finding the solutions to problems. In this way the subject matter became the vehicle for teaching learning and thinking skills.

How successful do you think this approach to teaching might be?

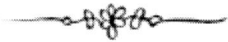

Broadening horizons

Is teaching for mastery a good way to meet standards?

I moved to another high school at the completion of my third year in the small one. This time I became the Head of Special Programs in a suburban high school. I was put in charge of two special classes of students with a history of low academic success. One was nominally at the ninth grade level, the other at the tenth grade level. The ninth grade class was functioning in the third grade in reading and the fourth in mathematics. To deal with students who were this far behind I needed to know, *how much my students really understood or what specifically they could and/or could not do.*

To get around this problem, I looked for the point(s) of breakdown in understanding. I then taught toward these identifiable students' weaknesses. As I taught them these skills and understandings, they gained competence and confidence until many of them became independent learners. I used a *mastery* approach to teaching. Insisting on nearly perfect test results allowed me to be certain that they had these missing elements mastered. Only then could I let them move on.

When working toward the in-depth remediation of missing parts of learning, the timetable goes out the window. There is no point in leaving learning unfinished to cause students to stall once again. However, mastery-level standards must be much higher than 50%. Students should be approaching 100% accuracy in the skills they can use with understanding. If I then used these higher scores for our reporting, my marks would become "too high" to reflect reasonably how they compare with others in the same grade level and school system.[29]

Here also, is where I strengthened my suspicion that *lower scores might sometimes mean higher performance.* What happens when most students respond as though the question is straightforward, but a few find it ambiguous? As teachers we all encounter the classroom lawyers who defend vehemently and well the appropriateness of an answer we intended to consider "wrong." They are often defending a *valid* alternative interpretation, which needs encouragement, not rejection.

My special-classes students were past masters at being wrong. Their self-confidence was out the window as a result. I had to follow their reasoning to their answers to understand where they had gone astray. In many cases, they often interpreted the question differently and answered this different question appropriately.

Are different answers always "wrong" or might they also be examples of "creative insight" like the insight I had about the propagation of sound?

A Learning Environment

What about classroom atmosphere?

For many years my friend and colleague, Tom McCord, has sensed the problem of "atmosphere" within the classroom.

This atmosphere can have either positive or negative effects upon everyone concerned (including the teacher). We need to look at issues such as peer pressure, trust, acceptance, safety (physical, emotional, intellectual) and intimidation in its various forms. It also involves the backgrounds of both teachers and their students, styles of dress, socialization pressures, and many other concerns.

Less successful students, who depart from the mainstream in any of these areas and therefore don't "fit in," have an additional set of problems with which to deal in school. Most of the letters of thanks Tom McCord has received over the years have come from students he has helped to realize their personal worthiness as he tried to help them become valued members of their class. The more successful students often also get pressured to achieve less than their potential as they attempt to become a part of the mainstream peer group.

Both the less and more successful groups may be subjected to being bullied, snubbed, teased, or otherwise ostracized. The socially inept students are often the most tormented.

How do we use procedures like the one to develop self-worth in an accepting and cooperative manner?

The teaching act under a microscope[30]

What is happening during teaching-learning interactions?

Ms. Wilson had written two sentences on the chalkboard before her eighth grade class had assembled. These sentences were:

John hit the ball.
The ball went through the window.

Once they were settled she began:

"All right class, I want you to get out your Language Arts notebooks. On a fresh page use these two sentences to make a single sentence in at least three different ways."

The class members began this assignment and Ms. Wilson moved around the room to observe their progress. When most of them had at least two sentences she returned to the front of the room and said, "Now then, Bill, give me one of your sentences."

Bill replied, "John hit the ball through the window." She wrote this sentence beside the initial ones.

"Very good," she then redirected her attention. "Mary?"

Mary replied, "When John hit the ball, it went through the window."

"Well done." This sentence was added to the list of samples.

"Hugh?"

"John hit the ball through the window."

"We already have that one. Do you have a different one?"

"John hit the ball and it went through the window." This sentence was added to the samples.

"Bertha?"

"The ball went through the window when John hit it."

"Good. Notice how changing of the order of the words or phrases in this way doesn't change the meaning." This sentence was also added to the samples.

"Does anyone have anything different?"

Larry raised his hand, waving his arm with enthusiasm. "Yes, Larry?"

"John hit the ball *after* it went through the window."

There was general laughter among the class members.

First alternative ending   "Doing to"

Ms. Wilson also laughed at Larry's answer.

"Now really, Larry, isn't that an absurd possibility?'

Returning to her lesson she continued, "Which one of these examples is a simple sentence? Gretchen? …"

Gretchen replied, "The second one?"

"That is the easiest way of combining these two sentences. Is it a simple sentence, George?"

"The first one?"

"That's right. Why is it a simple sentence? Frances? ..."

Her lesson continued, establishing sentence types until either all examples were classified, or until she had the types she wishes to represent. Then she gave them a follow-up assignment.

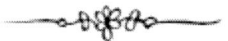

If Larry has a reputation for being the class clown, Ms. Wilson's first thought might be, "Was Larry trying to divert attention from me to him?" If Larry is playing to an appreciative audience, he has successfully diverted attention to him. The fact that she laughed may indicate that she did not recognize his answer was a correct solution to her assigned task.

What she *does to* these students to keep them with her, is part of her skill as a teacher. What she has *done to* Larry, by putting his answer down, is another matter. Her message to him is, "Don't give me off-the-wall answers." Mr. Franklin did the same to me when I asked about the inconsistency of his explanation of how sound is produced.

Second Alternative Ending   "Doing for"

Ms. Wilson waited for the laughter to subside, accepts Larry's contribution without laughter or comment and continues. In this way she modeled accepting behavior to the class. More important for Larry, she tacitly supported his correct answer.

"Now I want you to notice the ways in which these samples differ. In the shortest sentence, some words were left out and part of the second sentence was added to the first one." She then reviewed with the class the characteristics of a *simple* sentence.

She used different colors to mark the subject 'John,' the verb 'hit,' the object 'ball,' and the preposition 'through'. "Such sentences are called 'simple' because they have only one verb part in them." She labeled it accordingly.

"Roberta, please explain to me how our second sample When John hit the ball, it went through the window is different from the first one."

"The second sentence keeps both verbs, changes the second 'ball' to 'it,' joining them together."

"Is there any other difference?"

"Yes, the word 'when' is added to the beginning of the sentence."

Ms. Wilson had Carmen color-code Roberta's sentence.

While Carmen did this, Ms. Wilson asked, "Can anyone tell me what we call 'when?'"

After a period of silence, she continued, "Words like 'when' and 'after' are called *subordinating conjunctions*. These are called 'conjunctions' because they join ideas together. They are called 'subordinating' because they make one part of a sentence less important than another.

"Mary's sentence showed that the ball going through the window is more important than John hitting it, so she put 'when' in front of the first part of her sentence. Such sentences are called 'complex' because they have more than one verb part (or clause) with different levels of importance." She had Rodrigo label this sentence accordingly.

"Would someone like to try a similar analysis of Hugh's sentence?" Ms. Wilson points to the sentence, 'John hit the ball and it went through the window.'

Janice volunteered, "The two sentences are joined by 'and' using 'it' for 'the ball' in the second sentence."

"Excellent! And which part of the new sentence is more important?"

"I don't know," Janice replied.

"Anyone?"

Roberta offered, "Aren't both parts of equal importance?"

"Well done, Roberta!" Ms. Wilson continued. "The 'and,' which is a 'coordinating conjunction,' makes them equal. Such sentences are called 'compound' because they have more than one clause of equal importance." She had Karl label this sentence accordingly.

"Larry, would your example be considered simple, complex or compound?

"Complex," he replied.

"That is correct, good for you."

She reviewed the characteristics of the sentence types with further questioning before continuing with the next part of her lesson. She then passed out a guide sheet that defined each type of sentence, with examples, and reviewed the examples with the class.

The fact that Ms. Wilson did not laugh could mean that she saw the validity of Larry's answer. She didn't want to go there. It would have changed the direction of her lesson. Her intention, to help the class with editing skills overrode the option of exploring ideas.

Third alternative ending "Doing with"

Ms. Wilson continues:

"Please explain, Larry, how you arrived at this sentence."

"Well, Ms. Wilson, you said 'different' and I suddenly realized that the order of these events does not need to be the order you used when you wrote them on the board."

"You are quite right, Larry. That was very insightful. Please go on."

"So I thought of putting 'after' in the place of 'when'."

"But it couldn't happen that way!" Frank objected.

"Why not?" Ms. Wilson asked.

Frank was bemused. Somewhat reluctantly he admitted, "Well, I guess it could, but …"

"Remember," Ms. Wilson went on, "I said to make at least three sentences. I didn't exclude what might seem to be unlikely events.

"Can anyone suggest how Larry's alternative might have happened?"

Larry waved his hand. She smiled at him. "Please let the others think it through."

There was a pause and then Frank raised his hand tentatively. "Suppose the ball was inside the room and someone threw it out through the window so the others could play with it?" His statement sounded more like a question.

"What do you think?"

Frank beamed. "Yes, that would work!"

The enthusiasm spread.

Sarah suggested that the ball in the first sentence and the one in the second might be different.

"What would your sentence be like then?"

Sarah struggled with the wording so, Ms. Wilson had others help her.

They finally came up with, "The ball that went through the window was not the one that John hit."

"What happened to the window?" she finally asked.

"It broke," Richard blurted.

"Did it? Where in the two sentences do we have evidence for that outcome?"

"You're right, Ms. Wilson, we don't," he replied.

"What did Larry's contribution do for us?" she asked.

"It gives us many more sentences to make," Roberta beamed.

"Very insightful, Roberta! Now notice how the assumptions we make about these events influenced our choices. If we assume the order of the events *must be as given*, we severely *limit the number of sentences* we can produce."

Remarks

If we look more deeply and realize there are a number of links between these two sentences that can be broken, then we can produce many more sentences. Is this one way that professional writers do their creative work? Would students learn to be more creative if more teaching like this were done? Is this the true strength of the "reading to write" program?

In this ending Ms. Wilson responds to Larry's enthusiasm. This way of teaching opens discussions to the dramatic impact of insight. Which of these three approaches to intellectual development is the most common in our schools? Which one is required when teaching facts?

Which is the most effective way to teach? How does this approach relate to my insight about how sound is propagated?

The next step

Where do we from here?

I left my position as a special programs teacher in high school in 1964 to begin work on a Ph.D. in educational measurement and child development. I knew I was onto something but was not quite sure what it was. Taking an advanced degree seemed the most logical next step.

It was then that I team-taught classes in excess of 500 students in a large auditorium. I ran a "dog and pony" show with multi-media presentations. I used two hours a week for presentations, and the third hour, with up to seven assistants, as a seminar to discuss issues and problems in more depth.

My research focus was upon the meaningful interpretation of "wrong" answer on multiple-choice tests. I will give more details about this work in Chapter 6 where I will discuss the results from this entire lifetime project.

After completing my Ph.D., I spent a year in a school system as a "Learning Disabilities Specialist" and a second year as a clinician in a psycho-educational clinic. Pertinent to this present discussion was my year in the school system.

There were four thrusts to this effort.

First, I tried to identify those students who needed special programs.

Second, I identified the special programs that were already in place and helped the teachers involved to assess their effectiveness.

Third, I tried to establish community liaison to get support for the valiant efforts being undertaken by the system.

Fourth, I set up a number of special programs that were designed to further enhance program offerings. Here are some examples.

Identifying needs

I went to each school in the system and looked at every student's files. I was looking for anomalies in their records.

Did students show widely different marks from year to year?

Did they show widely different marks among subjects in the year immediately past?

Did they have an intelligence estimate that disagreed with the marks they were getting?

Did they show frequent absences, poor-conduct reports or other characteristics that might require special attention?

Of the roughly 2,000 elementary school students in the system, I flagged a bit more than 500 students to look at in more detail. I then met with the teachers in each school and gave each my list for their classes. The first question I asked was for the teachers to shrink the list by telling me those among them who were not showing current problems and to add to the list the students who were of particular concern to them. This move reduced the list to about 200.

We then looked at ways the teachers might deal with the problems we had identified. Where additional resources seemed to be needed, I tried to find them.

Working with existing programs

Our largest elementary school had four fourth-grade teachers. Two of them were teaching the main stream. Two had special programs. A teacher trained in the use of Pitman's *Initial Teaching Alphabet* taught those who seemed to be having difficulty learning the phonetic approach to words. This is a program developed in the United Kingdom that uses a 36-character phonetic alphabet. As far as I could tell, this program worked very well. Both the teacher and the students were excited about it and their reading scores were improving dramatically.

The other teacher worked with the children who showed limited vocabulary skills. She had collected dolls and toys over the years to represent all of the characters, and objects that were in the reading series she was using. This approach provided concrete objects to help children build their vocabularies. Her thrust was the "whole word" approach. Aside from suggesting an enrichment of her creative writing part of her program, I was equally pleased with her efforts.

Many teachers wanted to be able to do more with the Science Research Associates (SRA)[31] reading laboratories. This is a self-monitoring program published by IBM. The school board treasurer vetoed the expenditure. I was able to work around this power conflict to some degree.

Community liaison

In the course of my clinical training I had found a couple of simple surveys that would help teachers catch problems early. After discussing the use of these with several of the school personnel, it became clear that, although a good idea, we did not have the personnel to do this screening.

I learned, however, that the local health department did immunization screening for all pre-school children. I talked to the nurses in the program and to the local physicians and found the money and the agreement to get this screening done at the time of the immunization clinics by the public-health nurses.

The "painting in black" incident illustrates how I worked with school-community relationships on a face-to-face basis.

Special projects

There were several special projects that are worth mentioning. I established a rotating library using publishers' introductory offers. There were 40 books in each of several boxes. Each box included comprehension checks. I took them to the fifth grade teachers and left them for six weeks. These were new books available in the classroom that would be removed in a short time. This situation seemed to motivate enthusiasm for reading. All the teachers reported a surge in voluntary reading. They had the comprehension checks to prove their claims.

We had one child in the fifth grade that was the sixth of thirteen children of a mostly absent father and an alcoholic mother. It was her lot to be substitute mother and to get the younger ones to school. Her school success was low and her attendance sporadic.

We enrolled her in the Alberta Correspondence courses. Her classroom teacher marked her work. This meant that she could work at her own pace and have her next piece of work awaiting her whenever she came to school. No longer missing the sequences of teaching by her absence, her schoolwork improved dramatically and her attendance improved substantially as well.

I also had a couple of the best teachers develop theme kits for our social studies program. Once they had used the kits themselves, I rotated them to other classrooms. These kits generated a great deal of enthusiasm.

The outcome

Unfortunately budgetary constraints and internal politics led to the discontinuance of this post after one year. There was a community outcry that led to their offering me a principalship. I chose instead to move to another community to work in a psycho-educational clinic. I thought that my services would be more effective being broadly distributed. That position also lasted for only one year. My work style and that of the department head clashed. I decided to leave teaching altogether and try my hand at business. I enrolled in an M.B.A. program at the University of Western Ontario.

The following year I began a 16-year stint in the Faculty of Education at the University of Windsor.

After more than forty years of life, had I found my niche as a teacher of teachers?

In the remainder of this chapter I will give a number of examples of classroom management techniques that I have conducted or collected. These are illustrative of how the approach I am recommending can be applied in a number of subject areas.

Multi-tasking

How might several learning goals be integrated into one activity?

Mr. McBain, a shop teacher, had his students, in groups of four, build a ramp of their own design. These consisted of a platform, a series of vertical supports, and a trough made of cardboard. The ramp could curl in any fashion but could not be straight.

Once the ramp had been completed, the students let a marble roll down the ramp and time the duration of the roll. Typically, the first attempt is unsuccessful because obstacles of one sort or another prevented the marble from completing the trip. At this point, trouble-shooting skills come into play. In the best case, the students, working in teams, log their attempts at fixing the problems and the results of these attempts.

Observation of the pathway shows that sharp corners absorb momentum and cause the marble to be sensitive to minor incline changes or surface obstructions. Solving the problem of how to make the corners more rounded can be a good exercise in creative group-problem-solving.

The next step was to measure the lengths and heights of the ramps of several such projects and to get the average run time on several runs. From here the mean velocities as a function of the slope of the ramps can be determined. Students can then try to develop a mathematical equation for this relationship.

How might a similar approach be developed in book-based subject areas?

Listening skills

Can we assess the effectiveness of our students' listening?

Mrs. Clements passed the plastic bowl around the room. "Each one of you, please select a slip of paper from the bowl and pass the bowl on. On that paper you will find a letter from "A" through "G." Once you have that letter, please move to the table that had the corresponding letter on it. This will be your working group for this class period."

She waited for the class members to rearrange themselves. "Will one person from each table come up to this table and pick up the folder that has your table's letter on it? Each folder contains some information for you to read. Every folder has something different in it. There should be enough copies of the item in each folder for everyone to have a copy to read.

"Once you have read the material I want you to discuss the contents of the item amongst yourselves and to develop a short summary of it."

"How long?" Jennifer asked.

"Fifty words or less – short enough to fit into one space in the summary sheets in your folder. When you have completed your summary, write it into the space for the letter of your group. Everyone in the group should have the same summary."

Mrs. Clements waited until they were busy discussing and writing their summaries.

"Now choose a spokesperson to read your summary to the rest of the class. Read it slowly enough that they can copy what you are reading. Tell the rest of the class the letter for your group so that they can know where to write the summary on their summary sheets."

Soon each group in turn was reading the summaries upon which they had agreed.

At the end of the period, Mrs. Clements concluded, "Make sure that your name and the letter of your group are on the top of your summary sheets, and then hand them in. I'll give them back to you tomorrow, when we will discuss the information you have summarized. Please also put the information sheets back into their folders and place them on the table as you leave."

Notice that the transcription of these summaries requires very careful listening.

How might this approach be applied to language arts?

The incredible shrinking log

How might we teach visual decoding of physical events?

"It's a lovely fire, Dad!" Shelly burst out with delight. "We ought to do this more often."

"You bet, Dad!" Brian rejoined as he carried his second armload of firewood to the site and dropped it on the heap.

"Mom, hurry up with those wieners, I'm really hungry," Freddie called.

All smiles, Mrs. Henry carried the hamper with the tableware from the van while Mr. Henry carried the cooler to the picnic table. The three children, Freddie, Shelly and Brian helped setting up the table. Brian and his dad made the fire ready to roast the wieners in the blaze.

Soon, they were wolfing down all the goodies and joking with each other.

Comfortably seated and searing marshmallows in the embers, they sat together contentedly on the benches beside the fire.

"What can you tell me about what you see as you watch the fire burn?" Mr. Henry, a high school chemistry teacher, asked.

The children knew this was the beginning of a 'thinking game' their dad often played. The end result was always something unexpected.

"The fire is hot," Freddie ventured.

"Of course, but when is it hottest?"

"When the flames are biggest," Shelly ventured hesitantly.

"That's another of your trick questions, isn't it?" Brian spoke with confidence. "I'll bet that the flames are all the same temperature, no matter how many there are."

"You're both right," Mr. Henry grinned. "The fire throws more heat with more flames, but the heat from the chemical reaction is constant. It depends how you define 'hottest'."

At that point there was a sharp 'crack' and one of the glowing logs threw a shower of sparks, broke and fell among the embers.

"What happened just then?" Mr. Henry asked.

"It sounded and looked like a small explosion," Shelly said puzzled. "But how could that happen?"

"What do you think?"

"It must have been an explosion."

Mr. Henry beamed at Shelly. "You are quite right. Do you want to explain how wood might explode?"

"I'm not sure …"

"Does it have something to do with the unevenness of wood's structure? What with the grains in the wood and all …" Brian proposed.

"And so?"

"I'm not sure …" Shelly remarked.

"What do you have to do to start wood burning in the first place?"

"You start it with something else, like paper," Freddie suggested.

"Doesn't it have to be at a certain temperature for it to burn?" Shelly was now catching a glimpse of the idea.

"Yes, that is known as the 'kindling temperature'."

"So the wood turns to a gas before it flames? And the unevenness of the wood makes for little pockets of gas before they burst into flame," Brian put in.

"And that's the source of these spark-producing explosions." It was not a question this time. Shelly's voice showed the certainty of understanding.

"Okay." Mr. Henry smiled. "Now for the key question; does wood get smaller and lighter, or larger and heavier as it burns?"

"Smaller and lighter," Freddie said with conviction.

"This is another one of your tricks, isn't it?" Brian asked. "If the burning wood is turning into a gas, it's increasing its volume."

"Yes, and …?

"If the wood is taking on oxygen, it is adding to its mass." Shelly was pleased at her cleverness.

"If it is larger and heavier, why can't you see it?" Freddie wanted to know.

"Because the gas is invisible," Brian said.

"Oh," Freddie replied somewhat puzzled at his brother's explanation.

"But can you see the process that produces this result, Freddie?" Shelly asked.

"In the flames and the explosions, I guess." Freddie seemed to grasp the idea now.

Similarly, how might we collect data in elementary school to prove that the world is a globe?

Concrete experiences from difficult language
How do we make words visual?

> Scene III. The open country.
> <u>Enter</u> EDGAR
> <u>Edg</u>. I heard myself proclaim'd
> And by the happy hollow of a tree
> Escap'd the hunt. No port is free; no place
> That guard and most unusual vigilance
> does not attend my taking. Whiles I may scape
> I will preserve myself; and am bethought
> to take the basest and most poorest shape
> That ever penury in contempt of man
> Brought near to beast. My face I'll grime with filth,

> Blanket my loins, elf my hairs in knots,
> And with presented nakedness outface
> The winds and persecutions of the sky.[32]

Franklin remarked. "Gee! What a funny way to talk." He screwed up his face in disgust as he looked away from these words on the overhead projector screen.

"What does 'penury' mean?" Clarissa asked.

"Poverty," Mr. Crooks replied.

"Now let us consider how we would stage this scene," he continued.

"What is happening here?"

"Is Edgar hiding from someone?" Pete enquired.

"Yes, but where? Franklin?" Mr. C. asked.

Franklin grimaced as he read the passage over. "A hollow tree?" he offered hesitantly.

"Very good, and if we were to stage this scene, how would we go about it?"

"We'll need a hollow tree," Franklin grinned.

"And a blanket," Phyllis rejoined.

"And some dirt," Pete added. ...

Where would we add a movie version of King Lear to a lesson like this for the "reading to write" approach?

The substitute teacher

Is it always necessary for students to test the skills of a substitute teacher?

It was the fall of 1963. I had been invited to make a presentation at a conference and would be away from my classroom for three days.

I was teaching two groups of special program students, a group of ninth graders and a group of tenth graders. The former was new to me this year and the latter was a group I had also taught the previous year.

Making Peasants into Kings

To develop self-confidence in my two groups, I had them do most of the classroom management work themselves. This included distribution and collecting work assignments, scoring these assignments and entering the results on each person's progress charts.

Each student's program was individualized and drawn from sequential programs that required reading short explanations and providing written responses. There was little need for up-front teaching except when group activities were involved.

Upon my return, I asked the principal how things had gone. The substitute teacher was serving another class that day so the principal suggested I talk to her. I found her in the staff room.

"How did things go in my class, Mrs. Jones?"

"I've never seen anything like it," she replied. "I was never so bored in my life. I borrowed a book from the library the first day and brought one from home the other two days.

"How do you manage to do that with young people who are so far behind in school?"

"They may be behind academically," I replied, "mostly through no fault of their own, but socially they are just normal teenagers. They can take considerable personal responsibility when challenged to do so. They are proud of the fact that they can do so much for themselves. Once people have learned how to learn, they can teach themselves nearly everything they need to know.'

"Do you ever meet as a group?"

"Yes, on a regularly scheduled basis. When we are scoring their weekly compositions as a group, we meet on Thursdays. When something comes up that requires a group resolution, we meet in caucus to work through that problem. Otherwise they work mostly by themselves. They are too spread out in their skills to try to teach them all the same thing. That only bores some of them to death and goes over the heads of others."

"I've known this problem exists for most of my teaching career," she said, "but I was never able to figure out how to solve it."

"All you do is to stop using the 'assembly-line' approach to teaching. You use the 'job-shop' industrial model instead. And you teach the students how to help each other. The unevenness of his or her skills means that someone is better at something than the rest. This brings consultation into the picture. It's something like the old fashioned one-room school house."

"I think I understand. My mother attended a one-room school during her elementary school years. She said that she learned more there than anywhere else in school."

"At its best, the one-room school, that required students to learn how to learn, has provided the best education ever achieved in North America. At its worst, no one learned much of anything."

"Well, you certainly seem to have something going well for you, Mr. Powell," she concluded as the bell rang for the next class period.

Does getting students to help each other lead to appreciating each other? Does this positive interaction remove the destructive aspects of interpersonal competitions that pervade our schools?

Is this approach a better basis for effective teaching than trying to make everyone learn the same thing at the same pace?

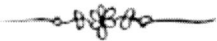

Our present position is insufficient. We must move beyond cooperation and even compassion into a mutual understanding of the interconnectedness of everything. I develop the reasons for this shift in our interpersonal relationships and our relationship with our environment in the next chapter.

Chapter 5: Developing connectedness

In classical physics all things vary in a continuous manner, but in quantum physics things change in both continuous and discontinuous ways.

Amit Goswami[33]

Going beyond the material

We return to the issue of connectedness raised by the Old One. Just what does the idea of connectedness mean? Here is what Thomas Moore[34] has to say about the soul.

I suspect further that if we come to appreciate the archetypal child whom we feel within ourselves, we have a more open and appreciative relationship to actual children. For example, an eternal question about children is, how should we educate them? Politicians and educators consider more school days in the year, more science and math, the use of computers and other technology in the classroom, more exams and tests, more certifications for teachers, and less money for art. All these responses come from a place where we can make the child into the best adult possible, not in the ancient Greek sense of serious and wise, but in the sense of one who is an efficient part of the machinery of society. But in all these counts, soul is neglected. We want to prepare the ego for the struggle for survival, but we overlook the needs of the soul.

Education means, "To lead out." We seem to understand it as a leading away from childhood but maybe we could think of it as eliciting the wisdom and the talents of childhood itself. As A. S. Neale, founder of the Summerhill School, taught many years ago, we can trust that the child already has talents and intelligence. We believe that the child intellectually is a tabula rasa, a blank blackboard, but maybe the child knows more than we suspect. Child wisdom is different from adult wisdom, but it has its place. Any move against the archetypal child is a move against the soul because this child is a face of a soul, and whatever aspect of the soul we neglect becomes a source of suffering. We are a society that finds it difficult to discover the exuberant joy and spontaneity of childhood; instead we spend great sums of money on electronic entertainment centers that don't speak to the soul's need for childlike direct pleasure.

Here then is the central theme of this book. "Should we educate towards the imperatives of the society as we extend humanity into an uncertain future, or should we educate with the imperatives of the soul as the core focus, with the assurance that the resulting connection with the universal part of each of us assures the future?"

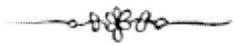

What is Reality?

To explain my understanding we will need to look briefly at quantum mechanics. Recent scientific research inside the atom has produced a remarkable picture of subatomic reality. Four characteristics of this strange reality are of interest here. These are:

1. Existence is non-local.
2. Matter is mostly "empty" space and is transient and discontinuous in nature. That is, events are only possibilities and are not predetermined. Particles appear and disappear instead of being "solid" matter.
3. Events precipitate into what we consider common reality because of the presence of a conscious observer.
4. At the subatomic level, the Zero-point Field, the potential power present is astronomical.

Let us consider each of these four aspects of reality to better understand what the soul might be and why it is important to effective education.

What is non-locality?

It is easier to understand what non-locality is not than what it is. This is what I mean:

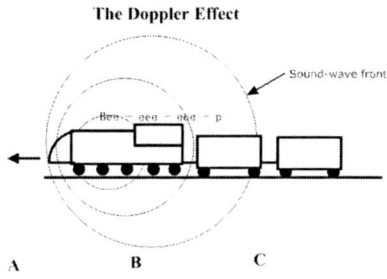

This is a picture of a moving train sounding its horn. The circles represent the wave fronts of the noise made by the horn. Because the train is moving, the point of release of each wave front moves with it.

A person standing at position "A" will hear a note higher than the actual note of the horn. The movement of the train toward that position shortens its wavelength. This is why the circles each have different center with a narrower space between them to the left and a broader one to the right.

The person at position "C" will hear a lower note because the wavelength is increased by the speed of its departure. This phenomenon is known as the Doppler Effect, named after the scientist who first described it accurately.

Notice that this effect occurs because the point of origin of the sound is localized on the train as it moves in space-time. All matter and energy displays this localization at the microcosmic level. Scientists assume it also occurs on the macrocosmic level, but it may not.[35]

Similarly, because our superficial consciousness appears to be in our heads behind our eyes, we regard ourselves as localized phenomena. This is what produces our sense of separateness.

In contrast, non-local phenomena exist outside of space-time. If sound were a non-local, we would hear the same note without regard to where we stood or the velocity of the train. In a non-local universe everything is occurring simultaneously and everything is interconnected. These interconnections are instantaneous across the entire universe, not constrained by the speed of light.

The nearest mundane thing we have on earth to non-local phenomena is the Internet. It is still confined in time, but it is not confined in space. Because electronic speeds are so great in the tiny space of the earth, response times on the Internet can be almost instantaneous. We can send and receive messages from anywhere to anywhere on earth as long as a connection into the web is available. Messages are slowed noticeably at either end of the transmission by processing them.

In the case of non-local events, the transmission is instantaneous throughout the entire Universe. Objects maintain their integrity as they appear and disappear, shifting from one plane of existence to another. In addition these objects can be modified by deliberate intervention.

Does the same thing happen with our consciousness?

The transient nature of matter

Back in the 1920s, Werner Heisenberg[36] was deeply involved in theoretical physics. At that time there was a huge argument going on about whether the lowly electron was a particle or a wave. He reviewed the research and he found that those researchers who were claiming it to be a wave performed their research in a particular way. Those who claimed that it was a particle performed their experiments in a quite different way. The two procedures were incompatible.

He concluded that the way we observe predetermines the conclusions we draw. Here we have a good example of making the data fit the interpretation. They were arguing from their results, which were true, without comparing procedures. Both groups had only part of the picture.

Heisenberg, in his now famous "Uncertainty Principle," first identified this strangeness about subatomic reality. The apparent solidity of our physical reality is an illusion produced by our physical size compared to the size of atoms and subatomic particles. Also involved is the wavelength of light as compared to the size of atoms. Since atoms are smaller than the wavelength of visible light, light is reflected from them.

Another of the surprises that physicists encountered when studying subatomic events was the fact that when an electron changes orbit as an atom heats up or cools down is that it jumps from orbit to orbit without leaving a trail across the intervening space. Further investigation has shown that this appearance and disappearance occurs with all particles, not just electrons.

The role of the observer

As we have just seen from our train horn illustration, observers in different places see or hear different things. If we were deeply absorbed in some activity, we might not even hear the horn. What we observe depends upon our attention, our intention, and our observation skills. If we were sitting on the tracks we had better hear the train!

How does intention fit into reality? How would you view a stand of trees as a(n)?

1. Farmer in need of more land to farm,
2. Conservationist trying to protect the environment,
3. Artist or photographer looking for a subject to commemorate,
4. Land developer planning to build a new suburb, or
5. Forester looking for hardwood to buy?

Obviously, the interpretation of this stand of trees will be different for each, according to their several or individual intentions. The outcome will depend upon which of these intentions triumphs. Notice that each of these intentions is self-serving toward their differing objectives.

Quantum mechanics goes further. The way we observe predetermines the conclusions we draw. Whenever these conclusions are converted to action, our observations predetermine the outcomes *as we observe them*. Unless we are very careful observers, unexpected or undesirable outcomes may be missed. If we do not coordinate our observation, or if they are inaccurate, the outcomes are bound to do harm. Such is the issue behind global warming. This is why teamwork is so important. Shared perceptions are more accurate than individual viewpoints.

Energy resources

I am told that Nickoli Tesla discovered how to tap the unlimited resources in the Zero-point Field more than 70 years ago. What happened to his discovery? We are uncertain. I have seen the results of others who have attained this same effect. A source of unlimited quantities of inexpensive non-polluting energy would solve many of today's problems.

This possibility is the second of three essential parts to the restoration of earth to the Eden state. Extracting energy from this source would eliminate the need for a philosophy of scarcity that is the *fear*-based driving force behind our sense of separation from each other and from the Universe and the *greed* that drives our economic system.

How are we going to learn to live with each other in ways that "do no harm?" We need to add another concept, the concept of *consciousness* to come to grips with this question.

The role of consciousness

Because Christianity often works to enrich life in the culture that spawned it, we are told that this is the only way to believe. When the same results come from a different culture, these results are assumed to be of diabolical origin. We need to look more deeply into the nature of reality. Science is uncovering a way to resolve this dilemma. It is fascinating that the *Course in Miracles* says the same thing. "Your thoughts determine the world you see (Workbook, Lesson 11; 1:3)."

Quantum physics has gone even further. Subatomic research has shown that;

1. Time, as we usually conceive of it, does not exist.
2. Matter, as we usually conceive of it, does not exist.

3. Space, as we usually conceive of it, does not exist.

4. Consciousness is also quite different from our superficial sense of immediate awareness.

I will not spend time telling you the details of the research that has led to these conclusions. Instead, I will merely put forward the suggestion that can be found in Amit Goswami's[37] enlightening book, *The Visionary Window*. In this, he proposes that the event that turns possibilities into realities is the application of consciousness to situations. In his terms, there are two levels of consciousness. There is the ordinary level in which we usually live, and a higher form of Consciousness that creatively precipitates material reality.

What if time, matter, space and consciousness are not what we think they are? What evidence do we have on a scale larger than the atom?

For most people the evidence we best understand is our own personal experience. Mathematics and physics are something "out there," done by strangers. Research seems to be an esoteric pursuit that is divorced from the real world.

Here, then, is my speculation. We start with the idea that there are two levels of consciousness. The mundane or superficial level is ego-driven, supports the fear-driven separation concept, and exists at the materialistic level. The deep level of Consciousness is part of the "Ultimate Observer" and is a non-local phenomenon that exists timelessly throughout the entire universe.

Each of us is a unique fragment of this Ultimate (or Christ) Consciousness. Being non-local, we also exist outside of space and time. This is how I define "Soul." It was never born, can never die but can extend itself indefinitely in space-time in accordance with the uniqueness of each fragment.

As such, we are both local and non-local. Our function is to bring to various localities the Universal Power from the Source of All to wherever it is needed. Our uniqueness enhances the effectiveness of the delivery system. Each of us is "God's Gift to the Universe."

Our problem is that we are too dominated by our sense of separateness. We respond to life from the superficial level of ego, where fear reigns, force is the basis for control and greed the basis of identity. Most of us live by the dictates of our heritages and not by the imperatives of our Souls. Our Souls have Infinite power and unlimited possibilities making fear and greed unnecessary.

This speculation has solid evidence coming from quantum mechanics.

Does the bigger picture conform to these tiny subatomic events?

A life beyond belief[38]

What conclusions can we draw about reality if we try to link spirituality with quantum physics?

I would like to begin with a short passage from *A Course in Miracles*[39]. This is from the Workbook, Lesson 121 (6:1-3).

> Forgiveness is acquired. It is not inherent in the mind, which cannot sin. As sin is an idea you taught yourself, forgiveness must be learned by you as well, but from a teacher other than yourself, who represents the other deeper Self in you.

Escape from logic

What happens when people try to make the data fit the interpretation?

On many occasions, I have had some interesting discussions with a wide variety of people. These discussions can become very frustrating when someone gets stuck on a particular point of view. Here is an amusing story that illustrates this point.

It seems that St. Peter and Lucifer were involved in such a discussion just after Gutenberg invented the printing press.

"Aren't you afraid," St. Peter asked, "Now that people can read Scripture for themselves you will be put out of business?"

"Not at all," Lucifer replied. "All I need to do is to help them interpret it."

The two basic principles of compassion (unconditional love) and expanded awareness (enlightenment) are common elements to all major religions. The rest may be window dressing.

Is this problem, of acting from superficial understanding, the source of the divergent positions among organized religion? Why else would they stress the uniqueness of their particular viewpoint?

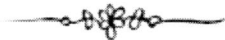

Genealogy of Jesus

What happens when we encourage students to think for themselves?

"Dad," Philip interjected. "Can I talk to you for a minute?"

His father turned away from the TV and replied, "Of course, son."

"No, I mean *really* talk; with the TV off. This is *important*."

Rev. Günter was now concerned. "What could be this serious?" he mused.

"I know, Dad. You took me out of Westend High, partly because of the drugs, but mainly because you wanted a more Christian atmosphere for my education. We discussed this and I agreed with you."

"Do you want to go back to that school?"

"No, that's not it. It's more serious than that."

"Okay, son, tell me about it; some girl perhaps?"

"No, Dad. Listen to me! You suggested that, in my home schooling I should examine issues carefully, get the evidence, and come to my own conclusions — right?"

"Yes, of course, son."

"And you often said that there are no inconsistencies and contradictions in the Bible."

"Yes, that is our belief. As Lutherans we regard the Bible as the Inspired Word of God, so it can contain no inconsistencies or contradictions."

"Well, that's my problem. I don't know why I decided to try comparisons of text as an exercise in getting some experience in these skills, but I did. And..." Phil's voice trailed off.

"What did you find?" His father was now very concerned. It was most important that nothing shake his son's faith in God.

"Well, I thought that it would be easy to find absolute consistency in the genealogy of Jesus, so I looked up the passages in Matthew and Luke that gives this information. Once I got past the fact that the orders were reversed in the two Gospels, I was shocked at what I found!"

"Which was?"

"Well, both genealogies lead to Joseph, who is supposed not to have had sex with Mary until after Jesus was born. Isn't that inconsistent? Shouldn't the genealogies have led to Mary?"

"I'm not sure, son. I don't think that the Hebrews kept track of the lineage of the females in their society."

"Yes, but isn't that inconsistent?"

"I guess it could be. We'll have to ask Rev. Schmidt, Dean of Theology at Brotherhood University, about that."

"But that is not all!" Phil's voice was almost frantic. "There is exact agreement from Abraham to David. But after David the next in line, in Matthew is Solomon and, in Luke, the next

Making Peasants into Kings

in line is Nathan. In fact, there is very little similarity in the two lists between David and Joseph. Isn't this a contradiction? Doesn't this make the claim that there are no contradictions in the Scriptures *false?*"

If you were Rev. Schmidt, how would you answer this question? Which matters more, what Jesus demonstrated about human potentials for all Faiths and Creeds or the polemics of literalists about details?

Does time as we usually conceive of it actually exist?

Baby robin

How might a four-year-old respond to death?

It was the spring of 1935. My sister Grace had just been born. I recall being awestruck at how tiny she was. Babies are miracles.

We lived in a California style stucco cottage on the outskirts of the City of Edmonton, in Alberta. I have many fond recollections of that lovely little house. The frost ferns that formed on the windows of the front porch where I slept are still vivid in my mind. The goldfish we bought, that died because we didn't know that they needed air in their water, awakened my interest in science.

But the strongest and most personal recollection I have of our time in that house in Edmonton is the day I was walking along our front fence. Our house was on three lots. The westerly lot consisted of a lawn and kitchen garden of which my father took meticulous care. This was where I watched Daddy use the lawn mower that I tried to replicate with my Mechano˙ set.

The eastern lot was thickly wooded with aspen and poplar trees that I loved to climb. Our house stood proudly in the middle lot in front of which was a small but immaculate lawn that added to the welcoming atmosphere.

The house faced north and on the northern edge of the three lots there was a row of large fir trees. Because these trees shed acid needles, there was no lawn under them. To help make this area more useful, Daddy had spread furnace ash along under the trees to make a firm walkway.

I loved to stroll along this walk, peering through the fence to the road beyond and imagining all sorts of wonderful adventures.

One bright and fresh spring day, as I walked my circuit, I found the body of a baby robin in the walkway. Its beak was as big as its head and its body had only a few feathers. I remember feeling sad, more for the mother robin than for the baby.

I remember digging a small hole with my pocketknife, saying a few words of prayer and burying the bird during a very private and discreet personal ceremony at the foot of the tree where the nest had adorned a branch. This act brought me a deep sense of inner peace.

I don't know how I knew that I should do this. We had thrown the goldfish into the garbage. There seemed to be a memory from long before I was born that this ceremony was what *we* did for the bodies of dead creatures.

This event was the point where my sense of my Soul's imperatives began to awaken. I have never related this event to anyone before now. It is important now because of the other events I want to relate to you in this chapter. How could a three-year-old have known what to do, if I had never lived before my present birth? Is there a *part* of each of us that exists outside of space-time?

How many other people have had a similar sense of deep awareness at such a young age, only to lose it as they matured? Should we help them recapture it if we can? Should we help those who still have it to retain it?

Prophetic dreams

Does the Universal Consciousness speak to us in our dreams?

I do not remember whether I had some invisible playmates. I do remember some of the children I played with before going to school. Many people commented upon the imagination I showed in play. I recall one incident where several of us had put some boxes in a row. We were sitting in them, pretending that we were in an airplane. I recall calling a warning that another plane was coming close and we all ducked our heads on cue.

Was this a voice from the past?

The things I remember most about my childhood and adolescence were the vivid dreams I had. One of the early ones was when I was eight years old. I seemed to be about the same age. I was living in a hot climate and wearing loose-fitting garments. My father at that time was getting ready to make a journey to the big city. I didn't want him to go. I was frightened. I *knew* that I would never see him again because *they wanted to kill him!*

"Don't go, please don't go!" I pleaded.

"I must," he replied.

"Then take me with you." Tears were running hotly down my cheeks.

"No, you are too little."

He turned away and joined his traveling companions. I struggled to free myself from the firm grip of my mother's sister. It was no use. Before long they had rounded the corner and were lost to view.

In my dream, I moped around for about a week. Then about dusk, when the Sabbath began and I was getting ready for bed, I heard his voice. It seemed to be right beside me although I knew he was far away. His voice said, "Father forgive them, they know not what they do," (KJV: Lu. 23.34.)

I awoke from that dream in a cold sweat. My pillowcase was wet with tears. The powerful reality of that dream still haunts me.

My family was not big on church attendance. It was several years before I discovered where this quote came from. Was this a figment of my imagination? How then do I account for the vivid reality of that dream?

Or was this the point in time that sent me on my mission?

Knowing a military secret?

As I approached adolescence there was a period of time when I had many such vivid dreams. Three in particular seem very important. In the early spring of 1944 I had a dream where I saw a large number of people in uniform. They were helping to build a floating harbor. It was to go across a short body of water with these uniformed people. On this occasion I awoke with a feeling of excitement.

My mother ridiculed the idea at the time. My father said nothing. I later discovered that he couldn't defend me. He was in the Royal Canadian Mounted Police As head of the Canadian secret service for western Canada at the time, he was aware of the preparations for the invasion of Normandy beaches on D-day (June 6th, 1944), but it was a military secret.

Did my consciousness connect across space-time to get this vision?

Who took a moonwalk?

About five years later, I saw in my dreams a man in a white suit that resembled the divers' suits I had seen in Bermuda. The difference was that this suit had what looked like an inverted goldfish bowl for a helmet. He was walking awkwardly in a barren landscape with a very black sky behind him even though he was in bright sunlight. I had the impression that he was walking on the moon. The dream was coupled with a strong sense of satisfaction. I remember telling my family that humans would visit the moon before the end of the 1960s.

This dream has also proven to be true. Was this prophecy? Was it another non-local event? Such events are easily explainable, if our consciousness is non-local.

My mother's concern increased to a point where she discussed getting me psychological help. Then, as a number of these dreams began to come true, she changed her approach. After that, she tried to get me to stop having these dreams. She was soon joined by my sister; both of them constantly challenged my emerging sense of Infinite Connection.

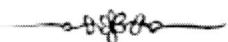

The cave of challenge and mystery

Movies enthralled me. After seeing one about Aladdin's lamp, I had a complex dream about entering a cave. A seer in a turban gave me some advice before I entered. Of particular importance were three pieces of advice.

First, I was to take the sword and not the ax.

Second, I was to ignore the advice of women.

Third, I was to draw my strength from the light.

As I wandered from chamber to chamber, having several adventures, I came upon an alcove where a sword and an ax were hanging side by side. The sword had the word "Wisdom" engraved on its handle.

The ax had the word "Rules" engraved on its handle. I took hold of the sword and lifted it from its scabbard. The ax came at me with a vengeance. Somehow I managed to cut it to pieces. This part of the dream reminds me of my endless, but mostly successful, battles with bureaucracy.

Moving on, I encountered a chamber full of women. They were dressed in Hollywood style Middle Eastern costumes.

They were chained to each other and to the ground. In a chorus they cried, "Strike here, strike here!"

All except one, that is. Her costume was more tasteful and less seductive than the rest. She said nothing. I struck the anchoring point between her and the ground. The chains fell away from all the women, who promptly departed in all directions except the quiet one. She remained standing by her fallen chains. She accompanied me along the corridor in front of us. I recall a soft but strong flow between us, though no words were exchanged.

This corridor was brightly lit with torches. One of them had the word "Strength" on it. I hung the sword on the hook where this torch had been and continued on down the corridor toward a huge black door. As we approached, it swung silently open. Still silent, she gestured that I enter and stepped back as though she could not enter with me.

As soon as I was inside, the door slammed shut. In the dim light of the single torch I saw a low large circular black table in the middle of the chamber. As I approached the table dark shapes attacked me and tried to overwhelm me. I stretched out my arm and touched the surface of the table with the flaming torch. Immediately the entire surface erupted into a brilliant white light.

Suddenly I was strong. The strength seemed to come from the light. I grabbed the dark forces with an unbelievably strong grip and hurled them into the brilliant disk, where they were consumed. At this point I woke up. Even though my sheet and blanket were in a tangle around me I felt triumphant and vindicated.

The corridor of torches seems to me to have been my education after beginning university.

I know that the demure silent woman who accompanied me when I fought the darkness was my lovely first wife, Frances. Since then I've had several other encounters with the darkness.

God's strength in me seems to have grown stronger with each encounter. That strength is always victorious.

Am I unusual in the fact that I have been able to interpret the symbolism behind many of these figurative dreams? My contacts with others who have "awakened" would say that this ability is a common part of human potential. Should we be trying to help others interpret their vivid dreams as well? Does everyone come here with a contract from Heaven, too often to lose touch with it?

If future events can be seen in such detail before they happen, can time flow in either direction?

The impossible trip

My first wife, Frances, and I spent about seven years in the mid 1970s to early 1980s traveling from Windsor, Ontario to Port Huron, Michigan nearly every Tuesday evening. We were attending a Spiritualist sitting at the home of the late Rev. Ray Seaton.

At one of these meetings I got into a discussion about some spiritual matters that seemed to involve some vital information being channeled through me. My mundane consciousness was becoming concerned because I needed to arise at six the next morning to do some practice teaching supervision at Wallaceburg (an hour's drive northeast of Windsor). I needed enough rest to be alert for a day of supervising student teachers. The observation I made that day is "Hiding behind coats."

Understand that it was 63 miles from the Seaton's house to ours, the last three of which were from the south end of I-375 at Jefferson, through the Detroit – Windsor tunnel to home.

The clock was ticking away, 10:10, 10:20, and 10:30 PM …

The session finally ended and we left the Seaton house at 10:34. Deciding not to be more exhausted than need be I set the cruise control at 64 mph. and drove at this "leisurely" pace (being passed by nearly everyone on the road) toward Detroit.

At the foot of I-375 on a billboard that we face as we turn onto Jefferson is a digital clock. This clock said 11:04 as we passed it. I remarked to Frances at the time that the power must have been off in Detroit for a half hour. I couldn't see the clock in the car because I had dimmed the dash lights to reduce the glare of night driving.

When we reached our home it was still only 11:15! The clock in the car, my wristwatch, and the three clocks in the house all agreed! To say that I was flabbergasted would put it mildly.

How could I possibly have driven 60 miles in 30 minutes, an average speed of 120 mph with the cruise reading 64 and most cars passing me? My sole witness is now in Heaven, but I have described this event on many occasions. Are there any *scriptural* examples of time anomalies? I have heard many contemporary stories of similar events.

Notice that this was a generous and thoughtful Gift from the Universe. Have you also had strange shifts of or gaps in time with similar beneficial consequences? Quantum mechanics research answers "Yes" to the question above about whether such time shift anomalies are possible. Perhaps such time dislocations are more common than many might suppose.

Could other strange events happen if time and space are <u>not</u> the uniform linear progression of classical physics?

Does matter actually exist?

Where did the bell come from?

I was giving a sermon in one of the several churches I once served. It was close to Christmas and my sermon was discussing the nature of Spiritual Guidance, as Spiritualists perceive it. One of these concepts is that of the "Joy Guide." He or she is often a bit of a prankster, pulling silly but lovely practical jokes to help lighten up tense situations.

Mine was a fairy. Fairies are *happy thoughts*. I used the word "was" because as I began to move away from the Spiritualist perception of reality, I found someone who needed a joy guide more than I. I invited her to serve this person with a greater need. She still visits me from time to time.

She was still with me at the time of that sermon and was helping with its delivery. The podium was a rectangular wooden box with a sloping lid. It was bare except for a light and the order of service taped to its surface. I had the Bible I was using sitting open at my Scriptural Reading in front of me. This was all that was on the podium

When the service was finished I picked up my Bible. Just above where I had placed my Bible was a little ornamental bell of the sort used to decorate Christmas packages.

This Gift from Spirit was appropriate both for the season and for the fact that I had nicknamed my Joy Guide "Tinkerbell." There was no way that some member of the congregation could have placed this there clandestinely. It was, without question, a materialized Love Gift from Spirit. I still have it among my trophies. It still gives me a leap of joy every time I look at it.

Frances and I were already familiar with apports (objects appearing from nowhere) because we were receiving them regularly at the Seaton's. This experience tells us is that *Consciousness* can produce objects from "thin air!" Notice the strong *Love* connection.[40]

How many of you dear readers have had some object, like a set of keys disappear, only to have them reappear in plain sight, exactly where you had left them? Could it be that you were having the good fortune of receiving a magnificent gift from "Heaven?"

My most recent experience of this sort of occurrence was early in December of 2006. When I moved to my new home after Mary, my second wife, passed in March. I took with me a letter opener she had given me for Christmas the year before she became ill. It is a beautiful instrument, with a wood-grained handle and superb balance.

About a month after getting settled in my new home the opener disappeared. I looked everywhere for it. I grieved its loss. It meant so much to me. Anyway, I was invited to have supper with some friends, and I left the mail strewn on the dining room table and went out for the evening.

When I returned the opener was lying on top of the mail in plain sight. *Mary was learning how to create apports!* It still brings tears to my eyes at the love she was expressing with this return of my favorite gift from her.

The best Biblical examples of material appearing out of nowhere are the account of the feeding of the Children of Israel in the desert (Ex: 16.15) and Jesus feeding the multitude (Mt: 14.15; Mk: 6.41; Lu: 9.12; and Jn: 6.5).

Could this sort of event happen if matter were not subject to laws other than those we have assumed to be true from what we expect from Newtonian physics?

In quantum mechanics particles appear and disappear routinely in a "random" way.[41] *Apparently when conscious will is applied, much larger objects can disappear and reappear once the adept learns how to do it. Would it be possible to have the environmental degradation of earth resolved in this same way? I am told that this is the third phase in the restoration of Eden. However, just as it is pointless to clear out the lungs of heavy smokers until they quit smoking, so it is still premature to put psychic power to work on climate change. We need to undertake our Good-Faith actions first. Can such healing be achieved?*

A healing touch

Frances my first wife and I moved to Windsor in the mid 1970s. We became active participants in a Spiritualist church in that city. One Friday evening, while we were studying Catherine Ponder's[42] *The Dynamic Laws of Healing*, we decided, as a group, to try some of the things she suggested.

My healing partner was a lady who had recently moved from England. While I was extending power from the Universe to her, her eyes suddenly became as big as saucers.

"What's the matter?" I asked.

"It's amazing!" she replied. "When I was a little girl in England our school went on a field trip to an ice plant. I became separated from the rest of the group and was left behind in a room full of ammonia gas for about twenty minutes before they found me. I lost my sense of smell because of the caustic action of that ammonia. I just now got my sense of smell back!" To my knowledge she has retained this gift of Spirit to this day. *Universal Love can restore physical conditions instantaneously!*

My response to that event was calm satisfaction coupled with sharing her joy and amazement. By this time I had experienced so many extraordinary events in my life that the "Gee Whiz Factor" was fading to be replaced by the feeling that *miracles* were natural occurrences. The *Course in Miracles* tells us that if we are not experiencing miracles routinely, something is wrong.

As a spiritual healer I never know when such treatments are going to be this effective.

Much research has been conducted on the effectiveness and non-local properties of healing.

Is this event clear evidence that our usual conception of physical matter cannot be true if living tissue can sometimes be rearranged in such a way?

Does space actually exist?

Vinny's message

You will recall the adolescent bet between Vinny Walker and me about who went to heaven? He was the age peer playmate I had in Bermuda.

Nearly thirty years later, I attended an "all message" midweek service at a Spiritualist Church in Lansing, Michigan. There were several readers on the platform. I was unknown to any of the people in the church.

One of them had a message for me. "I have someone here for you with the name of … I think … Victor. I'm not quite sure of the name. Anyway it begins with the letter 'V'.

"What he is saying doesn't make any sense to me. He wants to tell you that there were *four apples on the pear tree*."[43]

This message could only have come from Vinny. He and I were the only ones who knew about the challenge. It meant that, in spite of his insistence to the contrary, Roman Catholics were not the only ones who went to Heaven! Later I learned that it is not exclusively a Christian event either.

Some Christians seem to insist that such an event, if possible at all, would have a diabolical source. That interpretation would mean that, unless they themselves were Roman Catholics, they had no hope of heaven either. This is why I find the St. Peter joke so amusing. When we put limits on what we believe God will do, it makes us look ridiculous in the eyes of many thoughtful people.

The Scriptures of many different religions are full of predictions that have come true. A famous one from the Old Testament was Joseph's interpretation of Pharaoh's dream (Ge: 41.25 ff.).

I have had many other such "precognitive" experiences. Some others of them have also involved military secrets ... In fact, precognitions are very common phenomena among the general public. How many in the present audience are prepared to admit to such an experience?

Is there a possible alternative? Is "prophecy," as Paul gave it to us, besides dreams and experiences another way that God talks to us? Do our souls live in the place where Souls originate, in the company of God? Is this the "connectedness" that the Old One was talking about?

What other explanation might there be?

Reconciliation
Must we believe for it to happen?

Even though she gave Frances and me an Ouija Board for Christmas of 1954, my mother maintained to her dying day that death was the end of existence.

It was about 10:00 AM April 1st, 1988. I was getting ready to start work on a chapter in the second version of this book when the phone rang.

As I reached for the phone I heard my mother's voice clearly shout, "I'm alive!" The exuberant excitement in her voice was thrilling. I was tingling all over, *as though I had just encountered an angel!*

"Good morning, Jay Powell speaking," I answered with my usual greeting when I wasn't sure who was calling.

"Hello, Jay? This is Grace. Mother passed away a few minutes ago."

Yes, it was a spirit from Heaven! It was nearly twenty-five years since we had left Edmonton to get away from the inevitable challenges to our convictions about life-after-life. Mother had come to me immediately to express her joy and relief that we had been "right" after all. Notice the Love!

Does the Soul exist in the non-local zone, making all souls immortal? If so, is there a huge underdeveloped dimension to most of our lives that we should be exploring?

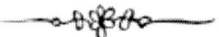

After Mother passed a problem arose with her will. Daddy passed late the previous September. They had assigned to me the face value of some Certificates of Deposit years before as my inheritance. They had not changed their wills to account for this gift. The will still gave a share of the estate to me.

I received a letter from a lawyer asking me to sign off on my inheritance. There was no explanation. I checked and found out the details, so I signed off.

Shortly thereafter, I received a letter from Grace expressing delight and bewilderment. "I thought you didn't like me," she said in her letter. "What happened between us?"

Back in 1957, a few days after we obtained a one-bedroom apartment in Toronto, Grace arrived there with a scholarship to the University of Toronto for her Master's degree. She expected Frances and me to provide accommodation during her stay. So did my Mother, who told us so before Grace arrived.

Grace had experienced a medical error, severely damaging her immune system. She needed a special diet. She took over the kitchen, saying some things to Frances that don't bear repeating.

Frances took me aside. She told me what Grace had said. She put it straight to me, "Either she goes or I go." I told Grace that we didn't have room for her; but not the whole story. Grace moved in with our cousin Joyce (Uncle Ted's daughter). They have been companions ever since.

This began twenty-five years of estrangement. In answer to her letter, I told her what had happened. We have had a close and loving relationship ever since.

How often does family estrangement arise from lack of open communication?

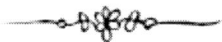

A spectacular display

My second wife, Mary, and I were driving to Lansing, Michigan from Flint, Michigan in the late summer about twenty years ago. This event occured before her cancer, which began in 1992. It was early morning and I was going to speak at a church in Lansing. Suddenly, the road in front of us was a network of luminous filaments. Every tree was connected to every other one. The grass was a mass of shimmering light. The cars coming and going were also linked into the network.

The effect lasted for several minutes from near Perry to about the Webster Road exit. It was not fog and the sun was too high for it to have been a trick of sunlight. We both saw it and were amazed. Is this what the world really looks like when we are completely "in the flow?" *A Course in Miracles* says that what we perceive is an illusion and that everything is connected; there is no separation. How many of you have had similar experiences?

Could such a shared observation have occurred if everything in physical reality were separated from every other thing?

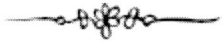

Passing through solid walls

How solid is matter?

Returning to the sittings with the Seaton's in Port Huron, we had several other astounding experiences there.

Being a Star Trek fan, one evening on the way home I asked Guidance whether living things could be transferred through space-time the way we were experiencing in the object materializations (apports) that were a regular feature of these meetings. With the phrase, "Beam me up, Scotty!" ringing in my ears, I quickly tried to cancel the request so that no damage or injury could occur.

The next Tuesday, the Seaton's ancient black Labrador struggled onto his favorite couch in the dining room and went to sleep. There was an unusually large group of sitters this evening, sixteen in all. Forming a circle around the living room for the sitting was a tight squeeze.

Their house was an old one, with the living room and dining room separated by an archway. On the south wall of the living room were two doors. One that led to a room that was being used as a library and the other that led to a vestibule and the front door.

The sitting was always held in complete darkness. Both the living room and dining room had blackout curtains. The library did not. For this reason, its door was always closed to prevent the glow from a nearby street light from disturbing the sitters.

We began our sitting with the dog asleep on the couch in the dining room. We had a ritual at the end of our sharing time in which Ray was the last to give messages to the sitters. We then sang his favorite song. And he would then say, "Let's eat." Upon this signal we would turn on the lights and retire to the dining room to enjoy a potluck luncheon and conversation.

On this particular evening, the moment he said, "Let's eat." There was a loud "Woof!" from behind the library door. We opened it and out trotted the dog, none the worse for being silently transported through "solid" walls. He had been moved from the dining room couch to behind the closed library door during the sitting. The dog eyed me with disgust as he ambled back to his resting place. I struggled to contain my laughter at that look. I didn't want to further embarrass the dog.

There are two notable examples of this same phenomenon in the New Testament. The first was the appearance of Jesus in the Upper Room after his Resurrection (Jn: 20.19), "The doors being closed." The second was the escape of Peter from prison (Ac: 12.9).

Ghosts are often depicted as being transparent and able to move through walls. Sometimes spirits can materialize enough to be fully physical. I know of several people who have had strange physical encounters with people who have been of extraordinary help, only to disappear. A number of books have been written about such encounters.

Yes, there are "Angels" and maybe even "aliens" among us. Love is Universal and *not* confined to the planet Earth.

Do such experiences actually happen? Can these events be explained by the transitory nature of matter under conscious control?

Did miracles actually end with the Resurrection of Jesus?

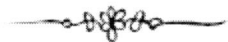

What does all this mean?

Are we created in God's image?

What does it mean to be creative?

While I was still working in Windsor and driving the car that I reported did 120 mph without appearing to do so, I was on the way to work one spring day when I passed my favorite auto dealer. In the lot was a beautiful light chocolate brown, metallic finished Lincoln Town Car. This vehicle was my all-time favorite.

I had just started to pull over to look at it when I heard a little voice in my head, "You're not going to trade me in are you? There's still a good year of service in me yet." That was saying quite a bit. The LTD had about 195,000 miles on it and, although we take excellent care of our vehicles, we were also putting 3,000 to 3,500 miles a *month* on this car.

"Okay," I replied. "I accept your wishes." I pulled into the left-turn lane to turn toward work.

The car was as good as its word. It was a year later on Easter Sunday when it died. We were in Lansing for a service, but that is another story. It was repaired and was running well, but it had lost its reliability so we decided to trade it.

The dealer told us that we had too many miles on it (now more than 250,000) and that we would do better in a private sale than in a trade. Our neighbor behind us needed transportation to and from work (about five miles) so we approached him with an offer that he accepted.

The following Saturday he rode with us to the dealership and he drove the LTD home. We negotiated its replacement.

When we got back to the house our neighbor was sitting in the car, with a face like a thundercloud. I went over to him and asked, "What's the matter?" He didn't say a word. He merely turned the ignition key. Nothing — not even a "click."

Then I heard that little voice again. "Oh, did you want me to stay with the car?"

"Yes, I did." I responded under my breath.

"That's fine, I will."

I chuckled to myself, knowing that my neighbor would never believe what had just transpired. I told him to pop the hood, fiddled with a wire or two, and said, "Try it now."

Varrooom!

He got three years out of it. Had our loving care of the car created a "consciousness" within the car that responded constructively to our thinking? Is this type of event a source for "new" Souls? There are more people in the world today than ever before in human history. From where did all these "new" souls come?

If simple "mechanical" objects can respond to Love, then is there not much more to "reality" than there seems to be?

Creating my own "hell"

I got my start in Spiritualism by going to a séance in April of 1969, about a year before I got my Ph.D. The clairvoyance I had experienced as a pre-teen and teen-ager came back with a vengeance. Suddenly, I had a whole range of "gifts" that were stupendous and exciting.

This rapid success went to my head. I began seeing myself as part of the "second coming." The energies were fierce, pushing me to more and more achievements. All the while there was a deep-seated burning in the pit of my stomach.

After several weeks, I began to realize that I was losing touch with reality. Eventually, about a week before my birthday in November, I hit bottom. I recall throwing myself down on the bed and putting out a desperate cry, "Dear God, whatever you might be, please remove this curse from me or I will institutionalize myself. Others around me are not safe with me in this condition."

It was gone! The burning, the pressure the snarling voices; all of it was *gone!*[44] In their place was a soft gentle voice that said, "You can rest now."

"What happened?"

"Later, rest now."

I was told later that I had gone upon an extreme *ego* trip. I had created an alter ego and had been at war with myself. As the spirit within the car mentioned above, had I created a new consciousness? Are our thoughts much more powerful than we realize.

Don't make a request of the Universe unless you are prepared to have it given to you.

Yes, we are that creative. We have created the "ego" that *A Course in Miracles* talks about, using the creative power, which God has given us. However, the products of the ego are *miscreations*.

The angels took that other *me* to the "hospital" in Heaven to recover. It was later born to appropriately supportive parents somewhere in Texas. Are the loving creations and the miscreations we inadvertently or intentionally produce a source of new souls entering the world?[45]

Could such misapplication of our creative potential be the source of all the misery and disease in the world? Are the problems of the world coming from our mundane consciousness, which has separated itself from our Soul Consciousness? The information that comes to us to explain about spirituality, revelation from many sources, such as *A Course in Miracles,* might quite literally be true.

This brief excerpting of the many miracles in my life suggests how I have been carried beyond "believing" (in the *faith* sense of *hoping it is true*) to the full knowledge that the Underlying Principles behind these discontinuities of time, space, matter and consciousness are the True Reality. There is Unity in this chaos.

As *A Course in Miracles* puts it in Workbook Lesson 167 (5:1-8):

Death cannot come from life. Ideas remain united to their source. They can extend all that their source contains. In that, they can go beyond themselves. But they cannot give birth to what was never given to them. As they are born, so will they give birth. And where they came from they will return.

More and more frequently people are having personal transformative experiences. Some of us have had awe inspiring near-death experience that begins the opening of our deeper selves. Many people today have started on a profound personal quest. Still there are people around us who, through lack of an awakening experience or through denial, insist that such experiences cannot happen. To resolve these conflicting perceptions, we need to put our understanding into action.

The *Other Self,* the Higher Consciousness, the Soul with which we began this discussion comes from the General

Operations Director (GOD). We cannot avoid returning to that source. We are not talking Religion here, or even, in its most mundane sense, Spirituality. We are talking about a layer of Reality that is deeper than, and beyond the comprehension of our superficial awareness.

The "evils" of the world come from the mischief we choose to create with our creative abilities. This is the source of our chaos. It returns to us, magnified by all of the extensions we have generated for these actions. Consider the current economic crisis as a prime example. Mortgage brokers are separated from mortgage lenders. When they close a loan and get their commissions, they are finished with the transaction. Low interest rate and lack of regulation encouraged excess. We all now know the results. Everything is interconnected and this excess spread around the world.

Alternatively, if we choose to align ourselves with the underlying dynamic of existence, we flourish and those around us prosper as well. Greed comes from fear of loss. It is Ego protective and hugely destructive. Love shares the connectivity of the Universe and is powerfully nourishing and dynamically productive. This is the choice the Universe gives us in the full knowledge that next to Love *fear* has no power.

We are all part of a cosmic network of "distributed Consciousness." We can live in Heaven right here and right now. We can become emissaries to the world with the knowledge that goes beyond ritual, dogma, creed, belief, and even hope — to the certainty of Truth. Once we step into the depths of Love, the world changes.

How do we access this awareness? I've been there on many occasions, as my brief autobiography indicates. But I haven't been able to *stay* there. When I get there, there is always an accompanying insight.

I understand Sai Baba is able to hold this level of awareness and Paramhansa Yogananda[46] was able to do it as well. It is obvious that such a level of attainment can be witnessed in the historical reports of Jesus.

I recognize in the writings of people, who have also been there, the fact that they have had similar experiences. A good example is Eckhart Tolle's[47] illuminating book, *The Power of Now* and Wayne Dyer's[48] more recent book, *The Power of Intention*. However, the *process* eludes me. I cannot even tell myself which "psychic" button to push. It seems that practicing the art of "Communion with Spirit," in its many forms, is the essential element in our personal transformation. We let the mundane get in the way; that is all.

I do know, however, that when we continue to ask questions and continue to explore, pushing back the envelope, that spectacular things happen. I also know that when we get our students to explore with us, spectacular things happen in the classroom.

Because these events happen, there must be a repeatable way of making these shifts at will. The Masters tell us that there is. But many of the disciples of these Masters do not have it, and the ability to transmit it seems to diminish with the passing of generations. Historically it has reemerged from time to time, sometimes within an established tradition, more often outside it.

However, all written accounts relate to the preconditions of these events and the outcome of the shift in consciousness, not the *process* itself. The various traditions of the world have developed rituals, ceremonies, initiations, formal philosophies and moderate or extreme dogmas around these events. These *artifacts* have not captured its *essence*.

Is this the explanation? Is the macrocosm identical to the microcosm? The discontinuities of time-space are well known to the subatomic physicist, where an electron changes orbit without crossing the intervening space. Can we make similar leaps across the Universe or among Universes at will, once we know how? The linear thinking of some people considers these possibilities to be preposterous. But are they? Are we on the leading edge of a major paradigm shift to a New Renaissance?

They are only preposterous if the Universe itself is linear. If it is not, then we may need a new science through which we might well discover how these events come about. When we do, then most of what we believe will need to be rethought and most our planned courses of action will need to be reworked. Is this also the message of the film, *"What the 'Bleep' Do We Know?"*[49] and Lynne McTaggart's[50] book *The Field?* Do these thoughts lend truth to the emergence of "A new Heaven and a new Earth?" Apparently the macrocosm conforms to the microcosm. If our theory of reality does not include discontinuities like driving 60 miles in 30 minutes, our theory must be *false!* These events did not end with Jesus.

"With God, are all things possible?"

Soul mates

How did I come to discover that connectedness is so important?

I indicated in the introduction that I have had a sense of mission all of my life. I am not sure where or when it started, but there are clear linkages that show a definite pattern. For instance, my experience with the baby robin now seems to me to have identified either with a past life or a connection with the collective unconsciousness of our culture, if not with that of the human race. The same thing might be said about my dream of hearing Jesus last words on the cross.[51]

There are several indications in the Bible that Jesus and Mary Magdalene were married. First, the *bridegroom* was traditionally responsible for the drinks at a wedding feast. Jesus was asked to supply more wine, leading to his first recorded miracle. Was he the bridegroom? Second, he is referred to as "Rabbi" on several occasions in the Gospels. To be a Rabbi, the person had to be *married*. Third, it was traditional that the bereaved *wife* was responsible for overseeing the embalming of her late husband. Mary Magdalene was the person who went to the tomb after the Sabbath.

These three instances may be circumstantial. Some of the Gospels that were not included are more specific that he was married to Mary. This information is put forward in the recent controversial book and film, *The Da Vinci Code*[52].

I do not wish to belabor this further except to say that from an early age I have sensed that I chose to come here with a job to do, with recurring events that seemed to give me this same message. I have been responding, as much as I am able, to my Soul's imperatives. Often when I did this, I was interrupted by society's imperatives. However, the pathway I am following has never been completely thwarted.

My interest in physics arose from the lesson on the propagation of sound in grade 6. This event is what insulated me from the disastrous educational career that had occurred to that point in my life. My dyslexia combined with the ridiculous demands of bureaucracy only served to heighten the ineffectiveness of institutional bureaucratic decisions upon me for most of my formal educational experiences.

These effects were diminished because I was able to learn how to read on my own and to learn how to learn through the home-schooling correspondence courses. My prophetic dreams also contributed to my sense that I was somehow different from others. I now know that most people have at least a few such dreams but they are not usually discussed openly in our closed-minded culture. Being "different" is not socially acceptable in many situations. The result is that many people sacrifice their uniqueness to be "politically correct," to abandon their basic humanity to fit their cultures demands upon them.

Each of the jobs that I have had has also taught me important lessons. As a pinsetter, I learned about being self-competitive. Setting difficult tasks for the purpose of honing

Making Peasants into Kings

my skills was the best way for me to ensure a life-long pattern of personal growth.

As I progressed, it seems that I knew what needed to be done and to do it without being told from an outside source. Call it intuition, or whatever you will, applying my self-competitiveness to my insights has moved me a long way in this lifetime.

A large part of this progress has come from getting control of my anger reflex. There is a progression from the box ends incident to the fight where I became the enforcer to the incident with Roger who wanted to fight and finally to being threatened with a Samurai sword. This sequence shows how experience, will power and my Inner Resources combined to bring tranquility to life. Behind each of these events and many of the others I have reported seems to carry this same message. Others around me have been finding the same outcomes.

This road has not been without its bumps. My attempt to become accepted by a peer group that was a closed community was a dismal failure. From this, I learned that I was better off not pretending to be something I am not. Being accepted in one's pretense is probably more dangerous than being rejected for one's best efforts. We would be better off if our schooling addressed pretense directly as it occurs, such as when Harry wrote the stories for everyone in the class.

Why do we remain silent about the deepest things in life?

Forming connections

Why do we feel so alone?

Up to that point, much of my life was a struggle to achieve and maintain my identity. This struggle had ranged from fistfights through trying to be a part of a family that found my emerging psychic abilities threatening and approaches to teaching that worked but were contra-cultural and cost me more than one job.

I was, by that time, in my second year of college. I was enjoying the lively discussions in the cafeteria of the Faculty of Education building. These discussions were so much fun that I often skipped classes. Somehow, telling students what the curriculum designers thought they needed to know didn't fit with me. The teaching I despised was being told what to know, the learning I loved was being encouraged to find out for myself. My experience in teacher training at that point was an overemphasis on telling and an under-emphasis on helping students to think it through.

November 11th, 1953, Canada's Memorial Day, was a holiday from both school and work. During the morning I had an engagement with the Canadian Navy. I was in the marching band and we had a parade to the Veterans' Memorial. I spent the rest of the day getting my assignments completed. After supper I was at loose ends. There was a theater on the South Side of the North Saskatchewan River that played British and foreign films. I liked these better than the Hollywood fare, so I decided to go to the show.

The movie was finished at about 9:45 PM. Going home would mean getting into another argument. I decided to go to a dance hall about six blocks away. I arrived at the 10:00 PM intermission.

One of my coworkers, a janitor at the Alberta Government Telephones (AGT), was a strange person. He was deeply committed to "conspiracy theory," which he reinforced by spending his days as a spectator in the local District Court. His attitude toward women was similarly angry.

As I walked into the hall, I saw him in the middle of the floor talking to an attractive woman. Knowing him, I understood, even at that distance, why she looked so upset. I decided she needed to be rescued.

I approached him. He recognized me and introduced me to Frances de Laura. It turned out that this was her married name. She was divorced and had decided to seek a little adventure by coming to Edmonton from Penticton, British Columbia where she and her mother shared an apartment.

We danced. We talked. I took her to an after-the-dance supper, where we talked some more. This woman was different. She had a gentle sweetness I had never encountered before. In addition, there was a sense of flow between us. It was as though we were connected at some deep level. I couldn't put it into words.

The flow was not sexual, although she was attractive enough. I always felt my sexual attraction in my genital area. This was more at my solar plexus. She seemed to be feeling it too, although she said nothing about it – neither did I.

We made a date for the weekend and I started seeing her on a regular basis. Then one morning in early January of 1954, I had no school and I needed some new shoes. I went downtown to my favorite shoe store.

While I was walking to the store from my parking spot, I met her on her way to work. We chatted briefly on the corner. As we parted, I was seized with an uncontrollable urge to take her into my arms and kiss her. She had moved on before I could act.

This was it! Here was the woman I loved. It didn't matter that she had been married unhappily before and that she was 23 years older than I. We were connected in a way that I didn't understand and I wanted desperately to build upon that connection.

To be absolutely certain that I was not deluding myself, I decided to buy her a ring and to say nothing about it until after I had asked her to marry me. This was the first truly independent action that involved another person I had ever taken in my life. I had just turned 23 the previous November.

One of my tasks at the AGT was to check all the light bulbs in the building and to replace those that needed it. Because I could not get to work at 4:00 PM (I could generally make it by 4:30 PM) I had arranged to do this task on Saturday morning to make up these 2 ½ hours each week.

On January 16th, 1954 I invited Frances to help me with this task. She didn't work on Saturdays. She only lived about three blocks away from where I worked. She put together a bag lunch and joined me at the AGT office building.

We finished the light inspection and replacement at about 11:30 and went to the staff lounge to eat lunch. After lunch, while we sat chatting for a few minutes I reached into my pocket and pulled out the little box with its ring.

She opened it. I couldn't read her expression as she looked at it. Our eyes met and the flow was stronger than ever. After a long moment, "Well, aren't you going to put it on my finger?"

I was still honoring my father's advice of keeping my options open. We had cuddled before this, but hadn't even kissed. That kiss was profound. It seemed that our Souls blended in that moment of ecstasy. Again it was nonsexual, but oh so right.

My father was hurt that I hadn't asked his permission before becoming engaged. I didn't realize the importance of his British heritage to him.

This act was my breaking out of the trap that some of the other women in my life were determined to lock around me. There was more than "escape" involved. There was this wonderful softness and gentleness to go to as well. Here was the outcome of the dream of the chains falling away and the silent one waiting patiently to move along with me. Once again Love from the Universe was filling my life.

Frances's father had passed away. Her mother was living upon a meager pension in Penticton so there was no way her family could afford the bill for our wedding. Frances was aware of my need to break from my family so she didn't want to accept anything from them. She had sat in our living room

Making Peasants into Kings

on many occasions listening in silence to their well meaning but misguided attacks on me.

She suggested that we "elope." I agreed and set up the adventure. I had been to Great Falls, Montana on a couple of occasions and that seemed to be adventurous enough for both of us with only a weekend available.

I contacted the County Clerk, obtained the necessary documents, arranged for a hotel, minister, one-way airline tickets down and Greyhound bus back. Yes we were that broke. The date was set for May 8th, 1954, just after the completion of my second year of classes.

When we arrived at the hotel, I was as nervous as a feral cat in a new household. Frances seemed to be so calm and collected that I couldn't understand it. Then she dropped her toothbrush into the toilet. She was nervous too! I went to get her another one, full of joy instead of anxiety.

Our first night together was awkward because I had never made love before. This got better as time passed. We set up housekeeping in a small basement apartment within a block of where I worked. Life became a dream.

She had two weeks vacation time coming that summer. I asked her what she would like to do. "I've always wanted to go hitch-hiking," she said, "but I've never had a companion to travel with." We packed two suitcases, large enough to sit on but small enough to carry in our laps. We bought two large straw hats to protect us from the sun. We took the city bus to the western end of the line, and set up station by the road heading from Edmonton toward Edson and Jasper, Alberta. Our destination was Vernon, British Columbia, where Frances was born and her older sister lived.

Our first trip together was a remarkable adventure. We were very lucky in the rides we picked up. We saw many elks and bighorn sheep around Jasper. The Columbia Ice Fields were magnificent. Lake Louise is undoubtedly the jewel it is reported to be. Vernon is a pretty mountain city in the midst of the most northerly extension of the fruit belt.

We had a good visit with Frances's sister, Josephine, who was far more welcoming than I had expected. We then headed south to Penticton to see her mother, and east toward Trail, Nelson and the Kootenays.

At Trail we had our first experience with television. A wholesale candy salesman gave us a ride. He stopped at every little roadside store, but called ahead to get us a room at the family rooming house where he would be staying. It was not a motel but a large old house that the owners, who had been traveling salespeople themselves, ran as a stopping point for fellow roadrunners.

Everyone gathered in the big living room after supper to watch TV. The feature that night was Liberace. He was so corny with his sparkling suit, his candelabra and his ingratiating voice that we decided not to bother with TV. We finally bought one to see the Royal Wedding several years later.

On the way to Nelson, we rode with a highway construction contractor in a bouncy pickup truck. He stopped to show us the house made entirely of embalming fluid bottles. It was built as a hobby and retirement home by a funeral director. This was my first encounter with recycling in any major way. I have been a supporter of the concept ever since.

From Nelson we went north to Radium Hot Springs, east to Calgary and back home in time for Frances to go back to work. The image of us two hobos, sitting on our luggage by the side of the road with our large colorful straw hats and pointing downstream with our thumbs is still endearing to me.

We must have been quite a sight to behold!

Becoming a scholar
What does it mean to be able to "Read between the lines?"

Back at college, I now had motivation to study hard. I also had access to the library bookshelves, a privilege denied to freshmen and sophomores at the University of Alberta at that time. Here was where the people after more than just a degree or a husband hung out. I learned who the best teachers on campus were during conversations among the books. I began to create my own multidisciplinary program.

I haunted the office of the Dean of Arts and Science and the Dean of Education until I got the best possible teachers to round out my education. What they taught was often less important than *how* they taught. Whether they ran effective group discussion session or told exciting and fascinating stories, or led us into blind alleys to spring intellectual surprises on us mattered more than their course content. Education came alive in their hands.

This was a far cry from the dull and droning explanations about laboratory safety with 47 points to memorize for the examination. This contrast to what I had experienced in my science methodology class was stark. Here people were excited about learning and it showed. Suddenly the interconnectedness of content began to dawn on me. Translating a story from German to English used substitution procedure rules that were similar to the use of substitution in mathematics. Both involve the idea of *meaningful equivalence.*

The construction of a generalization in science used the same logic as the construction of a generalization in history, or in anthropology or psychology. The facts used were different, which meant acquiring new vocabulary for each subject, but the procedures for organizing this information was closely parallel.

In my third year I took a course in remedial instruction. Not many students took it because the teacher was a tough taskmaster. We worked our buns off for middle-range grades.

We had to do something inspiring to get a good grade. However, the way she structured text materials to create open access to the layers of meaning behind the surface enthralled me. I used these ideas in my studying for the other subjects I was taking and my marks climbed out of the Ds and Cs into a solid B range for the first time in my learning career, except during correspondence school.

Taking correspondence courses in Bermuda taught me how to learn in an intuitive way. In that case, I followed my established interests. Now I was cracking the code of subjects that I would not previously have bothered about and finding them all fascinating. The key was the inter-connectedness of knowledge and the ability to transfer concepts and skills from one discipline to another. No learning is wasted when it can be cross-referenced and interconnected.

In the meantime, I was also developing a connectedness of a different sort with Frances. We were getting to the point where we often finished each other's sentences. She sensed my moods and helped me to deal with the chaos and pressure of a life with a fulltime job and fulltime study schedule. Her work was not as demanding and she was a good enough typist that, with her skill, I produced most of my assignments within ample time.

My encounter with Shakespeare's exchange of sonnets with the young man started me trying to work through ideas ahead of reading about them. This made it possible for me to produce much more than a standard analysis of trivia so often found among undergraduate writing. I started to become connected with the authors I was reading in the same way as I was becoming connected to other aspects of my life.

The janitor on the main floor of the AGT headquarters, who saw his job as the most important in the corporation, taught me another way to become connected.

We become connected to our work when it becomes a vocation (a calling). When this happens we do more than just a job. Everything to which we put our hands becomes an embodiment of our Soul. As a self-competitive person, I began to seek quality, not for the marks but for the satisfaction of having done the job well.

Some of this was already part of me from the enjoyment I had in making maps and other artistic pursuits, in the camaraderie of printing butter, in the inspiration of looking 50 years into the future with the Research Council. But this was different. On those occasions, I enjoyed these jobs. The pleasure came from outside of me, from my encounters with interesting others.

However, now I was seeking the pleasure from within, looking for it in the substance of the materials with which I was working, as my appreciation of the fundamental beauty of life grew. This was no longer an assembly line of widgets to pay the bills. This was the touch of the craftsman. This was the process of making a scholar. This was seeing the beauty in an idea before it was formed. This was seeing the beauty in people who couldn't see it in themselves.

Was this teacher preparation as it could and should be?

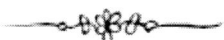

To hell and back

What can happen when we try to contact the world beyond?

Much to my surprise, for our first Christmas together, my mother gave us an Ouija Board. For the uninitiated, this is a game board, often about the size of a small coffee table with the letters of the alphabet, the ten digits from 0 through 9, and the four words "Yes" and "No," "Hello" and "Goodbye" painted or printed upon it. It comes with a small three-legged heart-shaped *planchette*. When our fingers are placed lightly upon it, it moves as if an independent force controls it. The point of the heart identifies letters, numbers or "Yes – No" to spell out messages in response to questions.

We both had a week off that Christmas and were quickly absorbed in the pursuit of information from "beyond the veil of death." We soon found that all Frances needed to do was to have one finger of one hand and I with only two fingers from each hand on the device and it would scurry around the board like a newly caged mouse.

This arrangement meant that she could transcribe everything that was spelled out. She wrote down the questions as well so that the conversation could be followed in its entirety.

It began by painting a pathetic picture of the "spirit" operator. As our discussions progresses it became meaner and more and more uncomplimentary toward Frances. That is what finally did it in. This was more than a parlor game. There was something *evil* behind what we were getting.

I recalled my dream of entering the room of darkness, fighting with the forces of darkness and winning. Our neighbor across the back lane had an incinerator. That is where the Ouija Board met its demise. The flaring of the flames was not as brilliant as in my dream, but it was very satisfying. Another prophetic dream had come true — or had it? In our later reading of the writing of Paramhansa Yogananda, he refers to "rogue spirits." This is a good description of what we had encountered.

Our initial spirit contact, who was a youth who had died in the 1500s in the tin mines of Cornwall, England, later became a good friend. He had no last name so we looked up Cornish names and found "Fogerty," which means "loud and boisterous." He liked it so he became Abe Fogerty.

About fifteen years later we had another series of strange encounters. It began in August of 1968. Coming back from our usual summer visit with Frances's sister in Vernon, B.C. we stopped to visit an old family friend in Calgary. This lady, Millicent (Scotty) Ogden had been the secretary for Fran's great uncle when he was Attorney General for British Columbia.

She was no slouch and always had fascinating adventures to relate.

This time she talked about a regular meeting she was having with a dozen other senior ladies. "We sit to develop our psychic abilities and to talk to Spirit," she explained. "I'm the only Protestant among them." She went on to relate some of the interesting things about the "after-life" they had been learning.

One thing she told us about was the hospital that was at the entrance to Heaven where those who passed with serious accident or illness went to recover before they were able to explore their reentered home. About a month later, we heard that Scotty had passed away.

Later that fall, I decided to hold my staff meeting at our home. I was teaching a class of 500+ students in an auditorium and had one hour of small-group seminars for each two hours of lecture. My seminar leaders provided an outlet for graduate student support. I had six of them.

We were living in a large living room with a screened off sleeping area, a comfortable kitchen and a bathroom we shared with an older lady who had a bed-sitting room and separate kitchen at the back of the house. We had bought the house with my pension refund from teaching in Ontario and had our space and three rental units in it.

Frances decided that she did not want to sit at the kitchen table by herself. She found an advertisement in the newspaper for a séance near us and decided to attend that instead.

She came back full of enthusiasm about the contact she had with Scotty. There was no doubt in her mind that this contact was genuine. The identifying evidence was too overwhelming to be denied.

She didn't like some of the other things that happened in the sitting. As a "recovered" Catholic, Jesus was her first Love. Spiritualists often do not honor Jesus because they believe in personal responsibility instead of vicarious atonement.

After his remarks to this effect, she decided that she would not go back. We found a Spiritualist Church listed, but it was in the poorest part of town, close to where I grew up during World War II, and she wouldn't go there by herself. We waited until April of 1969 so that we could both go together.

This church had a Friday evening "all message" service. We went first to that meeting. We were totally unknown to the group so I was surprised when one of the readers came to me with a message.

"I have a message for you," he said, as he stopped walking toward me from his seat in the circle across the room. "It's from — I believe a man named 'Edward,' something like that. Anyway, everyone called him 'Ted.' He had a bad right knee from an injury in World War I.

"He worked for a number of years for a government agency.

"He is saying that he is glad to see you here and you have no idea how profound the changes will be in your future."

I knew there would be changes because I was within 12 months of completing my Ph.D. My uncle's name was 'Edwin' and not 'Edward.' Aside from that, it was exactly accurate in details. He went by the nickname of 'Ted' and he had picked up a piece of shrapnel in his right knee in World War I. He was an installer and maintainer of equipment for the Manitoba Government Telephones for many years before his retirement.

The rest of the message also has proven to be true.

Intrigued by this event, Frances and I joined the group for coffee and doughnuts after the service. The minister lent me a book on the Spirit World and reminded us of a "teach-in" the following Tuesday evening. We went to the Sunday service but were not that impressed. He was not a dynamic speaker.

On Tuesday evening at the group meeting he darkened the room until no light, even from the Exit sign, was visible. The minister then began with a prayer for protection. Shortly thereafter he made some sounds that were gibberish to me and began leading the class in a voice that sounded Oriental.

I remember practically nothing of what he said. Almost as soon as the sitting began, I saw a light forming over my right shoulder. It moved slowly forward until it was directly in front of me and then disappeared. This pattern repeated several times. Each time I seemed to be lifted a little further out of my body.

There was no sense of fear attached to this feeling. From what I had read over the weekend, I knew I was being induced into trance. From deep inside of me, I knew that this was the wrong thing to do in someone else's séance. I stopped the process without difficulty.

Then I felt a hand placed on the top of my head and another under my chin. With a lift and a twist, there was a popping sound all the way down my spine. The twist occurred in the opposite direction. Sitting there in the dark, I was receiving a wonderful chiropractic treatment. I have had such superb treatments, so I can attest to this being a very good one. I left the meeting feeling awe at what had happened. I felt that God had intervened silently in my life to heal me.

As we left the meeting, I felt uplifted and more alive than I had felt in a long time. This was wonderful! The previous Friday I had received good confirmation of life after life. Now I had been healed of my back pains. Indeed, I had no idea that what already had transpired could happen. I shared my excitement with Frances and we agreed to explore these events further.

The following Friday Frances and I saw auras for the first time. Many of the people at the meeting had a visible glow around them. It was as though they were giving off a narrow band of a shimmering something that was similar in appearance to northern lights. With some of the people there was also a balloon-like glow above their left shoulders. When I put my eyes out of focus while looking at the balloon, I thought I saw a face in each. My love for sketching was reawakened.

The following Friday I took a sketchpad with me. I was able to capture the images in two of the balloons. One was a woman wearing a hat with an ostrich feather, ringlet curls behind her ears, and leg-o-mutton sleeves on her dress. This was a typical style from the Edwardian period.

When I showed it to her she gasped. "Why that is a perfect likeness of my grandmother!" she exclaimed. "We have a picture just like that we hung in the hallway of our new home yesterday."

The other drawing was a picture of an older man with steel-rimmed glasses and a large dark mark on his left cheek. I gave it to the man with whom I saw it. "That's my father," he remarked. "I don't know why he would bother coming to me. We didn't get along when he was here." The drawing of the woman could have been telepathy because of the recent connection with their life's activities. The drawing of the man could not have been telepathy because the thoughts of his father were not likely to have been close to him.

This was the beginning of our adventure into Spiritualism. Before long I had a list of guides as long as your arm and was giving messages of amazing accuracy. About 80% of them fitted the lives of the people to whom they were given to a remarkable extent.

During this process, I was reminded of my dream where I heard Jesus' last words on the cross from many miles away. At this point, these "guides" started to lead me down the garden path. They tried to make me believe that, as the physical and Soul son of Jesus, I was the new Messiah. The pressure to move toward the development of phenomena, like prophesying, manifesting and healing became great. The burning sensation in the pit of my stomach was almost unbearable.

I shared our Ouija story with some children and they began to show signs of a negative influence as well. Something was radically wrong. Was I at war with the dark forces again?

With that realization, I decided to stop these crazy voices in my head. There was a sudden shift in the battle. Now I had only one guide. It was trying to get me to violate all my moral principles. Every move I made to block this influence resulted in exactly the right counter move to prevent my success.

Finally, in November, about nine months after my awakening, I decided that I had lost it. I recall very distinctly throwing myself onto the bed in tears and saying, "Dear God, take this curse from me. If you cannot, I will voluntarily commit myself."

No sooner was this thought expressed and the horror was gone! The burning was replaced by comfort; the voice in my head was silent; agitation was replaced with calmness and a deep sense of peace. I had called upon God for help and had been helped. I later learned that the thought that I might be the Messiah had split my consciousness into two pieces. My ego had accepted this notion based upon my sense of mission and my dreams. My Soul stood firm in the connection we all have with God. I had been at war with myself. No wonder the being could counter my every move. It was the mean-minded other side of me!

Ever since then, those dark forces have tried on numerous occasions without success to intrude upon my sense of connectedness.

Frances was relieved. Was this why I had to marry her? She had an angelic innocence that came not from naivety, but from deep spirituality. She stood silently by me while I fought my greatest battle. And as prophesied, the Light won!

I could write a book entirely about this spiritual journey of mine. I've given you the highlights. From my study of quantum physics, I now know that our Soul is a non-local quantum phenomenon.

Does this mean that it exists outside of space and time and has a specific purpose created by God? If so, are not the implications of this realization for education stupendous?

The second love of my life

What happens to a person on a mission when his soul mate partner dies?

Finally, shortly after her eighty-fourth birthday, Frances's heart gave out on her and she joined her beloved sister in heaven. Her last few words to me were, "You are the most wonderful man I have ever met". Then, knowing more than I knew, as I prepared to leave for Windsor to get her clothes; she would not have been able to live in our apartment there; she sent me off with her favorite joke. "Be good, and if you cannot be good, be careful."

That was her farewell. She passed before I could return. This was February 10th, 1993.

In May of that same year I had one of my several Spirit visitations. This time it was Frances. She had Jesus with her. I was not surprised to have Jesus come with her because, although she had left the Catholic Church for personal reasons, he had always been her first Love.

Frances spoke first. "Hello, my love. I want you to know that I did everything for you that I could before I was called home. I was yearning to reunite with my sister, Josephine. You have accepted the task of building the bridge from the Continent of Turmoil across the Sea of Travail to the Island of Tranquility.

"You and I together built the approach and the continental anchor point for that bridge. Your task is not yet finished. You will need another helper."

"Would you help me find her?" I asked.

"Yes. That is why I came to visit you tonight."

"How will I know when I meet her?"

"You will have the same sense of flow with her as you had with me."

Then Jesus spoke, "It is important that you understand what is going on right now.

"As you are already aware the turning point for humanity was in 1985. This was the time when the amount of emanations flowing from the Universe began to exceed the amount of Life Force being expropriated from the Universe by humanity. What we are witnessing now are the last desperate efforts of the rogue forces miscreated by humanity to stay in control. (Witness the 9/11, the Iraq war and the financial crisis.)

"The key to this transformation, some are calling it the 'Second Coming' is spiritual unions like the one you had with Frances. When two Souls become that closely integrated, they can channel four times as much Love as either of them could by themselves. They need not be a man and a woman. They could be two men or two women. In your case it must be another woman.

"Later we will begin to link such couples into a network that will boost the channel capacity even further.[53]"

With these comments, the two of them disappeared.

I was planning a visit to England and Europe that summer. I was told by a good medium that I should be on the lookout for "Merry England."

On the lookout for this flow, I met a lovely lady in England. Her first name was "Marion." The two words "Merry" and "England" seemed to fit. I was too impetuous and scared her off, as was intended by the Universe. I reinforced, at that point, the need to pay close attention to women and to let them take the lead.

Upon returning to America, where I was now living since Frances's passing, I resumed my healing work with the wife of a good friend. In the course of this work, I reconnected with a woman whom Frances and I had met in 1980 named "Mary England." My friend's wife wanted to go off on her own, now that she was ordained, so Mary England (her last name by her second marriage) and I began working together with healing and workshops.

The church I was mentoring in Davison, Michigan decided to put on a Luau on October 16th of 1993, I asked Mary, my new partner to come to the affair. As we talked I recognized the *flow* with her!

She reminded me of our previous contact and told me that she had received a number of letters from Frances. She asked if I would like to read them. I agreed and we arranged to meet at her home in Lansing (about 50 miles away) on the next day, which was a Sunday.

Over the luncheon table she passed me the letters. Back in 1980, Frances and I had gone to a church in Jackson, Michigan on the "mistaken" perception that I was to speak there that Sunday.

Frances's letter said, "I had the same leap of euphoria when I met you (Mary) as I did when I met Jay. I do not think it was coincidence that we met. I have the feeling that somehow the Universe will make it possible for you and he to work together."

I told her about the visit of Jesus and Frances and the flow I had felt. I asked her to marry me. She accepted. We were married on December 5, 1993, after less than six weeks of engagement.

We began housekeeping in the cute little house she had in Lansing. With all my stuff, it was too small for the two of us. Fortunately, I was able to arrange to keep most of my stuff in the attic of where Frances and I had an apartment in Windsor.

Mary worked for the State of Michigan as an employment counselor. Her place of employment was about three blocks away from her house. I became househusband, cleaning, washing clothes, gardening, cooking the meals; the whole schmeer. On

Making Peasants into Kings

weekends when my ministerial work made it appropriate, we stayed at the small modular I had in Davison.

Getting acquainted was fun for both of us. We had many interests in common. We liked the same books, the same movies, and the same food. She wanted to become a spiritual healer so we arranged to have a person from England come over and teach an extensive healing class to twelve people. This was a very in-depth program, which led to the establishment of a center in Lansing and some worldwide contacts in the alternative medicine area.

Shortly after we were married Mary was transferred to the Flint office. We sold her house in Lansing too hastily, not getting enough for it, and moved into the modular in Davison, about 15 miles from her work. During that summer, the woman who owned the apartment where Frances and I had lived wanted the attic. We moved three truckloads of books, papers and other stuff from Windsor to Davison and put them into storage.

A year later, Mary was given a buy-out option to take early retirement. This seemed to give us a great deal more freedom. It soon was evident that our modular was far too small for two active people. We rented a house in the country, moved our junk into the basement and started a new life together with more room inside and outside.

The house we rented was actually the unused parsonage of a church. The church was to the north of us. The other three sides were cornfields. There we saw deer regularly along with many other creatures of the wild. One day we even saw an eagle. That was a thrill!

We started a daily routine of reading spiritual and inspirational books aloud, doing stretching exercises and experimenting with exotic foods. There was a closeness that was very different from the one I had with Frances.

Frances was quiet, Mary gregarious. We traveled a lot, visiting places like Jacksonville, Florida, where her stepdaughter lived, Ypsilanti, where her two sons lived with their wives, and Denver, Colorado, where her oldest son, her youngest brother and their family lived.

We took up camping as a recreation and rambled over much of Michigan. We visited her family a lot locally as well. It was different for me to have such a large extended family in close proximity. My only sibling, my sister, Grace, lived with our cousin, the daughter of Uncle Ted in California.

I continued my association with Dr. Norm Shklov. We had a publication in 1992,[54] and tried to carry the work further with no success in getting published.

I began trying to write what is now this book for the third time. This version is its tenth incarnation. Slowly and steadily our spiritual depth increased. Mary blossomed and life was beautiful.

After taking an extended camping trip to San Francisco where I attended a conference, we decided to buy a house. We spent many happy hours together making and remaking a list of what we wanted in our dream home.

We looked at many houses. In every one of them there were missing features. She laughed when I started to suggest how we might modify this or that house to fit. That lovely sense of humor carried us beyond quarreling into a deepening awareness of the needs and aspirations of each other.

The one we finally found was a large four-bedroom $2^1/_2$ bath suburban bi-level on a half acre of land. This led us to being more domestic – redecorating, house repairs, lawn mowing and so forth. Our closeness increased to the point where we were completing each other's sentences as had occurred between Frances and I. It was a good life.

Our main outside activity, apart from travel was healing and teaching healing. We both became Reiki Masters. She became ordained. I was ordained while I was married to Frances. Mary and I shared the speaking platform at a number of churches.

We worked with alternative therapies, settling her gall bladder problem without surgery, improving the circulation in her feet, resolving my lower back problems and conducting classes toward a healing ministry. She wanted to set up a practice but never managed to get it off the ground.

Then in late 2002 she had a severe breathing problem. They tapped her lungs and took off a liter and a half of fluid. The fluid had blood in it but no cancer cells. A second bout in February of 2003 also removed more than a liter; Still no cancer. This was followed by a bronchoscopy; still negative.

Finally, in March of 2003 a CAT scan showed something that looked suspicious. The team called in a thoracic surgeon who found lung cancer. By the time we began chemotherapy, Mary was at the fourth stage of the disease. She lost vitality slowly, being a very vibrant person. She took the hair loss in stride. The chemo didn't stop the progress of the disease and by March of 2005 she was to the point where she was going from the bed to her recliner in the living room and back to bed.

I almost completely discontinued my writing. Looking after her, the house and the yard occupied all of my time. We began some very deep conversations about life, death and our relationship with each other. Our relationship deepened. The flow between us grew stronger, even as she grew weaker. The family support was also tremendous.

Then early in May of 2005, a friend told us about the Born Clinic in Grand Rapids, Michigan. We called for an appointment and started immunotherapy immediately. Her turnaround was remarkable. Within a couple of weeks she was alive again. The tumors had shrunk by half from April to July.

We drove to Florida for our step grandson's wedding in August. We booked a windjammer cruise in Maine and had a wonderful time together with her sister, Jan, and a friend. It looked as though there was a future for us yet.

Then one night in October she fell on the way to the bathroom. An MRI of her brain showed two new tumors. Chemotherapy ceased in favor of radiation treatments. To prevent swelling of her brain she was put on steroids. These chemicals wound her up like the "energizer bunny." She took the kitchen apart and reorganized everything.

We had reduced the frequency of our trips to Grand Rapids to every other week. Her CAT scan in December showed the tumors progressing again. Our oncologist told us that he had tried everything he knew. Our family physician and the doctor in Grand Rapids both recommended the Cancer Treatment Centers of America in Zion, Illinois. We phoned and arranged for an appointment in December of 2005.

Our first visit was for five days during which time they did by far the most thorough study of her case she had yet received. Their treatment of their patients was wonderful. So was their treatment of me as her support person. We ended our stay with a different chemotherapy treatment.

Taking our luggage down to the van on our way home, I fell and broke some bones in my left hand. Mary insisted that I not drive, and she was too weak to spend six hours behind the wheel. We called her sons in Ypsilanti and they came to rescue us. Family support at this level of generosity is valuable beyond estimation.

We returned for a second treatment in February. She seemed to be coasting more than recovering. If this treatment was going to work, it was doing it very slowly. We tried to treat each other as though all was well.

Shortly before our return to Zion in March, she initiated sex with me. The event was amazing. As she told me later, she had never had so profound an experience either. It was like buttery syrup melting on waffles, smooth and sweet and luxurious, climaxed with ecstasy. Was she saying "Goodbye?"

At Zion, their CAT scan in March showed that the treatment was not working. At this point Mary said, "No more treatments."

She began to weaken rapidly. By the time we reached our home in Clio, Michigan she was too weak to climb the five stairs to our main living area unaided. She sat on a stair, put her arms around my neck and I lifted her stair by stair until I had lifted her to the main floor. I then helped her stand and supported her as she walked to her recliner.

I called upon a friend who worked with seriously ill people. She came to our house and looked at the situation. She took me aside and told me that Mary was dying. I already knew this. We called the hospice and an ambulance.

Within a week she began to spend much of her days with her eyes closed. Day-by-day she became less responsive. Her breathing developed a raspy sound, which was resolved with suction. By the end of the second week, we knew that her end was near.

Her family surrounded her. Even her stepdaughter and her family made it from Jacksonville, Florida to be there. Although she was almost totally unresponsive, with her eyes closed, a flick of her eyebrow told me she was aware when the family from Florida arrived.

She died peacefully 15 days after entering hospice on March 24th of 2006 at 6:04 AM after an all-night vigil. We had said our "Good-byes." I didn't want the continued torment of treatments any more than she did.

We have had a wonderful life together. She tells me that together we completed the support pylon in the middle of the Sea of Travail and the deck from the shore to the pylon. Apparently her physical assignment with me had been completed. Our love had blossomed into a deep spiritual bond. Maintaining contact has a great blessing of my life. The hardest part of it is remembering that sublime last physical encounter; knowing that it cannot happen again, at least not with her.

We were in contact almost immediately, and remained in contact on a daily basis for more than a year. Frances and Mary have agreed to work with me to help me find a third Soul Mate so that we can complete that bridge

This bridge is the approach to education I am presenting here, which I will describe in more detail in the last chapter. It is the first part of three phases in the transformation of humanity from fear to Love, from competition to cooperation. It is the form of education that gives the answer to Jesus plea, "… they do not understand." As warned by The Old One, humanity has lost its sense of connectedness.

The second phase is the development of a source of virtually free energy from the Zero point field so that scarcity can no longer be the basis of economic domination. Apparently, Nickoli Tesla had found this source. So, apparently have others, all is needed now is to make it public.

The third phase is the uniting of our intentions in the psychic field to remove the psychic and material pollution by which we are devastating our planet. With unlimited energy available, the earth an Eden and a restored sense of connectedness to keep it that way, fear and greed will no longer be necessary.

At this point in my life, I must conclude that I have lived a blessed and fulfilling life. Even when I was unaware of it, there has been a relatively silent partner through all this. This softly gentle and compassionate partner has been the General Operations Director itself.

Did I find and follow my Soul's imperatives?

Making Peasants into Kings

A message from Mary

What sort of a glimpse of the "beyond" can the departed give to us?

The drawing below was produced with the help of my artist guide in Heaven. It shows Mary with her hair returned, her weight back to normal and her youthful vigor restored. Below it is one of her first messages to me. It gives a picture of what it is like to be in Heaven. It shows that individuality is expanded and not lost by being connected into God's Will.

She does not need glasses in heaven. My angelic artist added them to make the picture more identifiable for those who knew her here.

You are coming out of it very well. I'm proud of you. I love you so much. But we must go on with the next phases of our lives. You were right. God expresses Itself here as tenderness, joy and peace.

We exchange thoughts more than words. Our actions get coordinated by the fact that our thoughts are coordinated. The joy and peace that is here is beyond description.

Dr. Jay C. Powell

This message came through me on March 30th, 2006, six days after she passed. It was delivered through "automatic writing" where a person in Heaven uses the hand of a person on Earth to write a message. Notice that her identity is not lost but her ability to cooperate is greatly increased. It is unusual for people to be able to communicate across the veil of death this quickly.

Does not this message sound familiar to all who study comparative religions? Is it not reassuring to know we go the same way, "According to our fruits?"

And now Valerie

The next chapter in this romantic part of the saga has now been unfolding. This time her name is Valerie and we were married on June 19th, 2007. She has a Ph.D., is teaching in Information Systems, including Health Information Systems. Her skills complement mine remarkably. Once again the flow between us was the key to the decision to marry.

She has been teaching at the college level for 50 years, is fluent in German as well as English, passably competent in Spanish and can get by in Russian and Arabic. Her skill as a human network builder will be essential as we tackle together the problems of education on a worldwide basis.

She is continuing her teaching career because she loves to teach. This has given me the opportunity to return to the college classroom after twenty years absence and to rediscover the delight of provoking flashes of insight once more.

Mary seemed to think that my editor, Roxane Christ[55] (Pronounced with a short "i") might be suitable, but like Marion in England, that didn't work out. There was an insurmountable "Yes but …" that came between us.

Peter, my senior guide in Heaven, suggested that I join a computer dating service with the suggestion that "Mrs. Right" had been persuaded to find a life companion through this means.

I followed this guidance and met Valerie online. Then the crisis came. Roxane called to tell me in February of 2007 that she had decided to accept my invitation to come to Michigan after all.

Feeling I had my first commitment to Roxane, and knowing there was a level of flow between us, I informed Valerie of the situation. In a message that evening, the General Operations Director put it straight to me, "It's your mess. You fix it!"

What to do? There could be only one solution, a Soul-to-Soul conversation. In deep meditation I tried to speak directly to Roxane's Soul and to Valerie's Soul; "Let the strength of our contracts with God prevail."

It worked. Roxane phoned me the next day to say that she was not coming. I contacted Valerie immediately, inviting her to visit me so that I could test the flow between us. The flow cannot be sensed in full intensity at a distance. This is the one exception to non-locality I know about and it is a safeguard against impetuosity for those who have decided to engage in following the plan.

She agreed, coming to Davison with a friend in the middle of May. The moment she walked into the manufactured home in Davison, the flow was like a hurricane. It nearly knocked me off my feet. I asked her to marry me. She hesitated, saying that she wanted to talk to me privately first. What she told me about herself was interesting, but only strengthened my resolve because she had followed her Soul's imperatives too.

We were married within a month and it has been wonderful! We are oh so right for each other! There are two remarkable things about this relationship. First, since Frances was born in 1908 and my parents were born in the 1890s, the entire setup must have been more than 100 years in the making.

Second, unlike the expectation that we subjugate our will to the Divine Will, as is taught in so many creeds of differing religions, we are expected to be cooperative participants in the planning and executing the transformation we need to take to bring Conscious Control to the Universe. "It's your mess! You fix it!"

What does this event tell us about surrendering to God's Will? Is it "surrender" or "creative participation?"

Responding to our Soul's imperatives

If we are extensions of God, does this mean that we all have a mission?

It is now time for us to return to the two types of learning introduced in Chapter 4. One is for the artisan, the other for the shaman. Where do these two fit and how do they work together?

It is simple. The training of the shaman occurs *after* the awakening, after the full realization that everything is connected. The hero of the introductory story had not yet achieved this sense of connectedness. He therefore considered the old one to be insane.

The loss of connectedness is the source of the turmoil in which we are living today. It is the basis behind social disorder, where we assume that people are interchangeable with each other and with machines.

It is the basis behind global warming, where we assumed that the environment would absorb our reckless exploitation of our Mother Earth's resources.

It is the basis of the current (2009) economic disaster, where unregulated greed replaced good judgment and fair treatment of others.

It is the basis of "9/11." Some of the disenfranchised found a way to protest the economic exploitation of the less developed countries by the developed ones that our social responsibility requires. We must "protect others from us," which is something we have not been doing.

The hero's number one wife was right that she stayed with her Soul's imperative of teaching crafts to the girls. That is were the future of society lies. His number two wife was right in following him to the lodge. He had not found connectedness, giving her the role of helping him to find it. That is also where the future of society lies. The material and the spiritual are inseparably connected. We must find this connectedness before we can advance beyond the superficiality of materialism.

The way of the artisan is one of working together for common goals and common gains. It is the way of sharing, and ultimately of connectedness. As each of us works to discover and develop our talents. In a cooperative setting, we learn to recognize and to honor capabilities in others and bonds of mutuality form.

These bonds can become as strong as those related to survival among soldiers on the battlefield. However, these can develop without the suspicions that inhabit warriors because they identify the "enemy" with apparent certainty. This paradox occurs because the enemy actually comes from deep within us, arising from our sense of separation. My battle with my alter ego has made this point abundantly clear to me.

Frances was my companion during my teaching career, helping me to hone my skills to the level of master craftsman. Mary walked with me on the shamanic road as I began to get past my anger at the abusiveness of schooling into an understanding of how wisdom is a constructive combination of interconnected knowledge and compassion.

I also needed to learn compassion for those who were unintentionally destroying everything they touched because, in the absence of connectedness, they were all doing the best they could with what they knew.

If we are going to make the disconnected people of this earth, the peasants who are the fodder for the cannon, into the kings who create the future, we need to use the education of the artisan instead of the shaman. Why? Because the education of the shaman can only be realized *after* the awakening has occurred.

We do not lose our identity with "death." We merely change our plane of residence. At any stage in the evolution of the universe we can deliberately change ourselves. These changes can be toward the underlying principle of *unconditional love* or away from it. Either way we live with the "karma" our intentions create. These acts of consciousness are the source of "good" and "evil" in the world. The universe supports loving acts and does not support selfish acts. Eventually all will be love, making "evil" a temporary aberration or "illusion" in the timelessness of eternity.

It is our careful observation of our intentions and their outcomes that is *crucial* to this whole process. Information is not enough. To release our inner potential we must expand and enhance our ability to observe and to connect what we observe with life's needs and purposes.

As we do this, our brain rewires itself to include our new understandings. Education's task is to empower students to discover their missions and to bring these forth so that all of us can fulfill our inherent roles.

We must abandon pursuing the imperatives of our cultures, which limits our awareness and separates us from others. Instead, we must pursue the Imperatives of our Souls, which will unite us into the Common Purpose.

This is the "Second Coming," the "New Renaissance." We must release the pent-up talents of all humanity by recreating ourselves. We then can follow our Divine Sparks and to fulfill our designated purposes as *full collaborators in the evolution of the universe!*

Are we about to discover and begin to realize the true depth of our humanity?

Making Peasants into Kings

In our final chapter, we will look at how I came to the educational conclusions that is building this bridge; guided and inspired by observation about learning and testing.

What should we be doing differently? How and why is this difference better?

Chapter 6: Developing Consciousness

Nothing is ever "true," except under certain circumstances, and then only from a particular viewpoint.

David Hawkins[56]

The meeting that changed the nation[57]

Why is testing an important part of teaching?

"The delegation from the colleges has arrived Mr. Mann," his secretary announced.

"Show them into the conference room, Helen," he instructed. Horace Mann had just been appointed Commissioner of Instruction for the Commonwealth of Massachusetts. He closed the dossier he had been studying and went through the richly paneled door to the adjoining conference room.

As soon as the six representatives of Massachusetts' major universities sat down and the introductions were complete, Mr. Mann enquired, "What can I do for you, gentlemen?"

"We have a serious problem. Perhaps you can help us?" the Chancellor of Yale began. "We are trying to make our admission standards more open. However, the transcripts of marks we get from different academies do not help us identify which students are likely to succeed."

"This problem is particularly acute for students from the smaller and newer academies," the President of Harvard observed.

"Are there students who do not present this problem?" Mr. Mann queried.

"Yes," the President of Dartmouth replied. "The sons of alumnae and the graduates of well established larger academies present few problems for us."

"How would you define your problem?"

"There seems to be a lack of uniformity of standards in the programs and in the reported grades," the Governor of Hampton College elaborated.

"I am in the process of defining a uniform curriculum based upon my study of the schools in Prussia," Mr. Mann explained. "In the meantime, is there anything else I might do to assist you?"

"We need a scientific basis for scoring tests," the President of the Massachusetts Institute of Technology proposed. "Could we do a study of the accuracy of teachers' marking?"

"That sounds like a good idea," they all agreed.

Thus, a proposal was put forward to conduct a study of scoring accuracy and they then moved on to the next issue on the agenda.

Horace Mann was as good as his word. He collected a number of student themes. He had them copied by some secretaries so that the students' handwriting could not be identified. He then had several teachers score each theme. As we now know, the marks given to each paper were all over the map. This was the beginning of high-stakes testing in America.

He concluded that a formal scoring system was needed to make sure that this variability did not happen for college admission. He did not realize that by disguising the handwriting and giving the same theme to several markers broke the link of understanding between teachers and their students. This error contributed to the score variability.

Does this research explain why we need uniform standards for assessing performance?

Should we be fighting the tests?[58]

"Perform the following thought experiment." Alfie Kohn directed his General Session audience at Association for Supervision and Curriculum Development's (ASCD) 2000 conference on Teaching and Learning. "Imagine that your state's test this spring is passed by almost every student who takes it. What is the likely response from your governors, state legislators, and newspapers? 'Damn, these teachers are good?'"

When the skeptical laughter from the audience greeted this suggestion, Kohn supplied a more plausible answer. "The test is too easy, the standards are too low; we need to raise the bar."

Given this likely response to universal scores, "High standards are, by definition, standards that not all children are able to meet ... This whole standards and accountability movement, stripped bare of its pleasant rhetoric about 'all kids can learn' is really a gigantic sorting device," said Kohn. "We can never in good conscience support even the more innocuous aspects of this movement because it all leads to that ultimate point. It's not just about 'harder is better.' It's about setting a bar where we can never allow all [children] to succeed."

Kohn continued that he was not necessarily against standards that allow teachers and students to move toward better learning.

Is it our intention to deliberately prevent some students from succeeding in school?

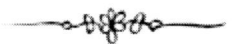

Discovering my mission

As *A Course in Miracles* puts it (ACIM; 1, II; 1.9 - 2.3):

You are free to believe what you choose, and what you do attests to what you believe.

Revelation is intensely personal and cannot be meaningfully translated. That is why any attempt to describe it in words is impossible. Revelation induces only experience.

I have suggested my sense of mission that has led to the writing of this book from my teaching experience and research results.[59] It is now time to bring everything together. I've told you what I have experienced as a teacher and as an explorer of the spiritual realms. What are the implications for effective education that we can draw from this combination of experiences?

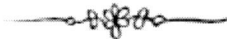

Robin's nest

What is a right answer?

"Why are you throwing that paper away?" Rickie's father asked.

"Oh, it's nuffin'," Rickie replied.

"Let me see it." Rickie reluctantly gave it to his father who uncrumpled it and examined it carefully.

"You got this answer marked wrong. What happened?"

"The teacher tells me to draw seven blue robin's eggs in the nest on that sheet."

"I see you drew only five, why?"

"Well … we know that robins lay three or four eggs. Never more than five, so I drew only five eggs!"

What would have happened if the teacher had asked Rickie, "Why only five eggs?"

So, what's the problem?

To begin with, Horace Mann's conclusion, that we need some form of systematic observation of student performance that has a uniform meaning in order to find out how well we are teaching, was perfectly correct, even though this approach has led to serious abuses.

We tend to have mixed feelings about testing itself. This is Alfie Kohn's point. The reason for this ambivalence is less clear, as I have illustrated in the "Robin's Nest" incident. The teacher was considering what she wanted Rickie to know. This is the shaman's approach to teaching. She did not consider what Rickie already knew. This would have been the artisan's approach to teaching. There are many examples in my narrative thus far that have shown how teachers' expectations can get in the way of learning. The account about "Painting in Black" is but one example.

Essentially, the discussion can be seen in how teachers relate to their students. Of the three models presented, "Doing to," "Doing for" and "Doing with." only the last one leaves room for teachers to discover and make full use of the resources students already have. However, in this approach, the curriculum emerges from the classroom interactions and cannot be directed from a document created outside of the room.

The middle ground, "Doing for" uses both the prescribed curriculum and accommodates some students' needs. It has the problem, however, of creating students that tend to be dependent upon teachers whenever they need to learn something.

I can now answer this question, "How then can we set standards of performance that we cannot document?"

Dr. Jay C. Powell

Plug-in theory of learning

How did current testing practices come into existence?

It was 1917. War had been raging in Europe for nearly three years. It was being fought to a stalemate. The United States was to be drawn into the conflict. With the sinking of the passenger ship *Lusitania* by a German U-boat, the battle lines were finally drawn. The United States joined the war on the side of the United Kingdom and her allies.

America had a small volunteer army that would be no match for the needs of the European front. A large number of troops would have to be enlisted and trained quickly. To find recruits with officer potential, the army asked Robert Yerkes, a prominent psychologist, to make a test that would screen many people quickly.

Yerkes called upon the wisdom of educational measurement at the time and his own inspiration. Microscopic examination of the brain showed networks of connections that resembled a telephone exchange. He had the idea that a person either knew the answer to a question or guessed blindly. Hence, a test that had options from which to choose seemed to be a simple and fast way to sort people into groups.

With this idea the *Army Alpha* group intelligence test was born. It proved remarkably successful for its purpose. The total score seemed to be a good estimate of how much the examinee knew. It revolutionized the way we tested large numbers of people. With only one right answer, it could be scored quickly and easily by clerks, and later by machines.

Of course, if people either knew the expected answer, or guessed blindly, the only meaningful information from the test would be how many "right" answers they gave. The other answers would be chosen by chance. They could be ignored.

However, if they were not chosen by chance, would ignoring them not be discarding information that might be useful?

The math behind the theory
Is the plug-in theory right?

Dr. Keeping, my statistics teacher at the University of Alberta, was one of the best teachers I ever had. He always took time to explain the "whys" behind any particular procedure. One day the class was discussing the bell-shaped (or *normal*) curve that is at the very center of all linear statistics.

"If you flip four unbiased coins, there are 16 possible combinations of heads and tails. These range from all heads, to all tails through every-possible combination in between. In the long run, the pattern HHHH will occur only once in 16 times. The pattern HTTT will occur four times. The pattern HHTT will occur six times. The pattern HHHT will occur four times. And the pattern TTTT will also occur only once. Does anyone recognize this sequence $1 - 4 - 6 - 4 - 1$?"

Having been a good student in high school math I raised my hand. "Yes, Mr. Powell?"

"It's the numerical coefficients of the expansion of $(a \pm b)^4$."

"That is correct. It is part of the series called the *binomial* expansion. The binomial comes from the two elements *a* and *b*. The expansion is the exponential number. Well, the normal curve is merely the limit when the exponent approaches infinity. There is a relatively simple solution to the calculus behind this relationship developed by Gauss more than 100 years ago.

"Notice that to use the normal curve, the data set *must* be binomial."

"What happens if the data set is not binomial?" my classmate, diagonally in front of me, asked.

"If multinomial or discontinuous data are collapsed into a binomial, the results will be a spurious distribution that has *no mathematical meaning*."

Wow! What a concept! Is it possible that we be getting *meaningless* information from our test scores?

More recently it has been realized that some "normal" distributions can have two parts; one is a set of specific states, the other is a set of links or movements among these states. This concept is best visualized as a number of self-contained blobs somehow connected by lines of linkage or flow.

One way of looking at this is to consider how an automatic transmission in a car works. Several sets of gears are organized into different drive ratios. The speed of the engine, the drag on the drive wheels and the load on the vehicle are measured by sensors. These sensors tell the transmission which set of gears to use. The gears are states the car can be in and the computer controlling them provides the linkage.

A form of analysis, developed by Georg Rasch in the 1960s is a basis for Item Response Theory (IRT). It identifies the scale positions of all alternative answers in multiple-choice tests along the item difficulty scale. In contrast, our research shows that *all* answers emerge and disappear along the scale of complexity to become the interconnected discrete elements in this *nonnormal* distribution.

Can we find a procedure to extract these components that shows how they are interrelated? Yes! Here is the story.

"X" marks the spot

Where did the information go?

I took this statistics course in my last year of my B.Ed. program as part of my math minor. This exchange has stuck with me all these 50+ years. My success in that course in statistics was the reason for my taking "Test preparation for teachers" and "The history of mathematical thought." as my first two courses toward my Masters degree in education, which I began in 1958.

This program required six weeks in the summer and a major assignment to be completed in the fall for each course. The measurement course required us to produce and evaluate a test using all the statistical techniques we had been taught.

This was a B.C. (before computers) course. The data analysis needed to be done by hand.

Try to visualize this process. I was to arrange the students' total scores across the top of a large spread sheet so that each score headed a column of entries. I was to arrange the test item numbers down the side of the sheet so that each row represented the answers to each item.

This gave me a large table into which I could record every answer from every student who took the test. My teacher said to leave the correct answers blank and to put an "X" into the small squares for the answers that were either wrong or omitted.

The table had two purposes. The total number of "right" answers in each item divided by the total number of students who took the test was to tell me how difficult or easy that item had been for these students. The more students who got it right, the easier the item.

I was then to count from the left the total number of "wrong" answers and to mark that square. A perfect question would have all the "wrong" answers below that mark and all the "right" answers above it. For questions less than perfect there is a way to use the number of right answers below the mark and the total number of right answers to determine how well this item measured the same thing that the test as a whole measured. We called this the "discrimination index." If it were larger than, say 0.30 we could consider it to be a "good" item. Values lower than this were "poor" items and needed to be revised or discarded.

Dr. Jay C. Powell

Simulated Sample Item Analysis Spreadsheet

Student Name	A	B	C	D	E	F	G	H	I	J	K	L	M	N	O	P	Q	R	S	T	U	V	W	X	Y	Z	Item Difficulty	Item Discrim.
Item Score =	3	4	4	5	5	5	5	6	6	6	6	6	6	6	7	7	7	7	7	7	8	8	8	8	9	9	P	D
No. Rt. Ans.																												
1 a				**B**																							0.96	0.17
2 b		a	a				a																				0.92	0.17
3 c	a	a		**B**	b			d	d																		0.73	0.67
4 c		b	d		a		d																				0.85	0.50
5 d	**B**	**B**			**B**	**B**		**B**	c			a	a c			a a											0.65	0.50
6 b	d		d	**A**	**C**	**C**	**C**		**C** a	**C** a	**C**	**C**	**C**					a	a	a							0.57	0.50
7 a	b	c		**B**					c		b			b				c								c	0.69	0.50
8 c	a		a		X	X							d					d	b b	b b			b				0.62	0.17
9 a	b	d	c	**D**	b	c		b	c	b	b	c	c	c	b	b		d	d	d	d	d		d			0.19	0.50
10 a	c	b	b		c	d	d	c	d	d	d	c	b	b	d	d		d	b	b	b	b c				0.15	0.33

STYLE 1: U. C.	The answer vector for student "D" was: B ABCD ABCD A	Average (mean) score = 6.35
Style 2: U. C.	Answers characteristic of LOW SCORERS	Average (mean) Difficulty (P) = 0.633
Style 3: U. C.	Answers characteristic of MIDDLE SCORERS	Standard deviation = 1.49
Style 4: l. e.	Answers Characteristic of HIGH SCORER Good Question Ranges = P 0.30 to 0.70; D 0.30 or larger.	
X	Omitted answers	
Blank	Right answers Item Analysis Formulae = 1. D = (Ur − Lr)/n Where: R= # of Right in item; N = # of Students	
	2. P = R/N	Ur = # R in Upper; Lr = # R in Lower and n = size used (6)

As you can see in item 9, a number of high scoring students chose the "wrong" answer "d" in the place of the "right" answer "a". However, only the high scorers got this answer "right." It was a difficult question but it measured strongly in the direction of the total scores.

This observation that particular "wrong" answers tend to be confined to specific score ranges was also observed by Georg Rasch[60] in Belgium at about the same time and has become the central approach for Item Response Theory (IRT) and is a central part of item design today.

Interestingly, attempts to *interpret* the *meaning* of these answers in order to identify and eliminate systematic errors have not, in the past 50 years, become a standard part of IRT. If there is anything meaningful in these obviously systematic choices it is ignored in current scoring practices.

With this information in mind, I produced a multiple-choice test for the end of the first term in my Grade 11 history class; the class where I was teaching my students to read the history text.

When I began entering their answers, I was troubled by the instructions to treat "wrong" answers the same as "omitted" answers. A little voice in my head told me that I would be losing information by doing this. I decided instead to put the letter for the actual answer in the small square and to reserve the "X" for omitted answers. My finished chart looked something like the chart on the facing page, only bigger.

The first benefit was that I discovered where I had scored items incorrectly. I don't remember how many times I had to redraw the sheet to get the order of the scores accurate; it was at least twice.

Once the chart was drawn, I noticed something unusual. Particular "wrong" answers tended to form fairly tight groups along the "total score" scale, as illustrated in the chart. This pattern was stronger with some items than others but it was a clear pattern over the whole table. This is a pattern that should not have happened if the selection of "wrong" answers were blind guesses!

So what was I to do? I asked some of the students why they chose particular answers. The explanations made sense, because it explained how they interpreted the question differently than I had intended for the "right" answer. A little thought on my part, and I could understand the nature of the mistakes they had made.

Sometimes they changed the meanings of the words in the question. Sometimes they left out a part of the problem, sometimes they added information to the idea that didn't belong. There is a whole series of logical error strategies that showed how they were thinking.

When I coupled this realization with the fact that they could not read their history text with understanding, I changed my teaching strategy in the way I described in Chapter 4. I was now paying careful attention to what each student was saying, the way I described Ms. Wilson responding in the "Doing with …" teaching strategy. As in that case, the response was electric.

There it was, in plain view! Answers on a four-item multiple-choice test were *not a true dichotomy!* Students select the best answer they can, based upon the way they interpret the question. From what Dr. Keeping had said about the *normal* distribution, the use of this curve for evaluating tests was invalid and the scores from this procedure *might be mathematically meaningless!*

Unlike the followers of Rasch, I chose a different route. When I decided to ask my students, who had given particular "wrong" answers, why they had chosen these answers, their explanations were always reasonable. In every case, they answered the question *the way they interpreted it*. Sometimes there was a clear error in their interpretation. More often, *accepting their interpretation* made their answers *valid* if not *right*.

This realization took me back to my own calamitous learning experiences, to the book by Dr. Leslie Bell and to my course in remediation. Finding out how they were thinking gave me a handle on their learning problems.

From here it was a short step to understand how to teach them. I was already using their book to teach them how to read a history text. I only needed to add how to think through and organize the information they were gathering and they should learn a great deal more rapidly.

At the end of the year I decided that I needed to validate the effectiveness of this approach. I arranged with the other history teacher, who was teaching the college-bound group, to give a common final exam to each of the two history classes. We agreed to share the marking as well. She marked the even numbered questions and I the odd numbered ones.

Here, my background in statistics came to the rescue. There is a procedure for determining how far apart two averages might be. The idea is to find out if the two distributions are from the same group or from two different ones.[61]

With this thought in mind, I compared the two average scores. The results? My diploma group scored significantly *higher* than her college-bound group. Since we were both second-year teachers, this difference must have come from the method of teaching and not from our experience.

Unfortunately, this procedure is based upon the normal distribution. It is a standard for current research procedures. I am, therefore, uncomfortable with the strength that would ordinarily be assigned to this result. I can say however, that the students who were taught how to read the text *seemed* to answer the questions on the content more thoroughly and effectively than those who were taught the content in the more usual manner. They also *seemed* to answer the more challenging questions more thoughtfully. The other teacher agreed with this interpretation. I knew that I was onto something.

From the point of view of the researcher, it is wonderful to find such strong intervention effects. From the point of view of the teacher, it generated considerable anger in me that these students' school experiences had lowered their expectations of themselves to a point where they no longer aspired to anything but a high-paying industrial job in a factory when they were at least as capable as the college-bound class if they had been taught differently. From such experiences grows crusades.

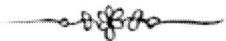

The reason I left that school that year is worth mentioning. In the "reading to write" approach to English literature I set a task of writing five pages of self-dialogue about a youth deciding to leave home. I was then going to introduce them to the chapter on that topic in Oliver Curwood's *Plains of Abraham*.[62]

One student handed me 89 typed pages of beautifully written introspective monologue. He had experienced a breakthrough in creative writing. Shortly thereafter my classes were rearranged and I no longer taught Language Arts to the college-bound tenth graders. At the end of the year the head of the English department took me aside.

"Jay, for most of the year I have disapproved of your teaching approach. The thing that turned me around was the play you put on."

"How so?"

"The person you had play the part of the villain was having terrible problems in school. A couple of years ago he stole a car and crashed it, giving him a severe brain injury. He has been the laughing stock of many of our better students ever since.

"But you pulled it off! I sat in the wings with a script in hand. He didn't miss a cue or a line. His performance in that dancing scene was exceptional. Why do you suppose that there was standing room only at the production, in spite of the curling tournament and other activities in town that night?

"Everyone wanted to see him fall flat on his face. Instead he astonished them all. I'm sorry to see you go. I couldn't persuade the board to change its mind.

"Do you remember Berry?"

"Yes. He's the one who gave me 89 beautifully written typed pages when I only asked for 5 hand-written ones."

"He is the son of the chairman of the school board. The family had an outing on that weekend and Berry refused to go because he had this assignment to do for you. It took him the entire weekend. His father decided that you were giving your classes altogether too much work to do; end of discussion."

Since this was also the school in which Roger challenged me to fisticuffs, I suspect that the "discipline problem" I had early in the year may also have contributed to this decision.

In retrospect, the realization that my students were thinking as they chose their answers and that the answers they chose showed *how* they were thinking was a *revelation* in the sense that is used in *A Course in Miracles* quoted above.

This "discovery" brought a new focus to my teaching and the understanding I had about this highly personal and deeply psychologically intimate act. I now knew my mission. My next step was to follow the trail of discovery to unravel the mystery of why our current way of teaching had been so ineffective with me and with so many others in the classrooms to which teacher were assigned. Was my success a fluke?

Where do you suppose this insight might lead me?

Dr. Jay C. Powell

Opening the door to post-secondary education

Are formal examinations a barrier to future academic success?

Here was the problem in the next school I taught at.

In the spring of 1959 and my third year of teaching, my Grade 13 students performed far below the expected standards for Ontario. What was I going to do about it?

This small high school had about 70 students from the ninth through the thirteenth grade. It had three full-time teachers and one half-time teacher. Each teacher was responsible for a cluster of subjects. I was responsible for all the science and mathematics subjects for the entire high school program.

To make this load more workable, each teacher taught a full ninth grade and tenth grade program. We each taught the eleventh grade and twelfth grade courses in alternate years.

This situation meant that I had seven preparations (including a course in business practice) in an eight-period day. Each full-time teacher had a similar course load.

At the end of my first year of teaching in this school I had taught two Grade 13 subjects (Chemistry and Analytical Geometry) to five students. Of these ten Grade 13 papers written by my students, only one student achieved a passing grade on the chemistry paper. The marks I estimated for my students were 30% higher than the scores they actually achieved from the government's high-stakes testing system.

I could not believe that I had taught them so poorly. When I looked up the marks of the school's principal, who had seven final papers written, his average decline in marks was 25%. Doing 5% more poorly than a teacher with many years experience was not quite as damning. The third fulltime teacher did about as poorly as I.

On the other hand, students could get into such professions as nursing or elementary-school teaching and the Provincial trade schools *without* Grade 13. This alternative, of trying to teach these advanced subjects on top of everything else, produced a ridiculously heavy workload.

I thought it would be a good idea to stop trying to teach these advanced-level subjects in such a small school. At the beginning of my second year there, the new principal, Mr. Jones, supported this suggestion and asked me, because of my statistical background, to present this suggestion to the local school board.

I arrived at the meeting armed with the massive notebook that contained all the marks for every student in the school since its founding in1905. It also included the Grade 13 final marks from the Province for everyone who wrote these exams. The picture just described was similar for more than 50 years, except for the period from 1939 to 1945; the time of World War II in Canada.

Rick Cuthbert, the board's secretary, asked, "How come our school has produced a number of professional people without transporting the college-prep students to another community?"

"Can you name them?" I returned.

"Well," said Ralph Kenney, the second trustee, "There's Jack McGregor, who is a physician in Highland."

"When did he graduate from our high school?"

"1944, I think."

I looked for Jack's record in the marks book. "You are quite right," I answered. "Here are his marks for 1939 through 1944. He had passing marks on all his Grade 13 courses."

"Then there is my niece, Sharon Hendricks," remarked Peter Bentley, the Board Chairman. "She's a chartered accountant with Granger, Gautier, and Musselman in Overton."

Her records showed that she graduated in 1945. This process continued to include a dentist, two more accountants, a lawyer, and several secondary school teachers.

I pointed out, "Every one of them had graduated during the time of World War II (1939–1945 in Canada) when the sons and daughters of fulltime farmers were excused from these Grade 13 examinations as part of the war effort.

"When our students have to take these exams they are at a distinct disadvantage. Of the 17 papers written this year only 4 received a passing grade. By teaching Grade 13 here we are overloading our teachers and disadvantaging our students!"

Some of the board members objected that these students would have to travel too far because they would be on the bus more than an extra hour for the round trip each day.

However, they finally agreed to transport the Grade 13 students 27 miles to the nearest full-service high school. As part of the agreement, we would endeavor to raise the achievement levels to a point where those students who wished to attempt Grade 13 would have a good chance of success in that full-service high school.

What does this anecdote tell us about high stakes testing?

Improving teaching effectiveness

Having stuck my neck out, what was I to do?

I was at that small high school for two more years. The Ministry of Education had inspectors who visited every school in Ontario at least once a year. These visits were to ensure that the quality standards expected by the people of the Province were being met.

The inspector for our district agreed to put the possibility of school closure on hold while we tried to raise the performance of the students in our school.

In those two years the Ontario Ministry of Education instituted some multiple-choice exams as part of their quality control in Ontario high schools. The subjects to be examined (algebra and physics) were both courses I taught. The fate of the school rested on my shoulders. The scores on these tests would be scaled across the entire province.[63]

Making Peasants into Kings

I spent the summer going over the tests I had given the previous year in both mathematics and science, looking for the places where a lack of understanding might be evident. It was immediately apparent in mathematics that the concepts of zero and of equality were not fully understood. In algebra these two concepts are closely related and of critical importance for success in mathematical learning.

I called upon my course in the nature of mathematics from my undergraduate days and the history of mathematic from my continuing M.Ed. program. I developed the approach to teaching math that I described in Chapter 4.

For equations, I showed them how to maintain equality by adding to or multiplying by the same value both sides of an equation in such a way that one of the variables on one side was forced to become zero, or one of the numerical coefficients become unity (1) when multiplied. We spent several weeks with me asking them to think through the problem until they figured out for themselves what they needed to do and why they needed to do it.

I estimated from my Grade 13 results that from their previous marks they were starting at a scaled score of 30. When their twelfth grade algebra average score came back at the end of the year the average was 46, I assumed that they had gained about two year's improvement in one year of teaching.[64]

In the second year, we had a new Principal who came from the Netherlands. He had two sons who lapped up the math taught my way. A math contest was advertised for the whole province. These were to provide recognition to outstanding students and schools. We entered the contest with four contestants. There were the two Dutch boys and a boy and a girl from the community. Our school came in 43rd from more than 450 schools across the Province. This would suggest that the program was a roaring success because the "locals" did as well as the "foreigners."

In the second year the eleventh grade physics was up for examination. I decided that I would make the program entirely hands-on with the students doing the demonstrations for each other, preparing and scoring the tests and then studying the tests' answers to find out what concepts had not been successfully communicated. They then conducted remedial sessions as needed.

When the government exam results came back with a class average of 55, I presumed that they had made *nearly four years of progress* (from a base score of 30) *in two years!* There were a couple of topics in the exam that we had not touched in depth, and there were some questions that my better students would have seen as being ambiguous. I figured that the school was now approaching the acceptable standards of the entire Province and may have gained about four years of skill in two school years. In any case, they were within 10 points of the Province's artificial standard.

Notice that I set up the structure and they did the work. What does this tell us about the best way to teach?

This is not the end of the story. Of the 12 students in that last twelfth grade class, none of them went on to Grade 13. Instead nine of them went to Teachers' College to become successful elementary school teachers. This occurred for two reasons. First, the Teachers' College did not require the thirteenth grade for admission. Second, they had enjoyed teaching their fellow students in my classes and by doing the teaching and the testing themselves, they had learned a lot about effective teaching.

Without experience in applying knowledge, no amount of theory will produce craftsmanship. The ability to do is more important than merely knowing what might be done. The teaching of the artisan must precede that of the shaman, remember?

Would you agree with this assessment of the gains they had made?

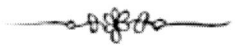

Students need two things to be successful in higher education. First, they need to have learned *how to think* and *how to learn*. Second, they need a strong desire to succeed as their studies advance. Do our schools effectively prepare them for college by teaching these skills and attitudes? How does emphasis upon *course content* in high-stakes testing impact upon their acquiring these profoundly powerful capabilities?

After teaching five semesters in two different universities in the United States in the last few years, I can ask exactly the same questions here. In fact I am just finishing a research project with my 2009 spring semester classes which seem to show support for this conclusion. All the results are not yet in.

In the Digital Age, should we be teaching by an exploratory approach instead of a didactic one?

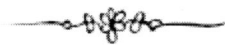

Becoming a special educator

What might follow from such success?

It is common for successes such as these to wash out in the school system when the person who achieved them moves to another setting.

What would have happened if I had become the principal of that small community school? During my third year there, being from Europe, the Principal was suspicious of the teaching methods I had been using. He said so to the inspector, which made the inspector suspicious as well. I received a poor rating.

Then the results of the math contest came in with his sons among the stars and the principal tried unsuccessfully to get the rating changed. To become principal I would have needed at least a permanent certificate. This required at least three years of good ratings from inspectors and principals. I had taught for five years, but had only two "good" ratings.

The principal of a full service high school heard about what I had accomplished. He had a problem he wished to solve. There were a number of students in his school and some others about to be admitted to his school who had not successfully completed their eighth grade but who were not yet old enough legally to leave school.

He was serving the middle-management community for a large international mining corporation. It was to the political advantage of the school board to have these students accommodated in high school for at least one or two more years.

He approached me with the offer to become the head of their new "special programs" department. I would have a free hand, teaching 40% of the time in each of the ninth and tenth grade special programs. Here was my big chance.

I taught at that school for two years. I had no discipline problems and the first year went reasonably well. My main achievement in the first year was the remedial math program I set up for the entire school. It was open to all students who failed their first term tests. In the first year it was voluntary. It lasted for six weeks, one after-school session each week.

Not all of the students stayed for all six sessions. For those that did, their average at Christmas was 38%. By Easter it had risen to 63% and by June to 68%. A year later this same group averaged 78% without further remediation. Apparently the learning they achieved from six one-hour sessions gave them the momentum to continue to make gains in their second year. This is the typical impact of "learning how to learn."

The principal was so delighted that he made the remedial program compulsory in the second year. It was nowhere near as effective when it was compulsory because the students resented being forced into an action that exposed their lack of ability to their peers.

By the time I had been there for a year, I had put together a fairly strong program. I have already described much of it

Making Peasants into Kings

in two incidents. The discussion of how the class resolved the issue of cheating when Harry wrote all the stories is one of them.

Their weekly writing progressed from a quarter of a page at the beginning of the year (marked out of 10) to a page and a half at the end of the year (marked out of 75). Although I still have some of these efforts as samples of their progress, I would sooner refer you to Herbert Kohl's account of his success in the Bronx in *36 Children*.[65] His account is so similar to mine that it would be redundant for me to tell the same story.

The second one was when Brian Richardson rose to the voluntary reading challenge.

At the beginning of the year, Brian was reading at the second grade level. By the end of the year, he was reading at the second year of college comprehension! He gained about one year in skill for each five books he read to a total of 13 years' gain in reading ability in 8 months!

The gains for the entire class in their reading ability were nowhere near as spectacular. The class average on this test in October was the sixth month in the third grade (3.6). The following May it was the second month in the seventh grade (7.2). This group had doubled its performance in one year of teaching. The gain of nearly four years in one speaks well for their willingness to learn, once they discovered that they were capable of learning. Once again I set up the program that encouraged them to do the work and to teach each other as they became more capable.

Their gains in mathematics were more modest (4.8 – 6.4). Perhaps this was because, to lighten my teaching load, I put them on the TEMAC* self-teaching program for mathematics developed by IBM and it was not as motivating as the way I taught math.

It was in this program that I began using standardized tests like the one illustrated below to determine my students' knowledge and skill levels.

Dr. Jay C. Powell

I used them to help with my diagnostic work. In the process of trying to assess the vocabulary levels of my special programs students, I discovered this *Full-Range Picture Vocabulary Test* by Ammons and Ammons[66] (1948). This test was better for my purposes than the Peabody because it tested more than preschool and early elementary school vocabulary.

Although the line drawings are now out of date in areas of transportation and dress, I found that I could easily adapt it for group administration, using an overhead projector and scanable answer sheets by adding an alphabetic label (a, b, c, d), for each drawing on each plate.

Plate 1 of the
Full Range Picture Vocabulary Test

pie	(1.7)
window	(1.7)
seed	(6.5)
sill	(6.7)
transparent	(13.3)
rectangular	(14.7)
sector	(16.0)
illumination	(16.0)
culinary	(17.2)
egress	(A6.3)

The words the students were to identify as I read them aloud for this plate in Form A are given above.

This test has a feature I liked. The numbers on the right represent the age levels at which these words enter the average person's vocabulary. With 16 plates and more than 80 words to identify for each form of the test, the extensiveness of my students' receptive vocabulary (hearing the word and knowing the meaning) was easy to estimate. In fact, it starts at preschool and went well into the adult range, hence the "A" for "egress." I assumed that my students' receptive vocabulary was about two years in advance of their reading vocabulary. This thought gave me a clue about the type of reading materials to select for them.

Let us suppose we had a student who missed the word "seed" and correctly identified every other word up to but not including "sector." That student then missed all the remaining words. We would say that this student had a language age was somewhere between 14 years and 7 months (rectangular) and 16 years (sector). We could then compare this estimate with that student's actual age to decide how advanced in language development he or she has become.

Of course, with all 80 words the estimate will be more accurate. We can assume that the student doesn't know that the kernels of corn are seeds, or we can ask that student for clarification. Either way, we have information that will cue us to places where a lack of language knowledge might interfere with learning.

This statement is a critical point in my entire argument. It is the nature and complexity of the errors students make that indicates the frontiers of their knowledge and their learning skills. This statement also helps to identify advanced thinkers who introduce valid complexities to what looks like straightforward questions. Recall David Hawkins' remark[67] that truth is situationally and personally dependent and is not absolute. Yes, 1 + 1 = 2 in the abstract, but put one male and one female rabbit into the same cage and we get multiplying, not adding. Tongue-in-cheek, I agree, but when we apply mathematics to practical situations we need to be certain that the application fits the circumstances.

Although mathematical terms are being introduced at an earlier age than when this test was prepared, meaning that new norms need to be established, it is obvious that a wide range of auditory receptive vocabulary is being assessed. The model is better, for today's use, than the product but it is serviceable as is. I have shared this information with the publishers.

I have also played around with these words, establishing categories like transportation and entertainment, or language of origin such as Latin or Greek. The profiles for these categories gave me additional information about home background, reading diversity and recreational interests.

I tended to use the age levels when each student's ability to recognize the words petered out instead of using the norms provided. The administration of tests like this one could be automated very easily and scored by patterns of response for as many considerations as would seem reasonable to the user. Here is a research project for someone with language-development interests. For instance, a student with a disproportionally high level of right recognitions related to athletic equipment or sports activities clearly identifies an interest in that area.

Is it likely that turning a test like this that is designed for individual administration into one for group administration and into a diagnostic test from a global assessment test would be helpful to teachers? This discussion illustrates what I am talking about in using testing to inform teaching. After 50 years of doing it I can say that it has worked for me. We now need the research to show that it works for more people than me and the few of my students who have bought into the idea.

I am now thinking in terms of comparing the frontiers of each student's knowledge with the activities of research scientists at the frontiers of human knowledge. In this latter case, their acknowledged ignorance does not deter them from trying things out and learning from their mistakes. The schools could be a place where students explore ideas and relationships in a physically and psychologically safe environment. There are no "wrong" answers in such environments, merely less or more effective approaches to the situations being examined.

Would you have liked your schooling experiences to have been like the ones being described here?

Beginning a research program

Knowing that total scores are of questionable value, what are the basic questions that need to be asked?

After two years in the special programs I created and seeing the sizes of the gains that occurred, I had more questions than answers. Clearly this was an approach that worked with a wide range of students, many of whom began with lowered expectations for themselves and from others. Also, it survived transplantation.

However, if total scores were of questionable value, what should we use instead? This global question raises a whole lot of other questions. What is the information we can recover from "wrong" answers? How stable and meaningful is this information? How do we recover and report it? How do we use it?

Up to this point, my focus had been on making a better mousetrap. The goal was to do a better job of delivering the *existing curriculum*. Was this the best goal for the students we are teaching? My efforts as a special programs teacher suggest that the best teaching identifies the interests and innate talents of students. Then it helps them to be more successful pursuing these potentials. Finally we need to broaden these interests to tap their inner resources. This last effort, when successful, as with my grade 12 math students who became successful teachers, puts them on the road to personal and professional success on their own initiative.

This approach worked well, especially when the students did most of the work after the background resources had been prepared. However, I sensed that this approach could exclude teachers from the process when I felt they had an essential role. I had more questions than answers;

What might this role be?

What would a curriculum, focused upon emerging talents instead of social norms, look like?

Who would design these curricula?

How would standards of effective performance be established?

On the move again

These were not questions a classroom teacher could answer unaided.

I made enquiries and found that the University of Alberta had the best Ph.D. program in educational psychology in Canada. I applied and was accepted.

To finance my first year in this program I took a half-time teaching position with the Edmonton Public School Board. The teachers they needed most were in vocational education. I had taught typing and shorthand to adults in night school and bookkeeping and business practice in the small high school. With that background and my experience as a bookkeeper in a bank I was hired to teach two sections of typing and two sections of bookkeeping in the afternoons at a vocational high school. In college, this confined me to morning classes in the first year -- awkward but workable.

Teaching bookkeeping

I taught bookkeeping as I had learned it in the bank. I gave the students a set of books to enter and balance from the outset. I then went into the details and the theory. Like my math program, those who obtained high scores in my weekly tests were asked to do some tutoring and not to disturb the rest of the class. They sat at the back of the room.

The ones who were struggling were at the front of the room. Their test results told me where they were having problems. The diagnosis and remediation pattern worked well. All seven sections of Bookkeeping 10 were given a common final exam that was marked collectively.

Once again, my students' combined average was statistically higher than the combination of the other five classes. The department head commented, "Your classes certainly know their bookkeeping." Notice that I used testing to inform teaching. Total-correct scores do not contain enough information to perform this service for teachers.

Teaching typing:

What is the impact of rescaling the marks of students?

Mr. Scott, the Principal of Northern Vocational School, motioned the typing teacher, Bert Gray, to take a seat. He made a big point of shuffling the papers on his desk. Finally, he leaned back in his chair and looked out of the office window. Without looking at Mr. Gray, he cleared his throat and said, "Bert, I asked you to come and see me about your typing marks." There was a long pause; although it was obvious he expected no reply. "They're too high. We cannot submit them as they are, can we?"

"Why not?" Bert replied. "My students earned them."

"But look at this one for Lugene Maxie. You gave him A-. He has never received a mark this high in his life."

"I'm new to this state, as you know," Bert explained. "So when I saw that the State Board of Education had a set of typing-performance standards in its curriculum guidelines, I was delighted. However, there were no suggestions for the October report, so I used the December standards instead. All my students took the five-minute test, as recommended by the state guidelines, and I scored them using December's standards. If anything, the standard I set *should have been* too difficult for them."

"I don't care how you arrived at these marks, they are too high!"

"But I've already published them. Do you expect me to lower them now, when it was a matter of personal pride among my students that they did so well? Will you take the responsibility for any negative fallout that might arise?"

"Of course not! You gave them these marks. They're too high. You lower them and face the consequences. You should not have published them before you submitted them for my approval."

Bert was perplexed. How could he have avoided giving them their tests back, with their scores on them until he had received approval of these marks from the principal? Were any other teachers expected to get his approval first? Was the principal a higher authority than the state document?

How are standards of excellence established in schools?

Are test-score standards all as arbitrary as those set by Mr. Scott?

This event, reported to me by a friend, with the names changed, was similar to my own experience. It is also similar to the issue raised by Alfie Kohn. In my case, I explained the situation to my two typing classes with the promise that I would restore these marks for their final marks if they maintained this quality of work.

One of the two classes rose to this challenge and one of them fell apart. They were restless for the balance of the year and, unlike the other typing class and the two bookkeeping classes, they did poorly on the final exam.

Is this a common result with students in vocational programs from the rescaling of marks? If we shouldn't rescale marks, what should we do instead?

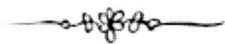

Now the fundamental question

Are "wrong" answers blind guesses or systematic choices of major educational importance?

I had just finished my pre-dissertation seminar. I walked with Dr. Steve Hunka back to his office. He was my number-one candidate as advisor for my Ph.D. Dissertation.

"That was an interesting seminar, Jay. But what makes you think that you will find something in 'wrong' answers when Kaiser, my Ph.D. mentor and top-notch people like Thorndike and Spearman did not?"

"Because I think that we need to use non-linear techniques to extract the information I found during my teaching."

"You'll have to do more than work from hunches to convince me. Let's see what you turn up in the literature before I agree to supervise your Dissertation. Why not choose something easier, more routine and less controversial for your topic?"

"I came here because of the Faculty's reputation, and you are its star. I came to study what's going on in 'wrong' answers. I'd like to give it a rigorous try before I change direction."

"Show me something worth my time and I'll change my mind."

There was nothing like a challenge to get me going. However, six months of intensive literature search led almost nowhere. Many tests in the mid 1960s were still applying the "correction for guessing" to their scores. A few were trying, with little success, to give partial credit for partial knowledge, adapting a common practice for written answers to multiple-choice tests. They were not having much success.

The deep underlying question seemed to be, "Are wrong answers blind guesses or systematic choices?" This thought gave me an idea. Could I gather the reasoning for answer choices as I had informally ever since the history test I gave in 1958? If so, could I predict somebody's answers from another person's reasoning?

I looked through my special-program files. I had come across a short test that might measure reading comprehension. It was called the *Proverbs Test*;[68] that was published by the same company as the *Full-Range Picture Vocabulary Test.*

The thing I liked about it was that it had two sets of "right" answers. One was for the common abstract translations of proverbs ascribed from our Anglo-Saxon culture. The second was a subset of the "wrong" answers that were treated as "concrete" answers. These answers were developed because schizophrenics tend to think concretely. The test was intended to be used as a quick initial clinical screening for this disorder.

However, I had developed a deep admiration for Jean Piaget's clinical observations and he discussed in detail how children move from concrete thinking to abstract thinking with a series of personal insights as they enter and emerge from puberty.[69] This test might give some clues about this transition, if the meaningfulness of "wrong" answers could be determined.

I did not have easy access to children, but I did have two classes of adults in a night-school course. There, 41 students in these classes (23 in one and 18 in the other), I approached them with the idea that I was interested in studying why people selected the answers they chose on multiple-choice tests. They agreed to help me with this study. I used an entire class period to have them answer the *Proverbs Test* and to take time to write an explanation of their reasoning for each answer.

Because they were mature adults, they did not have many "wrong" answers in common. I had to find a way around this problem. It struck me that there might be error types that could identify groups of "wrong" answers. I use one class to set up my classification system. For technical reasons,[70] I used only their "wrong" answers in a factor analysis. This produced four factors, one containing four answers, each from a different item, and three factors with three answers each.

I then found that the reported reasoning was quite similar within each factor and quite different between factors. This gave me 13 answers from 12 different items that seemed to be selected with some degree of consistency.

Now, I was ready for the acid test. Would the reasoning reports, for any of these answers given by members of the other class, predict the answers they chose? Just as the answers predicted the reasoning, so the reasoning should predict the answers.

I was testing the null hypothesis that wrong answers were blind guesses. The results were:

There was a direct, not a chance relationship, between the reported reasoning and the answer selected.

The answers that hung together statistically, but also hung together psychologically. The logic behind the selected answers in the reported reasoning was identical for every answer within a factor.

For answers to be blind guesses there should be little similarity in the reasoning reported within a factor and no similarity from one group to the other. In fact, the reported reasoning to establish selection in one group predicted the answers selected by the second group almost two thirds of the time. Chance would have predicted somewhere around one ninth of the answers between the two groups (1/3 by 1/3 because of there being three possible wrong answers and two groups). Choosing a particular answer required a similar interpretation of the question without regard to the person or group represented six times more frequently than chance.

Arranging these students by their total scores did not affect the conclusions drawn.

Apparently, the selection of answers on this multiple-choice test is *not* entirely a random event. Also, the answers given can be used to suggest the reasoning behind the answers chosen. This is the information I was using to sustain my successful teaching in multiple settings. It is information that is lost when a test is scored "right – wrong" because the scoring ignores *which* "wrong" answer was chosen.

I submitted this study to the journal of *Educational and Psychological Measurement*[71] and had it accepted for publication. I gave a copy of my paper along with the acceptance letter to Steve and he agreed to supervise my dissertation.

Apparently, getting published satisfied him that I might be onto something after all.

Breakthrough or disaster?

How do linear statistical procedures fare with non-linear data?

I still did not have easy access to groups of children to study the transition from concrete to abstract thinking. I did, however, have access to the large classes in Introductory Educational Psychology that I was teaching at the University of Alberta. I taught one section of this class of in excess of 500 students in each of the fall and spring semesters (Alberta does not admit to winters.)

For this reason I decided to try my hand at developing a test that would study the properties of the hierarchy of reasoning suggested by Benjamin Bloom.[72] His higher levels, (analysis, synthesis and evaluation) are rather challenging to write in multiple-choice format. I chose a number of short reading selections and wrote a test that asked the lower level question on each selection and provided questions that asked the readers to contrast (analysis) and compare (synthesis) the content among the selections. A final few items also combined several of the reading selections into evaluative probes.

I then did some extensive reading into logical fallacies and designed the alternative answers to reflect these fallacies. My classifications for these wrong answers was to be the fallacies employed in writing them and my classification for the right answers was to be Bloom's *Taxonomy*.

I gave this test to a fall class; factor-analyzed the right answers to determine whether they came out correctly in accordance with their Bloom's classification. They did quite well. The factor pattern for the logical fallacies' classification was less strong. I had to reword or rethink a number of the alternative answers.

With these changes, I needed to reevaluate my instrument, so I repeated the process during the following spring term. I was now entering the fourth year of my Ph. D. program. I had to complete my Dissertation within six years. I couldn't afford to wait until the fall to administer the test for my final data gathering. However, I had a very large group of adults to teach in an advanced educational psychology class that summer. I decided to use this group instead.

These were not a homogenous group of 18 – 19 year-olds. They were a very diverse group. The Bloom's classification held up fairly well but the fallacies' classification fell apart. I had about 140 people in each of two groups. The Group A was to validate the test, and Group B was to cross-validate it. I used half a dozen statistical procedures from the general linear model, such as factor analysis. Every approach I used to try to cross-validate these answers produced disappointingly low results.

Then I tried a simple non-linear tack. I arranged my wrong answer categories in a hierarchical order based upon how far they had moved out of the classification assigned to them. I shuffled the order until the sum of these migration distances was minimized. Although the validation values were still not strong, this reorganization proved to be the most stable cross-validation between groups.

That was all that I was able to salvage from the wrong-answer part of my study, a strong hint that these answers were non-linear.

Where the right answers were concerned, my results were much better.[73] I was able to show that Bloom's "Taxonomy" is not a true taxonomy where each category in the order subsumes all the lower levels. It is instead a hierarchy of complexity of solution strategies. In this, his order is almost correct. Analysis and synthesis

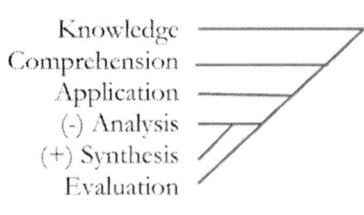

The Component Relationship Pattern in Bloom's Taxonomy

Knowledge
Comprehension
Application
(-) Analysis
(+) Synthesis
Evaluation

are opposite to each other. In my test at least they form a compare – contrast twin of strategies, one which combines by similarities, the other that separates by differences.

Notice that the order conforms to the one proposed by Bloom as they came from the analysis. However only Evaluation encompasses all the other processes and Analysis and Synthesis form the same branch with opposite directions for their factor loadings.

The tree gives both an order vertically and a relationship pattern horizontally.

Do we now have enough understanding to begin investigating how wrong answer s might indicate current learning?

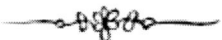

Studying children at last!

Does this approach identify the intellectual development of children?

I finally arrived in a permanent professorial appointment in the Faculty of Education at the University of Windsor, beginning in 1973. I approached a school system to study the transition from concrete to abstract thinking using the *Proverbs Test*. I began with all the children from the third through the eighth grades in three suburban schools of a uniform middle-class background.

I had 550 children in my group. I developed a team of graduate students to work with me and we took about half an hour in the afternoon in the fall in each school. The balance of the afternoon was spent taking a sample of the children from each classroom to represent the whole class. They interviewed these children about why they chose particular wrong answers. These interviews were tape-recorded, their reports transcribed and put aside for later use. I also collected the ages of the students I tested.

I used cluster analysis to identify subgroups among the wrong answers in their responses. For all clusters with four or more members I then developed sub-scores. I noticed that all the members of each cluster of answers had an interesting characteristic. Many of them were the same age. One of the subtests contained all the answers that had two age groups represented.

Dr. Jay C. Powell

I wanted to identify the order, if any, of their subset answer selections based upon their ages. I scored every child in the study on all twelve wrong answer subsets. Finally, I included in this list of scores their concrete and abstract right answer scores and ran the cluster analysis again.

A remarkably clean pattern emerged. My computing assistant was as astonished as I was. The order exactly followed the age levels assigned to the clusters! Concrete right answers were embedded with four others among the 8 year-olds. The nine year-old clusters were side by side. The rest climbed the age order exactly, with the bimodal one filled the hole between ages 11 and 13. At the high was the abstract right answer score. If I ever had any doubts there being meaningful information among the "wrong" answers, these were blown away.

The next step was to take the reasoning reports and try to classify the wrong-answer sub-scales by the reasoning that led to their choices. This approach had worked for the adults. Would it work for children? If it did not, all the other findings would be useless.

Several readers went through the transcriptions. First, I tried to pick up the most common explanation for each subset, and then I counted the frequency of this explanation for the answers in that cluster. If the students could not give an explanation, we counted it as a mismatch.

Can you guess the results? Their reasoning reports explained between 51% and 62% of the answer selections in each subset. By chance alone, this should have occured in one event in 81 or less. A strategy of *simplification* (leaving out some part of the proverb) occured at four differnt levels in the sequence. The conceptual omission was more subtle at each level. These children were thinking, not guessing!

Agreements among selection strategies were the lowest among the youngest children. These children also had the highest proportion of inability to explain their answers. The highest proportion was over 60% but not quite as high as for adults. Just like adults, children *do not* simply know or guess. They try to reason their way to an answer if they don't recognize it from experience. As expected, they are behaving exactly the way adults behave with varying levels of sophistication. The frontiers of their understandings are revealed by the wrong answers they select. This crucial information about learning *gets lost* when such tests are scored "right-wrong."

As a professional scorer of tests for a contract company, I observed that written-out answers supplied by students in both writing and mathematics showed similar orders of sophistication in these responses. When these answers are scored for partial credit, the specific nature of the errors made is also lost. The range of maturity of the solution strategies selected appears to be our best measure of their current thinking abilities.

However, teaching for the elimination of errors is quite different from teaching for right answers recognition or recitation. Error elimination requires a "Doing with ..." approach while recitation requires a "Doing to ..." approach. In the "Doing to ..." approach, we cannot distinguish between answers that were produced from memorization without understanding and those that came from some level of understanding including a very profound awareness that can often lead to different answers, which get classified as "wrong" when they are not!

There was one other observation that occurred in these results. The 8 year-olds responded egocentrically (in Piaget's terms). The 9 and 10 year-olds interpreted the proverbs literally. Literal interpretations would be considered *concrete* by Piaget. After that the sequence showed increasing skill at figurative interpretation. This is precisely the sequence Piaget's clinical observation revealed. The arguments that seem to have discredited Piaget over the years were based upon technical details that now seemed to me to be spurious nit-picking.

Among the adults in the first study, I found some reasoning that added more information to the question than was intended by the test designer, leading to a "wrong" answer that went beyond the intention of the question, making it a correct answer. I also observed this same problem with the profoundly informed when scoring supplied answers.

Does this mean that our most profound thinkers can do less well on tests of any type, when the expectations are narrowly defined, than the efficient memorizers? This observation addresses the issue of the quality of education more deeply than right-wrong scoring can resolve. To teach toward profound understanding requires the "Doing with ..." exploratory approach in which truth is situationally specific.

At the frontiers of human knowledge, the concept of a fixed and exact "right" answer disappears. This statement is the meaning behind the "Uncertainty Principle." When we teach how to think and how to learn, we are addressing the frontiers of our students' understandings. There appear to be no "right" answers here either.

Is teaching students how to identify and reduce their errors a profoundly different way of teaching from getting them to recite what we expect to hear?

The dilemma

Do the answering changes fit the pattern?

These findings had raised more questions than they had answered. I now knew that my approach to teaching from the reasoning of my students was a solid way to go. I had done all of this with individual students. The age match suggested a strong developmental sequence was present.

As so often happens when a breakthrough discovery is made, this study raised more questions than it answered. Here are the questions it raised:

Do the times of change from one wrong answer to another fit *between* the ages when these answers were chosen on a single administration or are chosen twice to reflect stable interpretations?

If these changes occur between these selections then the sequence observed is a genuine developmental pathway, indicating that this important development information is discarded when the "wrong" answers are reduced to zero (0) in the scoring process.

To investigate this possibility, the same test would need to be given to a group of students *twice*. The age range must be sufficiently broad that maturity levels can be identified. Furthermore, systematic shifts from one answer to another produces a discontinuous sequence among choices, not a linear one. Does the bell-shaped curve actually describe what is happening during learning? The very mathematical nature of this curve means that it cannot reveal such underlying complexity.

Is there only one pathway? Would a greater diversity of students taking the test expose a multiplicity of patters of development?

If there is more than one pathway then putting all the scores onto a single straight line does not capture this diversity. Discontinuities in response selection and multiplicity of pathways, if these are found together will invalidate the use of total-correct scores for diagnostic purposes. The study just reported was done on a relatively homogenous population with the test given only once. It was a snap-shot, not a movie. The changes can be observed only by moving from frame to frame.

How could we manage to go to the expense of norming tests using interviews?

We need to decide whether our purpose for testing is to get systematic observations to inform teaching or to ignore what current scoring doesn't measure and continue to rely upon whatever this current approach does measure to evaluate our schools' effectiveness.

How would we report the alternative reasoning or other aspects of error types to teachers in a way that was useful to them?

The metaphorical meaning behind the slogan "No Child Left Behind" seems to be the desire to give equal opportunity of education to all children without regard to creed, gender, race or socio-economic status. If these aspects of children create a diversity that gets lost using current scoring practices, the present method *cannot* achieve this admirable intended goal.

Are recall and understanding equivalent?

If not, should we be teaching for recall in the absence of understanding? Does such teaching contribute to leaving children behind? Does the need to be "right" discourage thoughtful diversity and create pressure towards memorization? If this latter proves true, scoring tests *right-wrong* might be destructive toward effective education instead of being helpful.

Thus far, my investigations had been following the conventional path using current practices. Dr. Keeping's remark about the misuse of the normal curve, and all of the linear models derived from it, was still ringing in my ears. Behind that was the ancient echo, "Father forgive them, they know not what they do." (KJV Lu. 23.24.)

Please understand, these observations show that students give the best answers they can based upon what they know. Multiple-choice test scoring is based upon the "Plugged-in" theory of learning. We cannot know whether this theory is true from the right answers alone. And the alternative answers, where the truth of this assumption lies, are removed in the scoring process before we begin interpreting the test results. Educational theorists and practitioners are doing the best they can from what they know as well. This issue is at the frontier of human knowledge

Hence, in order to establish the transition points between the ages of specific choices, I would have to give the *Proverbs Test* at least twice. In order to accommodate diversity, I would need to get a larger sample. In order to deal with the reasoning when expecting such diversity, I would need to find a way to identify the reasoning patterns, while avoided costly and time-consuming interviews.

To most people, these might seem insurmountable problems. To the mind of a researcher-scholar they are part of the excitement and challenge of investigating at the frontier of knowledge. The story has only just begun.

Where do we go from here?

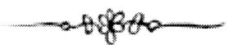

A leap into the possible
Is there more than one way to interpret reality?

Dr. R. A. Carlton[74] published an insightful article in the *Alberta Journal of Educational Research* in 1974. He had been reading a number of books on educational criticism. They all seemed to say that there are two ways to educate, "my way" and the wrong way. When he looked more closely there seemed to be more than one "my way." Upon detailed consideration he decided that these "my ways" actually represented seven different approaches to teaching. His article detailed the differing characteristics of each approach.

His article started the gears turning in my head. Then I reread a second article by H. Spears. This was in the *Phi Delta Kappa*[75] magazine regarding the goals for education. The members of this organization had ranked 18 goals of education in order of importance as they saw them. The ranking was then reported collectively as if there were one best way to state the outcomes of education.

I awoke at about three in the morning a couple of days later. That same little voice in my head that had suggested I would lose information by putting an "X" in my item analysis sheet was saying, "If there were more than one image of effective education, there should be more than one way of ranking of goals." My question now was, "Could I devise a survey instrument that would identify a person's image of schooling by having them rank their views of goals of education?"

I reread the Carlton paper, making careful notes of the ways each image differed. My notes condensed to three dimensions:

Dimension	Poles of the Dimension	
1. Approach to Motivation	Intrinsic	Extrinsic
2. Approach to Information	Knowing	Doing
3. Approach to Authority	Group	Individual

Each of these dimensions was bipolar as I showed above. This gave me 8 images. The missing one was the Intrinsic – Using – Individual combination that I am now calling "Humanistic."

I used Spears' 18 goals and added six more so that all 8 images could be represented in all three dimensions and began the technical process of trying it out. I called the resulting survey *Schools I Would Like to See*.[76] I enlisted a couple of my graduate students to help with the validation process.

The three dimensions emerged from a cluster analysis, the 8 images were validated, and the spanning tree gave two more dimensions. One was a People – Things dichotomy and the other was a four-level ordered sequence that resembles a Maslovian[77] scale. Scale 6 is a composite of scales 1, 2 & 3 that indicates the image being held.

Trials of it suggested that it is actually a probe into the ways people are viewing reality. It was, therefore, worth a trial as a substitute for interviewing that could be collected from all participants in a study. I approached the school officials in a small Midwestern industrial city with a local university and obtained permission to conduct a study from a representative sample of 20% of all of the students in that city. I used two high schools and 8 elementary schools in my sample.

Permission was granted and I collected, in less than one hour of testing for each student, in October and in the following March, a repeated-measures sample from more than 3,000 students. The *Schools* survey proved to be too difficult for the third and fourth graders. *Proverbs* responses were collected from these younger ones. Both instruments were collected from the balance.

Does this design address the several problems we recognized from giving the test only once?

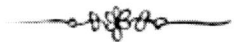

The end of an era

Alternative answers

How should I analyze these data?

The usual way to connect one test with another is either to correlate the total scores or to compare two administrations of the same test is to use analysis of variance to identify the degree of change. I could make this comparison with the entire test or compare age groups separately.

None of these procedures would tell me whether the changes from *one answer to another* occurred at ages between the points where students chose the same answers repeatedly, whether right or wrong. This was a longitudinal study that required point-by-point references. I scoured the literature to find such an algorithm without success. I then appealed to a mathematical statistician, Dr. Norm Shklov for help.

We tried several adaptations of the Chi Square (χ^2) statistic. No luck. We tried Darrel Bock's *Multiqual*.[78] That showed us that I needed curves of an order of x^3 or higher to describe these data. These data were non-linear and this meant that correlations and analysis of variance and such similar procedures did not apply.

We tried geometric and harmonic distributions. We tried log-linear procedures. Nothing worked. At the frontier of knowledge, trial and error eliminated possibilities, but takes time. It took us ten years. Then he suggested that we try the multinomial distribution[79].

Cross-tabulating each test on an answer-by-answer basis was easy. All we needed to do was to ask the computer to tell us how many times an answer pairing occurred. How many students chose the same answer both times and, if they changed answers, from which answer did they start and to which answer did they go?

This divided their answers into two groups, the unchanging group and the answer changing group. Hence we could look at the dynamics of learning.

The next issue was how to follow this process along the ages of the students. By dividing the students into five-month age intervals (because there was five months between the two administrations) we had a stack of 4-answer-by-4-answer answer-change tables, 27 age levels deep. Now we had a whole bunch of numbers, but what did they mean? How big did the numbers need to be to be meaningful?

To answer this question, we used the multinomial procedure to estimate the strength of every number in every cell. We plotted all the cells where the proportion of explained variance was less than 0.054 and greater than 0.945. This is a standard statistical way of determining meaningfulness. It means that there is one chance in 20 or less of the highest or lowest events being accidental. We have not determined the probability distributions for the proportions we were calculating. It seemed reasonable to consider only extremely high and extremely low proportions.

At this point the information we were seeking fell out into our laps. Indeed, the middle of the transitions between answers

Making Peasants into Kings

occurred *between* their repeated choices in more than 75% of the case for all 40 items on the test at all 27 levels! There was now no question about it. Intellectual development, as revealed by the "wrong" answers, is characterized by an observable sequence of *discrete response changes*. A dividend was that we also found more than one developmental pathway.

This means that the pathway described by Piaget is not the only one. We also found some older students moving systematically away from the right answer in some of the items. It looks like we have found a doorway into the dynamics of the learning process.[80]

If there is more than one reason for choosing a particular answer, then what is the reasoning that was used by the student that chose that answer?

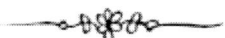

The extraordinary challenge
Why do students give "right" answers?

In our research program, it seemed that we should be able to determine the reasoning behind "right" answers more easily than the reasoning behind "wrong" ones. Harley Miki[81] and I conducted a simple experiment to this end.

Our thought was that there are two probable common sources for *right* answers. One is through simple *recall* without understanding. The other is through *understanding*. I raised this issue because my calculus teacher made the claim that if you understood, you didn't need to remember.

Harley was a mathematics teacher in a local middle school. We planned a study that fits the pattern of all our earlier studies. He was to pre-test and post-test a unit in math. Then we interviewed a group of volunteer students. We scored the tests of these students in the conventional way. We scored the interviews derived from the questions "understood the concept" and "did not understand the concept."

We then cross-tabulated the results for both scoring procedures into 2 by 2 (yes – no) discrepancy tables, using each score on the pre- and post-test independently. It is a simple statistical test using the *Phi* (ϕ) statistic to determine how closely the four pairs are related.

What were the results? For both tests, understanding the concept and giving right answers were statistically *unrelated* to each other! Both scores increased significantly from pre- to post-testing. The understanding score increased significantly more than the right answers score. However they remained unrelated. [82] This observation is an easy one to check out[83]. It is well within the scope of a classroom teacher in their first statistics course.

Is this yet another way in which our current test scoring practices provide questionable results?

The Souvenir Shop

Is there more than one way to find a "right" answer?

Mr. Rodriguez decided to use the grouping of students to show that there was more than one way to solve many mathematical problems. Here is the problem he gave them:

> Mary and Gladys have decided to open a small souvenir shop for their class to raise some money for the Junior Class Prom at Washington Heights High School. They can get class rings for $80 and pins for $30. They know that in the past three years, three times as many rings as pins were sold. If they have $3500 to buy these souvenirs, how many pins should they buy?

Statements: $80r + 30p \leq 3500$ (1)

$r = 3p$ (2)

He divided the class into four groups. Each group chose a leader and the leaders met to decide how to go about solving the problem. Francine's group was to use successive approximation (guess and check). Gregory's group was to use simple substitution to solve the problem. Abdul's group was to use the simultaneous solution of the two equations, and Amit's group agreed to solve the problem using graphs. The groups met and discussed their solutions.

I present the discussion of the solutions to this problem within each group in narrative form in the Appendix. I designed it for those with some interest in teaching high school algebra or those with some degree of mathematical sophistication.

Readers may want to follow up on it once you know what this presentation contains.

My design intention for this problem is to present the fact that there is more than one way to solve it. The "guess and check" approach is the least mature way to get the right answer. The "substitution" approach is intermediate in maturity and the "simultaneous equations" approach is the most mature. Giving full credit for a right answer hides the maturity of the solution. This major failing for right-wrong scoring explains my reason for including this discussion in this book.

Unless the teachers are encouraging the use of spreadsheets in the class, they seldom use the graphic approach. In this example, the computer gives a *wrong* answer. It is an error in the application of the program because the problem's answer has a "less than" constraint. The point I intend is that we cannot rely upon computers to give right answer all the time. I also have a student make this same mistake and that group missed the error.

For teacher interest, I illustrate different interaction styles within group activities.

In the recapitulation, I have the students challenge the reasonableness of the question and point out the error of treating an average from the past as an unqualified prediction of the future.

In all, I show that teaching how to think requires more than acquiring skills with procedures. Challenging authority is an essential part of learning how to think independently.

It is typical in rubric scoring to give full marks for "right" answers without regard for how the answer was achieved. This practice also loses vital information. Details about solution style are lost. Also, if the solution procedures display differing performance maturities, this information is also lost. An immature procedure tells us that this student has been left behind. An unusually advanced procedure tells us that the student has gone beyond the current teaching level.

Furthermore, too often in most classrooms, the logic of the questions is not challenged. Fake realism creates the impression that schooling has nothing to do with real life. Students who acquiesce to such inanities lose the opportunity to look beyond the surface of things. Students who raise such important issues are only accepted in the "doing with" context. Otherwise they are put down, to lose self-confidence or to become resentful and either rebel or become bored.

Like the "Doing with …" example in a Language Arts class with Ms. Wilson, this lesson illustrates the exploratory approach to teaching in a mathematics class. I have successfully applied this same approach in history, physics, typing, shorthand, bookkeeping, psychology and more recently, in four Environmental Science areas. The content does not need to dictate the approach.

Why not teach students how to think and how to learn?

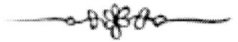

A new scoring technology

Can we interpret scores on one test from the results on another one?

I retired in 1989 and have had fewer resources for research since then. With two wives passing in the interim, I have had less time than I would have had as a college teacher. I have found Allan Clapp, a superb programmer who has, over the past 16 years, turned out a ton of code to carry the project forward.

With the multinomial procedure we can interconnect seemingly unrelated observations. For instance, *Proverbs* had 15 sub-sets across 4 alternatives in its 40 items (our research has now added three more scales). *Schools I Would Like to See* has an entry in any one of 3 score values for each of its 24 items. When these two instruments are given together and both are given an answer, these answer categories can be interconnected.

Using only the highest proportional explanations in the resulting tables, each *Proverbs* answer was assigned a score from all six scales from *Schools*. Our results are fascinating. For instance, scale 5 is a Maslow-like scale that forms a sequence from *self-protection* through *helping others to help each other* (Covey's 8th habit).[84]

Dr. Jay C. Powell

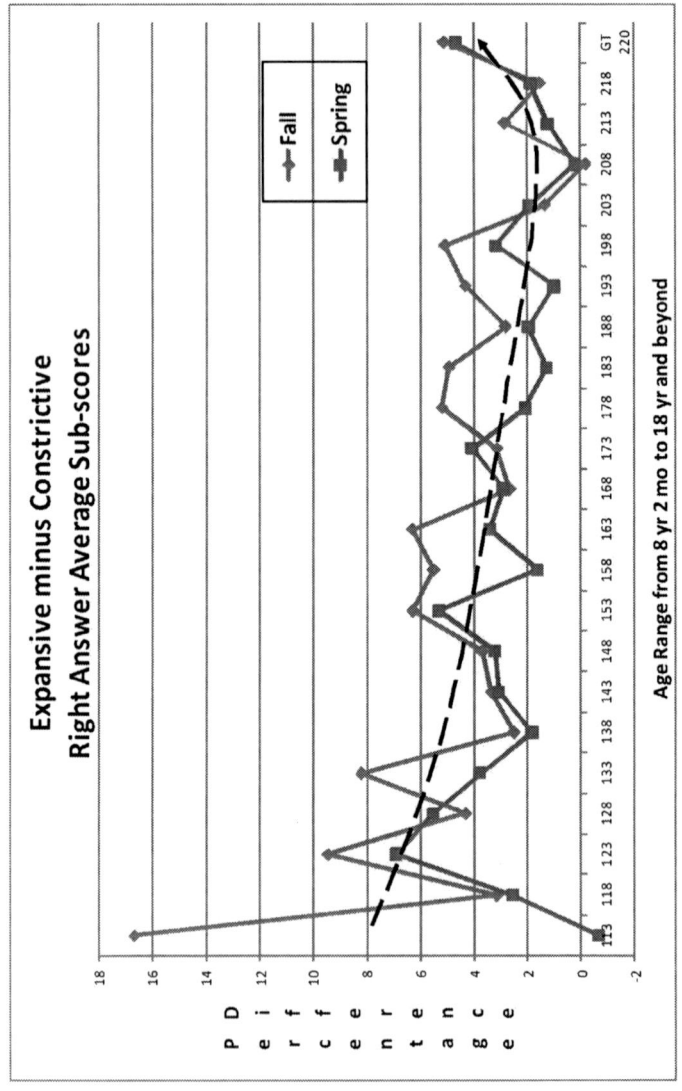

Making Peasants into Kings

We collapsed the bottom two categories (self-protection and self-indulgence), calling it "constrictive thinking." We collapsed the two higher categories (self-development and outreach) into "expansive thinking." We now had a new pair of possible values for each right answer on *Proverbs*. We hoped that this distinction might be similar to the "understand/did no understand" distinction that Harley Miki and I found in mathematics.

Using only the "right" answers we rescored *Proverbs*, giving every student a score for constrictive and expansive thinking based upon *Schools* calibration of the answers they chose. We can now ask, "What is the impact upon constrictive and expansive thinking of high-stakes testing in an established school system?" The *constrictive* subscale held 24 items and the *expansive* scale 16. To resolve this problem we used the selection proportions for our comparison.

Based upon the criticisms of education we have heard over the past 150 years, would you care to predict what we found? If you said that you would expect expansive thinking to decrease progressively from the third grade through the end of high school, you would be right. The arrowed black line shows this trend.

There are unexpected secondary impacts. Expansive thinking decreases dramatically with 9 year-olds. In most cases from October value (light grey line) is *above* the March value (dark grey line) with a general downward slope that only recovers somewhat after the school-leaving age of 16. Expansive thinking levels are higher in the fall than in the spring except for only five of the 23 age levels reported here. Apparently this decline in expansive thinking over the five months that school is in session implies that use high-stakes testing *causes the teaching of constrictive thinking* in order to get "right" answer on the high stakes tests?

It is interesting to note that, in many cases, this impact diminishes over the summer, but not completely so. This is the first time, to my knowledge, that there is clear empirical evidence that current schooling practices may be harming our children.

Is it not sad that this event occurs at all? However, is it not exciting that our procedure can probe this deeply into the impact of our schools?

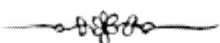

A light at the end of the tunnel

Who are the students least impacted by this mind-numbing impact of our schools?

The graph above includes all students. It seemed reasonable to probe deeper. Are there any students who are not influenced by this impact of the schools? I remember well the impact of my insight about the propagation of sound that ended this sort of impact upon me.

Hopefully our best students would show a smaller effect. To look at this issue, we selected the top 20% of these students based upon their total-correct scores in the fall. We combined the groups by age into elementary, middle and high school levels in order to obtain a large enough sample to avoid high proportions with small numbers. We then separated them into three groups:

1. Those students who were in the top group because they were very high in *constrictive* thinking,
2. Those students who were in the top group because they were very high in *expansive* thinking, and
3. Those students who were in the top group because they were very high in *both* constrictive and expansive thinking.

We then looked at the changes in their sub-test scores from fall to spring.

Making Peasants into Kings

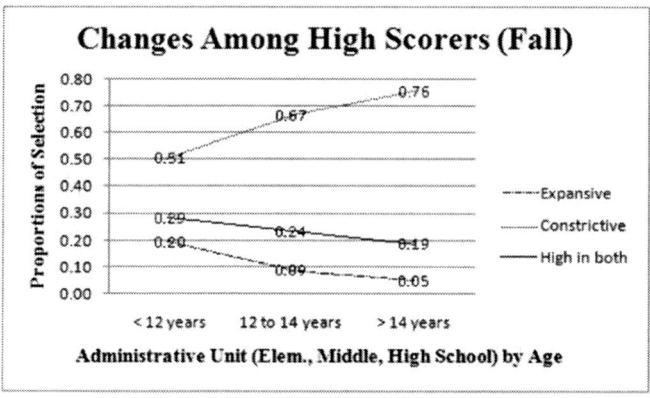

This chart looks at the top 20% of scores in the fall administration. Half these high scorers were Constrictive thinkers in the elementary school. This increased to become three quarters of our best high school students. This is the group that is either self-protective or self-indulgent.

One in five of our best students were Expansive thinkers in the elementary school, but only one in twenty remained this open minded in high school. This is the group who worldview focus is either personal development or service to others.

The best students who were high in both dimensions lost a third of their membership but were still one in five of our best students in high school. Except for the dramatic collapse in Expansive thinking among the 9 year-olds in the previous diagram, representing the fourth-grade slump, the average decline of these Expansive-thinking students was only about twice the 6% for all the students in these age groups.

These are the students, by being high in both scores, who have learned how to balance Constrictive and Expansive thinking. They declined about only about twice as much as the overall average. This skill they must have developed outside of school, as with my insight about sound. Are these the students, who by balancing the two perspectives, who become the "Elaborative" thinkers, and can respond to both the "big picture" and the "need for details?" Are they the ones who survive schooling with most of their creativity intact? Do these students the one-in-twenty, who provide all the major creative contributions to our society? Are the skills they have achieved independently of the overall impact of schooling teachable to many of the other students as well?

This school system had by far the most intellectually damaging effect upon its best students. This high level of cognitive destruction of the most visibly talented is a disgrace. Here, at last, is evidence from our research that the creativity-destruction claims our most severe critics have been making could actually be true.

Are there students who do not make the top 20% who have these same skills? Could these be students, like Chris Tramp, who is content to "get by" in school, because they have other aspirations and interests? Are they potential scholars like myself, who have gained a profound education in spite of and not because of, the schools through dogged persistence? Are they in the ranks of the dropouts who leave out of boredom but who later succeed in life?

We are now studying a fourth group who are 16 and older who changed their Constrictive right answers in October to particular wrong answers in March. This group may be breaking through the ceiling of the test. If so, they may be the most profoundly open-minded students in the group. The result of this answer change is a decline in their total correct scores.

Has the depth of penetration that our new procedure has achieved exposed a fundamental weakness in our schooling? If so, what is this weakness?

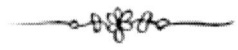

A paradigm shift

How good is our alternative?

One of the ways that we try to assure ourselves of the quality of our tests is referred to as test-retest reliability. The idea is that if we give the same test twice, a good test should give us a consistent message.

In our study, we used a tighter definition by asking the question, "Looking only at the high proportion cells (where $p ≥ 0.95$),[85] what proportion of all answers were a repetition of the "right" answer? We assume that, if the students knew the answer, they should get it right both times.

We could have added the portion of those students who moved from any wrong answer to the right one. In this case we would be assuming that they had learned the answer between the two tests. However, test-retest reliability requires that the answers are the same on both administrations.

We could also have subtracted a portion of those who moved from the "right" to a "wrong" answer. In this case we might assume that they didn't actually know the answer when they chose it correctly the first time or they wouldn't have chosen wrongly the second time.

These latter two arguments both come from the "plug-in" theory of learning that assumes no reasoning about the selection of "wrong" answers occurs. On the other hand, we have good evidence that as students become well informed they often read more into a question than was intended. In this case they may choose a "wrong" answer for a *better reason* than they needed to choose the right one.

In addition, we have no way of knowing how many students gave a right answer from rote memorization, superficial understanding, clear understanding or profound knowledge.[86]

Using *Schools* to classify the right answers as constrictive or expansive provides a partial solution. Increases in constrictive thinking indicate deterioration in cognitive performance unless their expansive thinking also increases. A decline in constrictive thinking by shifting to particular wrong answers can also indicate cognitive gain, even when total scores decline.

Perhaps the only students who knew the right answer at the expected level (not profound understanding) were those who chose it both times, which occurred for only 30% of the entire *Proverbs* test.

Using the same underlying idea, we can suggest that for *all the combinations* of answers, those answer pairs where the selection was high ($p \geq 0.95$) that these answers reflect thoughtful selection. When we do this within the items for *Proverbs* we discover that more than three quarters (76%) of them are "thoughtfully" chosen. This means that if we can identify the thinking used, we can now account for *more than three out of four* student responses.

Is this amount of increase in explanation large enough to be considered a breakthrough in scientific discovery? This increase comes entirely from within item interactions. It does not consider connections between items that we have already shown, which we used to identify the reasoning within "wrong" answer sub-scores. Nor does it take into account connections between different tests, that we have shown can lead to new categories of "right" answers.

All this success comes from *within-item* analysis. We have not yet established a satisfactory way to identify the interconnections *between items* in a manner similar to the cluster analysis approaches used with linear statistical models.

Now we can present the absolutely critical question. ***"Is there something fundamentally wrong with the way we are scoring tests?"***

Dr. Keeping pointed out that if the frequencies in an observation do not come from a true dichotomy, the analysis of these data using the normal distribution is mathematically inappropriate. Our work has shown that answers chosen for multiple-choice tests are not a true dichotomy. In the first place, such answers come from reasoning more than guessing blindly, making many of them psychologically and educationally meaningful.

In the second place, answers change as students learn. This fact produces discontinuities in both the right and wrong answer sequences, showing the learning process to be non-linear.

Third, the discovery of a second, reverse-order developmental pathway that can be concealed by increases in the selection of constrictive answers invalidates the "single pathway" assumption required for the use of linear statistical models.

Finally, thought-process meanings of the reasoning behind alternative-answers selection are educationally useful when the exploration of ideas and mind-opening processes are the educational objectives.

We have also shown that the emphasis upon being "right" on tests and in classroom interactions "Doing to ..." is destructive to the intellectual development of our students.

What should we be doing instead?

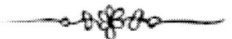

Dr. Jay C. Powell

A possible solution

How do we put the experience and research presented here into a solution for this problem?

To begin with, we need a different model to describe test-taking behavior. The current one is a coin-toss model in which one of the two sides (say heads) is acceptable while the other side not.

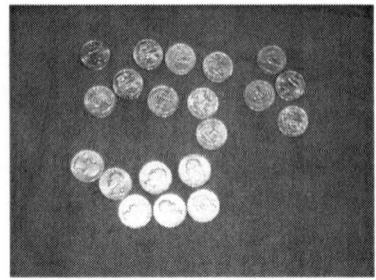

Currently, we count the number of "Heads" and the rest disappears in cyberspace. Once counted, we still know how many "Heads" we have but no longer *which* coins made up the sum. In the pictorial example we have seven "right" answers (using "heads" for the right ones) and 13 "wrong" answers, which, using electronic scoring, are removed from these data when we score this test. We know that there are seven "right" answers but not *which* of the 20 answers were "right."

The option we are proposing is a dice roll. Here we have six "right" answers. However, we know which of the six facets faced upward for each item and which item produced this particular display. We get the seventh "right" answer from the W_3+ breaking through the ceiling of the test.

A quick glance at these two illustrations make it abundantly evident which of these two models provides more information about this one student's response to this test. Is it any wonder that this alternative model, using the same items provided more than two and a half times the information about student performance?[87]

Also, we have observed that the nature of students' answers reveal their thought processes. We need to know what their thought processes are to be effective teachers. Using this information produces substantial improvements in learning effectiveness that is sustainable over time and transferable to many settings.

In the classroom, the "doing with" approach to teacher-student interaction gives access to students' thinking better than any other approach. It is a clearly definable approach for the teaching of thinking skills. We have also shown that when this approach is coupled with teaching students how to learn, the combination is powerfully effective.

How do we get the information we need to make this change from our tests? There are three ways our research has shown to collect these reasoning processes; 1) using interviews, 2) using external tests that can provide markers for the skills underlying their answer and 3) using psycholinguistic analysis of the stimulus-distracter relationships.

We have known for more than 40 years that the best test items, whether open response or multiple-choice, show a strong sequential pattern underlying the answer alternatives. Item Response Theory (IRT) was a major breakthrough in test construction. Unfortunately, the need to identify the reasons for this strong underlying force has not become a systematic quest because the way we are scoring tests wipes out our ability to find out what is happening in our students' minds.

In effect, we are replacing a psychological interpretation that is behavior-specific with a numerical interpretation that is less specific, simply to have these values capable of numerical and statistical manipulation. Information is lost. This insight was given to me when I made my spreadsheet to evaluate my history test.

More recently, we have begun establishing new norms for Proverbs using the fall administration. The linkages among the figurative transition have not held up completely. The three stages described by Piaget have remained almost entirely intact. This is the same outcome as the one I that occurred in my dissertation. These shifts may be caused by a diversity of pathways within a non-homogeneous group. We are currently conducting research designed to identify these pathways so that the performance levels within each pathway can be determined.

Changing the characteristics of the sample from a close-knit middleclass community to a representative sample of the entire city seems to have added to the diversity present. The same increase in diversity occurred with my Dissertation. Does this observation increase the importance of searching for multiple pathways and further indicate the non-linearity among these data?

We need to do three things. First, we need to identify the reasons why a behavior departs from expectation. These reasons could be the result of the observation style of the observer that leads to personal or scientific discoveries, as when I was playing in the water. The reprimand was based upon the Principal's perceived need for control of my actions.

The reasoning could come from contaminating prior knowledge, as with the Robins Nest. Eleanor Orr's[88] analysis of Black English clearly shows that the conceptual structure of that vernacular impedes the understanding of mathematics in school. Once again, we see the Uncertainty Principle in action, with the interpretation forcing the conclusion. War has been fought over less.

Second, we need to find out the learning characteristics of the various developmental pathways. Gardner[89] has provided seven forms of intelligence that each may represent a differing learning pathway. These pathways can be collected through clinical observation, such as Piaget conducted. They can be collected through an in-depth analysis of the answer transformation among repeated administrations of tests by applying our multinomial procedure.

They can be drawn from linking collateral tests of known observation properties as we did with associating *Proverbs* with *Schools*. The ultimate model may be much like a brook flowing among rocks, with forks, swirls and backflows that become identifiable impacts from the vicissitudes of life.

Third, we need to arrange these learning characteristics into the sequences that fit into the pathways we discover. We can then apply a scale, like age, that has the single dimensional property of all mathematically countable series. The illustration of the *Full Range Picture Vocabulary Test (FRPVT)* demonstrates how this norming might be done. We can place the errors in the appropriate positions in relation to the benchmarks established for the correct solutions, providing an enhanced basis for curriculum development.

Once we have age-based norms we can then apply linear statistical procedures to our heart's content on the identified ages and know exactly the progress that has been made by each student. The issue here is the need to translate our observation into a simple single scale of known characteristics to get meaningful results. Age is such a scale while the total-correct score scale is not appropriately homogeneous.

When I found a tight ordering of "wrong" answers by age, I remembered my experience with the *FRVPT*. Does it not seem reasonable that we could do this same age-based ordering with *any* answer that shows performance maturity? Could we not determine the median onset age of those who achieve each performance level? In this way we can observe gains based upon what students are actually doing when they answer instead of how many right answers they give. In this case, tests do not need to be made equivalent for different age levels to determine their progress.

The actual interpretation of change scores is illustrated on our Website,[90] and reported in my 2010 paper.[91]

We have the further advantage, in this approach. Once we now know *why* each student got the answer "wrong" We have a solid basis for planning interventions. This system gives two dimensions to our students' scores. First is the performance maturity in terms of expected age for what was observed. Second is a statement of the benchmarks achieved from both right and wrong answers. Does knowing *why* give us a good chance to help each student fix it? How might the entire educational research community proceed to find an answer to these questions?

By looking at four randomly selected students from our data set of about 3,000 we have found an instance where a student's:

1. Total score declined because of a drop in the number of constrictive answers selected but the changes among the alternative answers suggested a strong gain in cognitive performance. Lower level errors declined and higher level errors increased.
2. Total score increased but cognitive performance declined because of an increase in constrictive answers and a decline in expansive answers. Higher level errors declined and lower level errors increased.
3. Gain appeared to be about 20 months in five with little change in total correct score. This student was still about two years behind chronological age. Such large gains among children far behind are encouraging.
4. Immaturity on total scores showed normal gains even though this test appeared too difficult, considering only the total score. The wrong answers told a different picture with the child about a year in advance of age expectation.

Four single instances are insufficient to form any meaningful generalizations beyond the expectation that with 76% of the variability explained we should be able to get many precise interpretations. All four of these provide much more information than the total scores of these students and they all contradict the conclusions that would be drawn from the total scores alone. Those who would like to challenge this statement are welcome to perform these same analyses in the remaining students in the data set and tabulate the results for themselves.

This conclusion means that although right answers may be necessary for student assessment, these answers are not sufficient for this task. Researchers are encouraged to perform similar analyses with any equivalent data set to replicate these results.

Beyond this, we can associate tests from different subject areas. This approach might expose higher-order processes that could inform the nature of the thinking and learning dimensions of student performance at a transfer level. If such were to provide the nature of the balance between seeing the big picture and attending to details, the content-process controversy might be put to rest forever as we develop the science of teaching for elaborate thinking.

The history of science is replete with stories of new insights into old problems that have increased our ability to explain what is happening. We can look back into ancient times when people discovered that irrigation improved crop yield and enhanced and evened out food supplies. We can look back to the telescope that proved to Galileo that the earth was a ball that revolved on its axis and rotated around the sun. These insights have always made the world more understandable.

In scientific terms, they have explained more of the variability in a system, making for better understanding of the outcomes. Our research is no exception. This procedure successfully extracts the discrete and the continuous parts of a "random" distribution and *shows how these parts are related to each other.* [92]

The fundamental flaw in education, then, is the thinking that it leads to "You're right" or "you're wrong" assessment; however it is applied in schooling. Is it any wonder that more than 150 years of attempts at educational reform have been unsuccessful?

If this statement is true, what can we do about it?

The key to this approach

How does this approach work?

I started with hunches that led me to careful observations. For instance, in my special programs class in high school I confirmed my expectation that these were unsuccessful readers with a reading skills test. My idea was to provide them with many interesting stories that were easy to read. I needed to know that they had read these with understanding, hence the comprehension checks. For non-readers, five books in 13 weeks would be a dramatic change in their usual behavior. With my follow up testing, success could be achieved one book at a time.

Let's consider Brian's success. The three key factors in his success were:

1. I provided him with a challenge he thought he could achieve with small successive steps. I gave him a supportive environment where his successful progress would be acknowledged and recorded immediately.
2. I gave him enough practice in the skill he was acquiring that he could become aware of his own progress.
3. I let him participate in the self-challenging process by providing him with an opportunity to choose what he did next.

It is often the case that when the desire to learn comes from within, students make spectacular progress without regard to their previous achievement performance. His gains were the most spectacular. In October he was reading at the sixth month of the second grade (2.6). The following May, after reading 60 books in the year, he achieved, on the same broad-spectrum reading test, a performance of second-year college level. This represents a 13 grade-level gain in 8 months!

Brian's gains were the most spectacular. The average gain for the class was from the sixth month in the third grade (3.6) to the second month in the seventh grade (7.2). Two of the 16 students retest scores declined. It is important for us to realize that we cannot expect to reach everyone. These students in the ninth grade had averaged about one four tenths of a grade level gain (3.6 / 8) in their school careers. In their year with me they gained eight times as much, recovering about half of their deficiency in one year (going into the tenth grade reading at the seventh grade level).

Another aspect of systematic observation is that we may not reach the right conclusion on the first attempt at theory formulation. I had seen a movie about an airplane crash that involved metal fatigue. My theory suggested that the stress of the metal at the end of each swing sent out an energy pulse that produces the sound we hear. After further investigation, I discovered that my invented theory was also *wrong*. It was more accurate than the one Mr. Franklin gave because there was a pulse from each direction of swing (not just one for each cycle) but I needed to investigate further to discover my error. See how exploration works?

Thus, the four critical characteristics of learning how to think were to:
1. Follow a hunch because it may lead to an insight,
2. Pay close attention to what you are being told, because it could be wrong.
3. Look for inconsistencies or contradictions in the message, and
4. Investigate the situation thoroughly and carefully because our conclusions could be wrong.

This pattern worked for me and for many in my classrooms, and those of others from the days of Socrates. Is this a the new teaching paradigm?

What other factors might inhibit school success?

Dr. Lipton's research suggests that the protective mode shuts down the higher mental processes. It doesn't matter whether this shutdown comes from severe pain, substance abuse, loud noises, or emotional trauma – including giggling fits. By turning off our ability to think we can protect ourselves from excessive psychological demands being made upon us. Medication is not as successful in correcting this problem as is effective teaching, which enhances self-awareness and self-esteem because the success comes from inside the person and not from outside, like a pill.

We have just suggested that when people become self-protective, they shift from clear-headed thinking into a "fight or flight" mentality. Their emotions overwhelm their reason and they either rebel or withdraw. One common form of withdrawal is "going blank" as we saw with the student who doodled.

Psychologists are now calling this behavior "attention deficit disorder (ADD)" or "attention deficit hyperactive disorder (ADHD)." So what is ADD or ADHD anyway? Such labels often bewilder parents because their child's behavior in school is not what they observe at home.

Alternatively, the situation on the home front can provoke bizarre behavior, which can become quite perplexing to their teachers. Some students panic at being tested and under-perform. Recent research[93] has shown that this disorder comes from a disruption in the executive centers of our brains. Medication can help, but our brains can also be rewired through appropriately constructive experiences. This is what

Mrs. Fraser did with Bill's Individualized Educational Program (IEP) where Bill was doodling instead of drawing.

However, this 'going blank' behavior can also result from something teachers are doing, but of which they are unaware, including being boring. The 'painting with black' incident illustrates how teachers can unintentionally cause what appears to be bizarre behavior in students.

Classroom disturbances can be handled with "time-out" opportunities as in the "hiding behind coats" incident. They can also be handled by redirecting behavior, as I should have done when I caused Roger to challenge me or by anticipating outcomes proactively as in the "flight contest" event and I did successfully in the paper airplane situation.

Teaching deep relaxation techniques, helping students avoid "sugar highs" and recognizing their deep personal worth and that of others is essential to learning cooperative skills. We cannot begin to approach this level of humaneness as long as we assume that we are the ones who "know" and our job is to give *our* knowledge to others. We would be much further ahead if we assumed that everyone has come here on a mission. Our job becomes one of helping others to find their mission; enhancing the needed skills to fulfill it.

I found that I learned to be an effective teacher more rapidly once I had begun using the "doing with" teaching strategy. This action shares power in the classroom; encourages insightful thinking and encourages mutual respect among all class members. I have also found that when beginning teachers use this same pathway to their success they quickly become outstanding teachers.

The other branch of the process is the systematic observations that tests provide. Teachers need to be shown how to identify the reasoning processes that answers display. Once they can do this on paper, doing it in the classroom becomes easier.

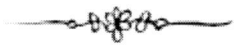

Dr. Jay C. Powell

The Heavenly Circle
What do others have to say about this process?

Here is a "meeting" that might have taken place among several individuals. Call it a "dream" or a figment of the imagination or whatever you wish. It expresses several important ideas that would take many more pages of philosophical or theoretical discussion to have accomplished.[94]

In attendance might have been:

Jay Powell, Mary Powell, Frances Powell, Peter Bar Jonah, John Dewey, Jean Piaget, B. F. (Ben) Skinner.

Arrived later: Maria Montessori —

Ben S: In your book your criticism of behaviorism is a bit harsh, but true. Reward systems are about external control and self-control is more important.

John D: Reward systems are also about communication, particularly with animals. With people, when mutual rewards are being sought, the resulting sharing leads to effective communication.

Jean P: However, communication relies upon mutual understanding and the communicators' worldview determines the nature and level of understanding that can be achieved.

Mary P: You gentlemen are talking about communication with your *heads* – your intellects. What about communication with your *hearts?*

Frances P: Deep communication is more than just *talk* – it also involves caring and sharing.

Jay: If this caring and sharing is to increase mutual understanding – it must occur in such a way that *insights* are achieved and shared. We must go beyond our current assumptions, preconceptions and prejudices to a new awareness for communication to genuinely occur. The rat in the maze must apprehend the pattern inherent

John:	Yes, expanding awareness is the basis for all effective education.
Jean:	More than this, awareness expands in phases and stages. There is an underlying sequence to the process.
Frances:	There is also an underlying *trust*. We cannot leave feelings out of the picture.
Mary:	Recognizing awareness requires more than hearing the words we want to hear. I'm trying to express a thought for which there are no words. My first few days here were profound because as I worked with my mentors to acclimatize myself, we shared visions, feelings and coordinated actions more than words.
Frances:	It was when Jay realized that he was robbing me of my individuality by doing too much for me that I was able to let my anger toward him go. This changed our relationship and I was able to die in peace.
Mary:	He was able to release me too. Love is empowering, not enabling.
Ben:	Do you mean that doing something for someone – helping him or her out – is not good enough?
Mary:	Even more so. When you do something for someone that they should be doing for themselves you are diminishing their value in your eyes and in theirs. Your message to them is that they are incompetent. This impression may be true momentarily, but if what you do is enabling, they need not undertake the personal responsibility of learning to do it for themselves.
John:	Is this where 'doing with' comes in?

(Maria Montessori joins the group.)

Maria: I was following your discussion and felt the need to join in. If you are going to try the 'doing with' approach, you have two options beyond sharing the workload among the group. One is to demonstrate the skill needed, using easy stages, and to have them practice it. The other is to create a situation where they can discover the skill or understanding for themselves. This latter method worked best for me.

Jay: This second approach is where a teacher's insight comes into the picture. As a helper we must have the insight that tells us the needs to be met by paying close attention to the hang-ups being shown in their attempts. We must then have enough understanding of learning sequences and processes to provide them with circumstances in which they can achieve the next step by themselves. We set things up so that they can do the work successfully. This is the 'doing with' approach to teaching.

'Doing for' is like feeding the hungry. 'Doing with' is teaching them to farm so that they can feed themselves.

Peter: But, as a fisherman, I can tell you that if they over-fish, the supplies of food will dwindle and they will be starving again. The same is true if they abuse the soil while farming. Their actions must consider the longer-term consequences beyond the immediate moment and their personal needs.

Mary: And beyond their immediate group as well. Jay's vision is for the whole of humanity. Mine was more family-oriented. It was not until after I died that I came to realize how narrow my perspective was. I could not have worked with him in the material existence very easily as he moved toward his mission because it would have taken me from family. Now I see that family, though important, is not enough. I now can enjoy my grandchildren by watching them from here at any time and as much as I wish.

On earth they seemed so far away and so busy with their own lives that I had very little contact with them. Once Jay gets his project going full blast this situation would have been even worse. I suspect that I would have become even more resentful towards his mission. I was already finding his working on the computer was isolating him from me until he started working with his laptop on the dining room table. This meant that we were in sight of each other while I read or crocheted in the recliner in the living room.

Jay: We were working out accommodations as we went. It might have been possible that we could have found ways to share each other's lives as we moved forward.

Peter: Yes, you could have, but it could have slowed your progress, Jay – and that might have led you into resentment. Now as an expanding team we can share our talents more broadly and with more focus. We can immerse ourselves in the project without having some emerging negativity interfere with it or with our love for each other.

We can give each other space without a sense of abandonment. In the mutual and personal gains thus made we can find the Joy of Service – and the true Peace that the Kingdom of God offers.

We all can know in our hearts that we are doing the very best we can at our current level of

	understanding. We can watch our understanding deepen because of the mutual sharing of purpose, of skills and of extending our knowledge from carefully watching the outcomes of our actions to be sure that all are thriving.
Mary:	I like the insight Jay has that he shared with Roxane. "Knowledge without Compassion lacks Wisdom."
Jay:	Thank you all of you for a most enlightening session. This is my first experience with a discussion circle from Heaven.

With God all things are possible because there is So Much Love.

(Signed) All

There are still several competing educational theories of learning in common use today. The constructivist, where we assume that students construct their own knowledge, is the closest to the one presented here. With a few adaptations it will fit. The assessment approach our research has develop suggests an underlying "reality" for each individual that requires going deeper than the *fear based* superficiality of the *ego*, which *A Course in Miracles* defines a common approach to life. This Love based approach would add that students should construct their own knowledge from their deep Consciousness, wherein their mission lies.

What did you do to my kid?

What is the impact that this approach to education is likely to have?

One day I was in a drug store close to the high school where I was running the special programs. A gentleman approached me.

"You're Mr. Powell, aren't you?" he asked.

"Yes."

"Well I'm Mr. Richardson, Brian's dad. What did you do to my kid?"

Taken aback, I didn't know what to say. "Is there a problem?" I stammered.

"Far from it! Brian is enjoying school for the first time in years. What's more, he is doing his homework and reading books when he gets home from school. He used to hang out with a bunch of older boys who are into drugs and are getting into trouble with the law. No longer. He is even more thoughtful and polite at home. We haven't had a shouting match in months. What did you do to my kid?"

"All I did was to challenge everyone in the class. He rose to that challenge and did the rest himself."

Is this the end or the beginning?

Epilogue: Unanswered Questions

Do not lose your sense of connectedness ...
This loss will be the cause of much sorrow.

The Old One

What can we now say about the questions raised throughout our discourse that we have not already answered?

A defining choice [95]

We face a defining choice between two contrasting models for organizing human affairs. Give them the generic names of Empire and Earth Community. Absent an understanding of the history of this choice, we may squander valuable time and resources on efforts to preserve or mend cultures and institutions that cannot be fixed and must be replaced.

Empire organizes by domination at all levels, from relations among nations to relations among family members. Empire brings fortune to the few, condemns the majority to misery and servitude, suppresses the creative potential of all, and appropriates much of the wealth of human societies to maintain the institutions of domination.

Earth Community, by contrast, organizes by partnership, unleashes the human potential for creative cooperation, and shares resources and surpluses for the good of all. Supporting evidence for the possibilities of Earth Community comes from the findings of quantum physics, evolutionary biology, developmental psychology, anthropology, archeology, and religious mysticism. It was the human way before Empire; we must make a choice to re-learn how to live by its principles.

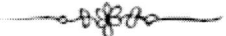

"Peasants" are people that are responding to the imperatives of their cultures. They have been dumbed down by their educational system (or lack thereof) to become vassals to the culture in which they live. They may be able to read but they don't. They may be able to think independently but they usually rely upon influential others to tell them what to think and what to do.

"Kings" are people that are responding to their Souls' imperatives; to the "Kingdom within." These are people whose talents have emerged to become gifts to others and a source for personal power. They create their own futures in concert with everyone and everything around them, recognizing and honoring the interconnectedness of all things.

If we intend to educate in a way that nearly all peasants can become kings, that is to provide equal opportunity, we need to do something different from what we are now doing. More of the same has not worked for more than 150 years and there is no good reason to expect it to work any better for the next 150.

This description returns us to the beginning. There we found a village living as Earth Community. We also heard rumblings of the beginnings of Empire with the threat of the Akkai and of disrespect for the wisdom of elderhood by the young shaman designate. The loss of our sense of connectedness that applies a "tooth and claw" interpretation upon Darwin's "survival of the fittest" is the source of the Empire model. Quantum physics has rediscovered connectedness in the concept of non-locality.

We can now add the evidence from educational research reported here to the list of sources for support of the Earth Community model. In addition, recent research[96] has shown that, for all its good intensions, the *No Child Left Behind* initiative has not worked to improve outcomes for the schools that were already ineffective. Without elaboration, we can state that this "No Effects" observation from attempted interventions has continued to be the results of research.

In the light of what Alfie Kohn had to say about testing, this observation is hardly surprising. Tests scored *right – wrong* are designed to identify the high performers for special recognition. Being a *linear* scale, used upon *non-linear* data, we cannot expect the scores on such tests to do anything else! The fact that there is a high correlation between socio-economic status and school success tells the story. Scoring tests *right-wrong* maintains the *status quo* and preserves success for the powerful elite of society and their families.

Such scoring and scaling of scores is essential for the Empire model to keep the "rabble" in their place. If we truly want to improve education, we need to do something very different than what we have been doing.

Look closely at the anecdotes I have related. If I had begun my educational journey as a top scholar, I would have had no reason to have followed the pathway I report. In order to realize my potential it was *absolutely necessary* that I do battle against the current system, not acquiesce to it.

Similarly, it was essential that I discover for myself that I could think, independent of the culture of "knowledge transmission." Also, being a non-normal learner, it was imperative that I learn how to learn *outside of the conventional schooling process*. Finally, my learning-how-to-learn had two distinct phases to it. The first was how to fill in the blanks that others provided. The second was how to fill in the blanks that I grew to identify within me and in the environment from a point-of-view from outside of the box.

I began my schooling career as a non-literate person, a "peasant" for whom the odds favored being non-literate all my life. My visual disability remains to this day. Amazingly, cataract surgery has given me clearer vision without glasses than I have ever had in my life.

On the other end, I am a profoundly literate person (a king) with more years of education after high school graduation than before it. More important than the time I have spent has been the depth of understanding I have achieved. This depth occurred because I sought it, driven by my sense of mission.

This is the transition from peasants to kings. It is the difference between a cook and a chef, a bookkeeper and an accountant. The cook throws things into a pan and serves what comes out. The chef creates a delectable experience. The bookkeeper enters numbers into a program. The accountant helps create and support a business operation. At the level of kings there is always a connectedness to others and to the environment. The concept of Earth Community always operates at the level of connectedness.

The theme of this book is that this "king" status need not be reserved to the select few. It is part of everyone's potential. It is the basis of vocation or mission. I know a Downs syndrome youth who is a superb spiritual healer. His ability to express uncluttered Love uplifts everyone he serves.

How should we teach what we teach?

More important than my life story is the fact that my teaching has demonstrated that the pathway I followed works equally well for other "peasants." Critical to this process is the need for information about those who start with any form of non-literate disability that is *not* provided by total scores on tests. The concept of "doing to – doing for – doing with" is no joke.[97]

We must go beyond content-area benchmarks and concept inventories because these do not interconnect thinking process across disciplines. The interconnection of all knowledge at the meta-cognition level is what gives education its true power.

"Doing to" is essentially an indoctrination strategy with its central thrust of control, originating external to the learner. Whatever this approach's intent, its effect is to disconnect each student from all other students and, more serious, from their inner or higher selves.

"Doing for" fosters codependency in which the domination is more covert, but nonetheless devastating to achieving our Souls' imperatives. It obstructs the creativity that lies beneath the surface for all but the most determined of students. Even these often emerge from schooling with a warped sense of their value towards humanity, seeing people as competitors or targets to exploit instead of helpers and friends. It makes helping each other into a contract instead of a service.

"Doing with" opens channels of communication and thus creates community. The interaction it fosters develops a deep appreciation of the talents and basic generosity of others. In the resulting "win – win" environment everyone thrives.

The critical first step is to foster an insight so that the excitement of learning can be initiated.

Then the more our students do for themselves, the more they learn and the more they learn how to learn. The better they become at self-instruction, the more flexible they become as learners. It is necessary to use hands-on and minds-on exploratory approaches until they are self-instructional.

The more they share what they are learning with each other the more connected into the emerging community they become. Their talents become part of a pool of services that is a resource for the entire community. For their contributions each member deserves recognition, respect and remuneration.

A retirement plan is not merely a way of farming out seniors to make way for younger blood. It is a way of recognizing elderhood. It makes it possible for matured talents to be provided more broadly than they could within a corporation, organization or particular community. The Internet and current transportation technology makes these services available globally and beyond.

In this respect we must create more than skilled machines. Of even greater importance from the quantum physics and the spiritual mysticism point-of-view, is becoming skilled intuitive observers and compassionate deliverers of service.

Beyond this point, the method of teaching the shaman works as well as any other. However, students must become scholars *before* they can learn with understanding from any form of teaching in which, on the surface, they appear to be passive receivers. This means that currently the only students we are really teaching are the ones who have become elaborative thinkers in spite of, and outside of, our current school systems. Our current approach is one that works for the few, not the many. This observation is why the NCLB initiative has failed.

We are inclined to be concerned about our standing educationally with other advanced countries. We need not be so concerned. First of all, we must be certain that we are comparing apples with apples. Some other countries may be producing a larger proportion of elaborative thinkers than we are producing. However, we are trying to provide a similar educational level of experience to everyone. Other countries often segregate the more successful early in their schooling.

There are a number of the more advanced countries, particularly in Europe where the climate is not as anti-intellectual as it is in North America. A good proportion of their elite had too much to lose to migrate to this side of the pond. In large part, initially, North America was settled by the misfits and the peasants. Both groups had more to gain and less to lose by migrating. Fortunately for us, these peasants were the ones willing to take huge risks under their own initiative.

Also, many of these countries make college-bound education available to a much smaller portion of their population than we are endeavoring to provide. In the developing countries, the superior education being offered is available to those who were already steeped in their own literate traditions. Education at this level is usually not even available to the "peasants" in these countries.

In developing countries, the emerging middle class probably comes from the small proportion of elaborative thinkers their culture has been able to produce. In both of these cases, we are not as badly off in the long run as it would seem. Also, our society is open enough that we may be able to adjust more quickly than most other countries, where tradition is a more powerful social force.

In all of the examples I have given, once we learned the secret, we all begin with a thought-problem *before* any explanation was given. We then worked through the explanation of this problem as a mind-game.

This approach contrasts sharply with the "I'll tell you all you need to know" approach to teaching. In "Castles in the sand" I began with a non-verbal demonstration of the skill. It was not necessary for me to be an expert for others to pick up on the idea.

Every teacher I have met, who enjoys teaching, has found some personal adaptation of this pattern. There is always a hands-on and a minds-on component to their approaches.

The third part of this process is the development of deeply powerful personal observation skills. Self-observation is at least as important as our ability to observe external events. This requirement occurs because events seem to transpire as we interpret them. We are the only ones we can change without domination or manipulation. The more constructive and helpful our actions, the more constructive and generally beneficial are the outcomes for everyone.

The fourth part of this process is openness to alternatives that encourages insightful mind stretching. My father talked in terms of "keeping my options open," when he discussed the birds and the bees with me.

Open-ended approaches need not be confined to sexual relationships. My entire teaching and research life has been built upon an open-minded approach to observing my own learning and the learning of others. When there is an error, there is always a missing piece, like the back of the hand while the palm was doing the compressing. Being alert for this missing piece is the route to insight and creative discovery. Teaching for insight provides students with the skills needed to identify missing pieces.

How about the teachers' workloads?
Who does the work?

There is no question whatsoever that no teacher can do all that is required for this approach to be successful. Fortunately, it is not necessary for teachers to do this. Teachers who are best at presenting ideas in an inspirational and thought-provoking manner need not change what they are doing now.

They can still turn much of the routine aspects of classroom management over to the class members. The grant structure in many school systems requires the keeping of daily attendance records. These need to be as accurate as possible. Every class I have ever taught has a number of trustworthy students who can do this unobtrusively for their teachers.

A routine I used in my special classes was to have my monitors for the week put the folders for the daily work on each student's desk. The unused folders at the empty desks told us immediately who was absent. Their names need merely be recorded in the register when these folders are returned to the files. At the end of the day these same monitors scored and recorded the scores (for the material that had scoring keys available) before they returned the folders to the files and were dismissed.

A list of the missed or questionable answers was attached to the assignment so that I didn't need to look beyond the list, unless I had some reason for so doing. In the simplest cases the red scoring marks were enough. Once my classes got beyond the sort of "helping each other" that Harry did in the writing assignment, the occasional quality check was enough. They realized that a "wrong" answer was more helpful to their classmates than an answer misclassified as "right."

This approach encourages risk-taking and takes most of the pressure off students' exams. The stakes are no longer high because exams are no longer hurdles to be jumped. Instead they become evidence about how close each student is to the skills and understandings required for the goals that they have set for themselves with the help and guidance of their teachers.

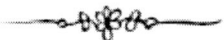

Marks and grades
What about marking to the curve?

Once we know the skills needed at the different cognitive levels, our analysis of student errors tells us their status in their cognitive progression. If we see them doing poorly, we use our assessment skills to find out the roadblocks and teach them how to do better. The only way to "fail" such a program is not to do any work.

We give them credit where they meet our expectations. It is unreasonable to disenfranchise them for being unable. If they cannot do something (like reading the textbook with comprehension) we should not classify them as non-academic students until we have tried, unsuccessfully to teach them how to read the textbook. If they have not yet come out of hiding, we teach them how to come out of hiding.

If there is something they cannot do, we do not despair and "mark them down." We redefine our expectations for them now and then teach them what is missing. We keep in mind the possibility that, once on fire, students most likely will surge far beyond our wildest expectations.

There is no "curve" to any of this. There are only skills and understandings that are present or are absent. They can acquire the understandings once they have the skills they need. So we teach them exploration, interpretation, integration and cooperation skills and they do all the rest of the work.

We then tell them the combination of skills and understandings they need to "pass" or to "graduate" or to get their "professional certificate" and with our skill-building support we leave the rest to them. Professions and employers may ask for grade-point averages and transcripts because, using right-wrong scoring we have nothing better to give them. What these people and agencies want is to know the skills and understandings possessed. This scoring system proposed herein can provide this information in whatever detail required.

We are still talking about standards of excellence and developed innate capabilities but now we use the artisan definition with precision. We know that the graduating brain surgeon is a superb and dedicated one before the qualification is awarded.

Because we are seeking our students' Souls' aspirations, we know that the level of competence and dedication to service to humanity is beyond anything most people now accomplish because these graduates are now champions in their chosen fields. I would reword the initiative to "No Child Left Underdeveloped."

I am suggesting an eight-part way of looking at social skills in the quest for understanding the connectedness of everything, including to both ideas and to other life-forms because each of us is an immortal idea in the consciousness of God.

There are four protective skills:
1. Protecting self from self, such as accepting instead of avoiding personal responsibilities.
2. Protecting self from others, such as blocking exploitation and changing our attitudes towards contentious issues.
3. Protecting others from us, such as observing, acknowledging and rectifying our errors and resolving conflicts non-violently.

4. Protecting others from each other, such as obviating unreasonable demands from people in authority and serving as mediators when unresolved issues arise.

There are four similar helping skills:
1. Helping us, such as learning how to observe our actions for errors and learning how to learn.
2. Helping others to help us, such as enlisting assistance from competent others and turning much of the teaching over to the students.
3. Helping others, such as dealing with emotional crises in stress-reducing ways and seeking win-win solutions to problems.
4. Helping others to help each other, such as teaching cooperation and compassion.

This model for social responsibility and social justice can best be described as the attainment of wisdom (knowledge tempered by compassion). It can be applied to all human activities within the global frame of reference.

If we assume, as our research evidence suggests, that we are all consciously thinking beings, then the quality of our thinking becomes the responsibility of the teaching profession. If our Souls emerge from the Inner Plane, the God space inside and between atoms and molecules, then our life's tasks are Divinely Ordained with our full participation and agreement (It's your mess, you fix it!). We deserve to be treated as such and are obliged to treat all others the same way.

To acknowledge that source is to imply that each of us comes with all the unique skills and abilities required to fulfill a mission for which our uniqueness was designed. Turning us into interchangeable economic slaves is a travesty and a violation of our Divine nature. We must instead help others to find and realize their missions by fulfilling the role that their missions' contracts intend. This is true education; this is "leading out the qualities from within."

We cannot trust our superficial consciousness because that part of us feels separated from all things. It is therefore deeply aware of its superficial limitations and it is driven to attack or to hide by its fear of being powerless. Our true power lies in our deeper natures where everything is inseparable from the Divine and expresses the Divine.

We are co-creators with God. When we choose to create vile or mischievous forces, we find that we must pay the price. Any harm we extend comes back to us multiplied by the law of "like attracts like." Any benefit we create returns in the same way. If we choose to do nothing, we are then subject to the impact of the actions of others upon us.

It need not be more complicated than this to explain all that we experience. Our intentions attract our consequences. There is no place to hide and there is no place to go where we can escape the uplifting impact of Unconditional Love and the distortions of this Love that fear creates.

Financial considerations

How much will this alternative approach cost?

The main up-front cost of this approach is the retraining of teachers to function differently. A second major cost will be the research expenditures needed to set up the alternative-answer benchmarks as part of the developmental sequences. We need to know the mistakes our students are making to help them to fix their misapprehensions.

Textbooks, courses of study, even the examinations themselves need not be changed. The changes come from the ways in which these media are used. Teacher assignments, class sizes, and other management and maintenance details need not be changed nor the school year lengthened or shortened. Once children get turned on to their emerging abilities, learning becomes a 365-24 operation under their own initiative.

We don't need to show a video presentation from beginning to end to make a particular point about it. We don't need to have the sound track running to study how the message is being delivered. Multi-media presentations are designed to control the input we receive. Breaking this control by removing one or more of the input channels opens us to deeper understanding, to the recognition of propaganda, to the identification of hidden assumptions – whether false or true.

After this the savings begin. My teaching and research has shown repeatedly that we can expect average students to learn about twice as much in one year with deep understanding, than when they learn superficially, and without much comprehension, using current practices. Students who are behind learn much more rapidly and often overtake their age peers in a year or two.

The last few words

Such gains mean that America could regain its standing and the respect it once had in the world. Our children would be able to create their own futures and live honorable and fulfilled lives. They could become the helpers of helpers on a worldwide basis; making life better for everyone everywhere they go. It would be a New Renaissance. It would be the emergence of the Earth Community.

The hearts of the American people are noble and generous. The fears we now carry are disconnecting us from our hearts and from each other. Change is in the wind. This turn around will cost us our greed, our self-indulgence and our egos but it could save our nation and the world.

As I said earlier, true education requires four things:
Hands on
Minds on
Eyes and ears open
Hearts open.
For this revolution to succeed, the last must come first.

Our company

Better Schooling Systems is a new not-for-profit 501(c)(3) operation that is prepared through grants and contracts to help make this transition possible anywhere in the world that requests it.

We will train your people to do the work and walk beside them to help them in their helping of others to learn how to help each other. As we become able we will also provide external media resources, including test-scoring and process-based critiques of existing media and materials to make the transformation easier, assuring its success.[98]

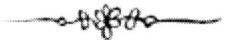

Afterword

It has yet to be determined whether or not this new mathematical approach has much broader applications than extracting diagnostic information from educational tests. The single attempt thus far undertaken gave some surprising results from the incidence of diabetes in the United States between 1901 and 2005. It could be that this approach might have value wherever a bell shaped curve is found using linear statistical approaches and researchers suspect more than pure chance is operating in the situation being studied.

Appendix A

There is how each of the groups went about their collective tasks.

> Mary and Gladys have decided to open a small souvenir shop for their class to raise some money for the Junior Class Prom at Washington Heights High School. They can get class rings for $80 and pins for $30. They know that in the past three years, three times as many rings as pins were sold. If they have $3500 to buy these souvenirs, how many pins should they buy?

Statements: $80r + 30p \leq 3500$ (1)

$r = 3p$ (2)

Francine's Group

Rudolpho suggested that they start with 18 pins and 6 rings.

Casey objected. "We need more rings than pins!"

"Oh, of course," Rudolpho replied. "I read the question wrong."

"Well then," Latisha rejoined. "Let's try 18 rings and 6 pins.

They got out their calculators.

18 by 80 plus 6 by 30 is 1620

"Wait a minute, Casey said, "I got 1710."

Francine looked at the two numbers. "Your answer is 90 more than ours. Did you hit a 6 for a 3? They are above each other on the calculator keyboard." Casey tried her calculation again. This time she agreed with the other three.

"Which pair of numbers should we try next?"

"It doesn't really matter," Rudolpho responded. "We are trying to get to something near, but less than 3500. How about 45 and 15?

This time they all agreed that 80 by 45 plus 30 by 15 is 4500.

"That's too big, how about 30 and 10?"

"Casey, you try this one," Francine suggested, and I'll check your work.

80 by 30 plus 30 by 10 is 2700

"That's a lot closer," Francine remarked.

"Let's try 36 and 12." Latisha was enjoying the group participation. "Rudolpho and I will calculate this one."

80 by 36 plus 30 by 12 is 3240.

Rudolpho shook his head. "3240 is a long way from 3500. Maybe we should try 39 and 13."

Francine said, "Okay, I'll try that one."

80 by 39 plus 30 by 13 is 3510.

"That's awfully close," Latisha observed. "We should check that to be sure there is no mistake." They found the calculations to be correct. They all agreed that the number of pins required was 12 because $3510 was more money than they had available.

Gregory's Group

"Where do you suggest we begin?" Gregory asked.

"Could we replace the r in the first equation with $3p$ from the second one?" Phyllis suggested.

"Why would you do that?" Minerva wanted to know.

Carlos replied that the second equation tells us that these two values are equal.

"Also, it is the value of p, the number of pins, that we want to find," Gregory added.

"If we do this we get:

"$80(3p) + 30p \leq 3500$," Phyllis continued, writing the new inequality on the chalkboard in their corner of the room.

"Why don't you show us the next step, Carlos?" Gregory suggested.

"It is:

"$240p + 30p \leq 3500$," Carlos wrote the new inequality below the one that Phyllis wrote.

"Oh, I see it now. This means that:

"$270p \leq 3500$," Minerva added this next step. Gregory got out his calculator and completed the solution.

"$p \leq 3500 / 270 = 12.964$, so we can round it up to 13."

(Did you detech the error just made?)

Abdul's Group

"Preston, you are our math whiz. Why don't you solve this for us the way Mr. Rodriguez showed us yesterday?"

"Okay," Preston agreed. "The first thing we do is to write down the two statements we are to work with." He copied them on to the chalkboard.

Statements:		$80r + 30p \leq 3500$	(1)
		$r = 3p$	(2)
"Now we:			
"Rearrange	(2)	$r - 3p = 0$	(3)
"Multiply	(3) by 10	$10r - 30p = 0$	(4)
	"Add (1)	$80r + 30p \leq 3500$	
	"Which gives	$90r + 0p \leq 3500$	(5)
	"or	$r \leq 3500 / 90$	
		$r \leq 38.89$	(6)
	"and	$p \leq 38.89 / 3$	
		$p \leq 12.96$	(7)

"The number of pins will be 12." As he talked he wrote the results on the chalkboard.

(Note* Preston did all the work for the group.)

Amit's Group

"I think we should try a graphical solution, as Mr. Rodriguez suggested," Amit began. "Myra, you are our computer expert. Why don't you walk us through it using Excel?"

"Okay. How many lines will we need?" Myra assumed the teaching role.

"Two," Sylvia said.

"Why?"

"Because we have two equations to graph," Theresa responded.

"Good. What values shall we use?"

"Well for the second one, any pair of numbers where one is three times the other will do for the second pair and 0,0 will be the first pair," Amit remarked

"Why?"

"There is nothing added to or subtracted from either side so that graph will go through the Origin." Amit was pleased that he was beginning to understand graphing.

"Good, what about the second pair?"

"It needs to be big enough that the other line will cross it. Today is the 13th so why not 13 and 39? We can make it bigger later if we need it," Myra suggested. She set up a table on the screen, with two columns labeled "r" and "p," two rows labeled "1" and "2" and entered the values agreed upon. "Now, how about the second line?"

"We need to find where this line crosses the axes," Amit explained.

"How do we do that?"

"I know," Sylvia said. "We find the value of each variable when the other is zero!"

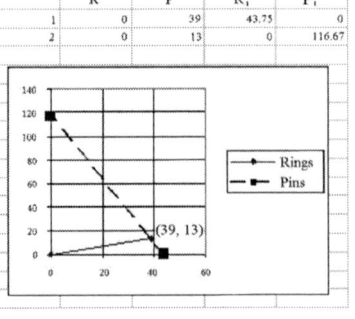

"Of course. Use your calculators to find these values."

They each found the value of 3500 / 30 and by 80, making the p crossing point 116.67 and the r intercept 43.75. Myra entered these new values in two new columns r1 and p1. She then set up the r and p values as Series 1 and the r1, p1 values as Series 2 and had the program draw the line graphs.

The results of this work appeared on the screen as shown in the graph.

When she pointed the arrow at the intersection of the two lines the values given on the chart appeared.

"I guess they will buy 13 pins," Amit concluded and the rest agreed.

Recapitulation

Once they had all found their answers, Mr. Rodriguez brought them back together to share their results.

"They would get 12 pins," Francine said.

"We agree," Abdul chimed in.

"We don't agree," Gregory challenged. "We think it should have been 13 pins."

"That's what we got on the computer," Amit joined in.

"This is interesting." Mr. Rodriguez smiled. "Two different answers are given to the same problem. How could this happen?"

"It has to be 12," Francine insisted, "Because 13 pins and 39 rings costs $3510, which is more money than they have to spend."

"Well then, Gregory," Mr. Rodriguez enquired, "Did your group check your answer?"

"Er, no …"

"The answer was almost 13," Carlos defended. "Gregory said that we should round the answer up."

"Let's look at your work." Mr. Rodriguez suggested. "There you are. Look at your last line. It says:

"$p \leq 3500 / 270 = 12.964$"

"Why did you change the less than or equal to sign ($\leq$) to an equal to ($=$) sign?"

"Carelessness I guess."

"If you had used the signs correctly they would have told you that the answer would have to be smaller than 12.964. Your answer had to be a whole number."

"Why a whole number?" Casey asked.

"Anyone?"

"Because you cannot buy a part of a pin." Preston chuckled.

"I still don't understand," Casey objected. "What's less than or equal to got to do with it?"

"I get it!" Minerva exclaimed. "We are solving a story problem and the wording requires a whole number answer."

Casey frowned for a moment and then nodded in agreement.

"In that case, why did the computer give us 13?" Sylvia asked.

"What do you think?"

"It must be programmed to round up," Sylvia mused.

"Does this mean that you cannot trust computer answers?" Phyllis asked.

"Not without checking them," Preston remarked.

"Is this true, Mr. R?" Minerva asked.

"Yes, computers do not think for themselves. They merely follow the rules the programmer gave them. If the rules do not apply, the computer can be exactly wrong."

"Jacques, did you follow what Preston said?"

"No."

"I didn't either," Cynthia agreed, as did Abdul's nod.

"What does this tell you, Preston?"

"I thought they understood," Preston defended himself. "It was clear to me."

"Yes, but …"

"I asked because it seemed that you were doing all the work," Mr. Rodriguez explained. "To teach effectively, your students must be with you, participating in the thinking."

"I'm sorry, I didn't realize." Preston's downcast look spoke volumes.

"Do you now understand why, in our tutorials, I have stressed 'Ask, don't tell?'"

"If others don't follow you, they don't learn." Preston looked up with a smile of relief.

"I have a problem with that solution," Theresa interjected.

"Oh?" came from several people in the room.

"Yes," she continued. "They have $260 they did not spend. They cannot make any profit on this money. They could buy three more rings and have $20 left, or two rings and three pins and have only $10 left."

"Maybe they can find $10 somewhere," Latisha suggested. "Then they could buy 39 rings and 13 pins and spend all their money."

"What if they cannot find the extra money?" Mr. Rodriguez continued probing.

"What about the three-to-one ratio?" Latisha asked.

Preston did a quick calculation in his head. "Or if they changed the ratio to four-to-one," he proposed, "They could buy forty rings and ten pins and spend all their money."

"Well, what about it?" Mr. Rodriguez prodded their thinking.

"Looking at the problem," Myra offered, "Makes me think that as store keepers they should spend as much money as they can."

"But what can we do about the ratio?" Mr. Rodriguez saw that they were going deeper.

"The question says 'in the past.' Does this mean that this is an average?"

"So?"

"Doesn't an average come from several numbers? It is not a discrete number like twelve rings."

"That is correct," Mr. Rodriguez agreed. "An average is a composite number that smoothes out all the variations from past events. What else is it?

"They were making a (hesitation) guess about the future?" Amit hesitated.

"In this case, yes." Mr. Rodriguez was delighted at their insight. "The girls will need to use their best judgment. If, on a high-stakes test, you choose to answer a similar question in a logical way that modifies the structure of the question, be sure to explain your reasoning and *hope* that the scoring rules permit such insights."[99]

Endnotes

1. Words that are in *Italics* in (or in this case underlined) the King James Version were added by the translator and were not in the original text.
2. Piaget, J. (1926). *The language and thought of the child.* New York, Harcourt, Brace. In this book Piaget makes the suggestion that this realization is what triggers the shift from egocentric thinking to concrete thinking.
3. These were drawn from the *Longman's Simplified Series* that were developed in the United Kingdom for use with non-English-speaking adult immigrants.
4. They could choose any of the 80 books in the set for which I had prepared comprehension checks during the previous summer.
5. Tannen, D. (1990). *You Just Don't Understand: Women and Men in Conversation.* New York, Morrow.
6. Lipton, B. H. (2005), *The Biology of Belief: Unleashing the power of consciousness, matter and Miracles.* Santa Rosa, CA. Mountain of Love / Elite Books.
7. An IEP or Individualized Educational Plan (sometimes going by other names) is often provided to students with specialized learning problems. This is an incident reported by a friend, whose name and personal history are fictitious.
8. Alcott, L. M. (1880). *Jack and Jill.* Nelson, Doubleday, Inc. Garden City, NY, 1957, p. 292. The issues being addressed by the "No Child Left Behind" initiative is well over a century old. The proposed solution, then as now, was to test more rigorously. It did not work then and it cannot work now.
9. Tramp, C., personal conversation, December 26th, 1997.

10. Drawn from Goleman, D. (1995) *Emotional Intelligence: Why it can matter more than IQ.* New York, Bantam Books, pages 62, 63.
11. I consider myself extraordinarily fortunate or "Blessed" to have married three times to three wonderful women. It is saddening that two of them are now in Heaven (Frances in 1993 and Mary in 2006), but our good relationships continue.
12. St. Paul's statement about this issue is, "Let every man abide in the same calling wherein he was called." (KJV: I Cor. 7.20).
13. In our program, Fridays were spent on work-experience activities at various businesses in the community.
14. Kessler, R. (2000). *The Soul of Education: Helping Students Find Connection, Compassion, and Character at School.* Alexandria, VA Association for Supervision and Curriculum Development (pages 2 – 5).
15. Holmes, E. (1984). *Living the Science of Mind.* Del Ray, CA DeVorss, page 409.
16. A search of the Library of Congress and Canadian Parliamentary catalogues provided some musical works by Leslie R. Bell but did not give the particular title for which I was looking.
17. See: Lakoff, G. & Núñez, Rafael, (2000). *Where Mathematics Comes From: How the Embodied Mind Brings Mathematics into Being.* New York, Basic Books. This book completes the picture that I formed and used successfully as a high school mathematics teacher. Mathematics, when taught appropriately, emerges from children's natural abilities to combine and compare small groups of objects.
18. Powell, J. C. (1973). Castles in the Sand. *The OECTA Review.* XXXIII, 2. A few minor editorial changes have been made to this document.
19. The reference to forty years indicates that I was 42 years old at the time of publication.

20. Carr, J F., and Harris, D (2001). *Succeeding with standards: Linking curriculum, assessment, and action planning.* Alexandria, VA. ASCD; (page 1).
21. This event occurred in Ontario where the underlying approach to teaching was borrowed from Prussia by Egerton Ryerson at about the same time as Horace Mann introduced this same schooling system to Massachusetts.
22. These levels of understanding are: Information extraction (Knowledge), Comprehension, Application, Analysis, Synthesis, and later Evaluation come from Bloom's (1956).*A Taxonomy of Educational Objectives: Handbook I; Cognitive Domain.* New York, David Mackay.
23. I am currently using this approach with undergraduate students at the college level in such subjects as Astronomy, Environmental Science, Climatology and Nutrition.
24. Pryor, K. W., Haag, R. & O'Reilly, J. (1969). The creative porpoise, Training for novel behavior. *Journal of the Experimental Analysis of Behavior 12.* 653 - 661.
25. Typical of the stories told about such events is the movie The *Dead Poets Society* starring Robin Williams. I was deeply disappointed in this movie because the suicide in the story was unnecessary. A courtroom lawyer needs acting skills and the boy's father would have approved of that vocation.
26. Once again the teaching model is "Hands on – Minds on – Eyes and Ears open – Heart open."
27. To achieve this goal we need to break the numeral into parts. V by X is L. (Five tens are fifty) III by X is XXX (Three tens are thirty) the sum so far is LXXX (or eighty). Because we had IX and not X we must subtract VIII from LXXX, which gives LXXII. (That is, 8 by 9 is 72.)
28. Another innovation of mine was to recycle problem types from earlier weeks on my weekly tests. In this way I assured myself that their skills were being maintained.

29 Instead of test scores I gave marks based upon the number of lessons mastered, similar to the way I used comprehension checks in their voluntary reading.

30 I first used this sequence in a demonstration of effective teaching with an eighth grade class. In this case, I used the third alternative ending. Subsequently I have used all three approaches to demonstrate the differences in student responses to teachers I was training. The discussions following these demonstrations were fascinating. Better Schooling and Information Systems hopes to prepare a DVD of this approach for mentoring purposes when funds become available.

31 Science Research Associates, 259 East Erie Street, Chicago, IL 60611.

32 Shakespeare, William. (1599 –1607) *King Lear*. Act 2, Scene II, Lines 1 – 13. Copied from Alexander, Peter. (1953). *William Shakespeare: The Complete Works*. London, UK, Collins, page 1087.

33 Goswami, A. (2000). *The Visionary Window: A Quantum Physicist's Guide to Enlightenment*. Wheaton, IL, Quest Books, Page 2. Author's emphasis has been added.

34 Moore, T. (1992). *Care of the Soul: Guide to cultivating and sacredness in everyday life...* New York, Harper Perennial, pages 52-54.

35 If energy and matter were localized at the macrocosmic level, then the universe is expanding at an increasing rate *proportional* to the distance objects are away from us. Shrapnel leaves an explosion at a constant velocity without regard to size. From whence is the energy coming that is causing this acceleration? There is a contradiction here. Astronomers now assume that the Universe itself is expanding, perhaps for reasons unknown. Is it possible that this part of the Universe is a "white hole?"

36 Heisenberg, W. (1927) *The Uncertainty Principle*.

37 Goswami, A. (2000). *Op. cit*.

38 In its original version, some of the material in this chapter was presented as a sermon at the Life Enrichment Center in Flint, Michigan in October of 2002.

39 ACIM. (1992) *A Course in Miracles.* Mill Valley, CA Foundation for Inner Peace.

40 These are solid objects that appear out of "thin air" and are known as "apports" in the Spiritualist community.

41 The term "random" in physics means "unpredictable." Such inability to predict may simple mean that the mechanism behind the event is not yet know. In this sense, many Conscious acts from the Universe (often called "Miracles") are *unpredictable* because it is outside much current scientific practice to accept the idea that there is a Consciousness behind existence. A common property of such "random" events is the appearance of the bell-shaped curve. The mathematical procedure we are developing seems to be able to reach behind this curve to reveal the underlying *non-random* structure.

42 Ponder, C. (1966). *The Dynamic Laws of Healing.* West Nyack, NY Parker.

43 I quoted St. Paul earlier on this matter (see: footnote 12) A more precise statement can be found in my translation of this passage, "Do not try to change the pathway of a person responding to the call, but let each keep God's commandments. Powell, J. C. (Unpublished). *The Craftsman's Way: The First Epistle of the Apostle Paul to the Corinthians* 7.20.

44 How then do we explain "evil" haunting and vile or "familiar" spirits? Could it be that when we die we carry with us the attitudes, desires and intentions we had while living here on earth? If we are unwilling to correct our misconceptions and miscreations, do we condemn ourselves to a "hell" of our own making? Is God offering us Unconditional Love and waiting patiently for us to

become willing to change? *A Course in Miracles* spells this all out in great detail.

45 Since there are more people alive today (about 6 billion) than the total of all the people who had lived from the beginning of humankind to about 1600, new souls must come from somewhere. Telling this story is another book.

46 Yogananda, P., (1997). *The Autobiography of a Yoga.* Los Angeles, CA. Self-Realization Fellowship.

47 Tolle, E. (1999). *The Power of Now: A Guide to Enlightenment.* Novato, CA. New World Library.

48 Dyer, W. W. (2004). *The Power of Intention: Learning to Co-create Your World Your Way.* Carlsbad, CA. Hay House.

49 *What the "Bleep" Do We Know?* (2004) Lord of the Winds Films.

50 McTaggart, L. (2002). *The Field: The quest for the secret force of the universe.* New York, Harper Collins.

51 Did Jesus have three children, two sons and a daughter? Was this daughter who was born after his Crucifixion the only off-spring recorded? See: Brown, S. (2007). *Secret Societies – And How They Affect Our Lives Today.* Carlsbad, CA. Hay House. Although of historical interest, if true, none of these possibilities have much bearing on the message I am trying to deliver of the non-locality of our Souls. What we may actually be, and where these concepts lead us is much more important than details about the past.

52 Brown, D. (2004). *The Da Vinci Code* New York, Doubleday.

53 For more details about this transformation see Hawkins book, referenced in endnote 57.

54 Powell, J. C., and Shklov, N. (1992) Obtaining information about learners' thinking strategies from wrong answers

on multiple-choice tests *Educational and Psychological Measurement 52*, 847 – 865.

[55] Roxane Christ is a superb contract editor who can be reached at (604) 844 – 7603.

[56] Hawkins, D. R. (2002). *Power vs. Force; The Hidden Determinants of Human Behavior.* Carlsbad, CA. Hay House. He presents a case by using kinesiology that he argues is a procedure that assures Truth, the picture he paints is a new science for Life. He confirms my other sources that the turnaround occurred in 1985.

[57] The following incident is fictional but the outcome is not. Horace Mann initiated the use of college entrance examination in the United States in the last half of the 1800s for the reasons presented.

[58] Kohn, A. (2001). Education in a dark time. *Education Update. 43*, 1, (1, 4). Association for Supervision and Curriculum Development.

[59] For a current presentation of my research results see: Powell, J. C. (2010). Testing as feedback to inform teaching. Chapter 3 in *Learning and Instruction in the Digital Age: Making a Difference through Cognitive Approaches.* New York: Springer. (In press).

[60] Rasch, G. (1960). *Probabilistic models for some intelligence and attainment tests.* (Copenhagen, Danish Institute for Educational Research).

[61] The procedure I used was the t test for differences between the means of two independent distributions.

[62] Curwood, J. O. (1928). *The Plains of Abraham* Garden City, NY Doubleday.

[63] Their scaling procedure was to set the average (mean) score at 65 and the spread score (standard deviation) at 15 for the entire Province. This means that about one student in six will fail and a similar number will get 80 or better. This approach is the same as the one that sets the average for IQ scores at 100 or SAT scores at 500. The resulting numbers look like percentage scores but they are not. This

approach is justified to the degree that totals scores are valid measures of achievement.

64 This claim is based upon the argument that if they had learned as much as they would normally have done, their score would have remained at 30. The standard deviation is often used in commercially prepared standardized tests to represent one year of progress in the norms provided. Hence, a gain of slightly more than one standard deviation would represent a second year of gain in one year.

65 Kohl, H. (1967). *36 Children* New York, New American Library.

66 Ammons, R. B. & Ammons, H. S. (1948). *Full-Range Picture Vocabulary Test.* Missoula, MT Psychological Test Specialists.

67 Hawkins, D. (*Op. Cit.*, sub-title text for Chapter 6).

68 Gorham, D. R. (1957). *The Proverbs Test.* Missoula, Montana Psychological Test Specialists.

69 Inhelder, B & Piaget, J. (1958). *The Growth of Logical Thinking from Childhood to Adolescence.* (A. Parsons & S. Milgram, Trans.) London: Routledge & Kegan Paul. (Original work published in 1955.)

70 When every person taking a test answers every question, the number of wrong answers is always equal to the total number of items minus the number of right answers ($w = t - r$). This produces a mathematical relationship known as linear dependency. It produces an effect like dividing by zero (0) in the computation of linear relationships of any kind, causing either nonsense or no solution. Rasch developed a scaling procedure that provided a partial way around the problem by scaling the "wrong" answers against item difficulty instead of total score and used a different base curve from the bell-shaped one. He showed that alternative answers are often sequential on this scale but no one, other than me, seems to have tried to find out why this sequencing might be occurring.

71 Powell, J. C. (1968). The interpretation of wrong answers from a multiple-choice test *Educational and Psychological Measurement, 28,* 403-412.

72 Bloom, B. S. (Ed.) (1956) *A Taxonomy of Educational Objectives, Handbook I: Cognitive Domain.* New York, David MacKay

73 Powell, J. C. and Isbister, Alvin G. (1974) A comparison between right and wrong answers on a multiple choice test *Educational and Psychological Measurement 34,* 499 – 509.

74 Carlton, R. A. (1974). Popular images of the school. *Alberta Journal of Educational Research 20* (1) 59 – 74.

75 Spears, H. (1973). Kappans ponder the goals of education. *Phi Delta Kappan 55* (1) *29* – 32.

76 Powell, J. C., Cottrell, D. J. and Lever, Margaret (1977) Schools I Would Like to See: An opinion survey with interesting possibilities. *Alberta Journal of Educational Research XXIII* (3) 226 – 241.

77 Maslow, A. H. (1968). (Second Edition). *Toward a psychology of being.* New York, Van Nostran.

78 Bock, R. Darrel, Yates, George (1973) Multiqual: Log-linear analysis of nominal or ordinal qualitative data by the method of maximum likelihood Chicago, IL National Educational Resources.

79 The multinomial distribution is like the binomial except that the expansion can have any number of terms greater than two. Its calculation gives the probability of any single value in any single cell in a table, taking into account all the other values in that table. The table can have any number of dimensions as long as the cells are frequencies.

80 The fact that more than one pathway was found logically is the necessary and sufficient condition to invalidate *right-wrong* scoring as a test-scoring as a test interpreting procedure when we are trying to use test results to inform teaching.

81 Powell, J. C. and Miki, H. (1985) Answer anomalies, how serious? Paper presented to the *Psychometric Society* Nashville, TN.

82 This finding resolves the conflict between teaching for rote and superficial understanding and teaching for profound understanding raised by the Old One. Acquiring information without substantial understanding unintentionally leaves students behind. It is unintentional because scoring "right – wrong" fails to collect the reasoning behind answers. We cannot therefore know that the students did not master some course material until later in their educational careers. This observation is the major psychological flaw in current scoring practice. It explains why NCLB is not working.

83 It is interesting to note that the paper reporting these results was submitted to several journals and was rejected by each. Finally, in 2008 a reviewer recognized the importance of by-passing linear dependency and accepted a paper for a major international conference.

84 Covey, S. R. (2004). *The 8th Habit: From effectiveness to greatness.* New York, Free Press.

85 I am using the symbol *p* to stand for the proportion of explained variability provided by each cell.

86 Willingham, D. J. (2009). *Why Don't Students Like School.* San Francisco, CA: Jossey-Bass. This book relates current brain research to classroom practice. From this perspective, constrictive right answers can reflect two aspects of learning, rote memorization and superficial understanding. Expansive right answers can reflect deeper understanding. Profound understanding can lead to either right or wrong answers. A wrong answer is more likely when the right answer is trivial and a more complex perspective is closer to one of the alternative answers.

87 The code on these dice is: R_m for a right answer from rote or superficial understanding; R_u for a right answer with

understanding; $W_{1, 2 \& 3}$ for various levels of alternative interpretation and W_{3+} for the reading more into the question than intended by the test preparer. The $W_{1, 2 \& 3}$ refers to the within item alternatives. *Proverbs* now has 18 such layers between items. The result is a substantial broadening of the measurement spectrum for the test. The numbering of each die provides an answer-by-answer interpretation, hence the increase in explained variability.

[88] Orr, Eleanor (1997 Twice as Less: Black English and the performances of Black students in mathematics and science. New York, Norton.

[89] Gardner, James (1983) Frames of Mind: The Theory of Multiple Intelligences New York, Basic Books.

[90] www.betterschoolingsystems.org Then select Excerpts from Writing: Models and review these sections.

[91] Powell, J. C. (2010). *Op. Cit.* (Reference 59)

[92] Powell, J. C. (2008) *Applying the multinomial procedure to medical data.* Paper presented to a meeting of the WorldVistA Association meeting, Pittsburgh, PA. Some surprising results cam from this study as well.

[93] Brown, T. E. (2007). A new approach to attention deficit disorder. *Educational Leadership 64* (5) 22 – 27.

[94] Transcribed: August 7th, 2006.

[95] Korten, D. (2006). The great turning: from Empire to Earth Community. *Yes: A Journal of Possible Future.* (Summer).

[96] Teicher, S. A. and Arnoldy, B. (2007) Hard recovery for failed schools *Christian Science Monitor* (March 1, p. 1, 3)

[97] This Spring, as a college teacher, I have established an approved research program in my two classes that is following the exploratory learning approach and using my classroom testing to inform my teaching. I am also trying to set up a consortium to seek research funding for the use of the multinomial procedure, which may be able to

pull details of dynamic systems in all research areas, into the establishment of an alternative mathematical way to conduct analytical studies that can combine quantitative and qualitative approaches to research.

[98] Contact information:
Jay Powell, Ph.D., Founder
Better Schooling Systems
P.O. Box 12833
Pittsburgh, PA 15241
Phone: (412) 835 – 2116
Website: better-schooling-systems.org
Email: jpowell@better-schooling-systems.org

[99] This incident is a fictional account based upon actual scoring practices. It illustrates how teaching in mathematics can be conducted in small groups to broaden insight. It illustrates that more than one procedure can be used to get a "right" answer. It illustrates differing modes of interacting during group discussions. It illustrates how the wording of questions affects answers and the need therefore to verify results, even from computers. Finally, it illustrates solving the same problem using differing levels of performance complexity. Considering only whether answers "right" captures none of this diversity.